The Great Depression and the New Deal

Recent Titles in the Unlocking American History Series

The Industrial Revolution: Key Themes and Documents
James S. Olson with Shannon L. Kenny

THE GREAT DEPRESSION AND THE NEW DEAL

Key Themes and Documents

James S. Olson with Mariah Gumpert

Unlocking American History

An Imprint of ABC-CLIO, LLC
Santa Barbara, California • Denver, Colorado

Copyright © 2017 by ABC-CLIO, LLC

All rights reserved. No part of this publication may be reproduced, stored in a retrieval system, or transmitted, in any form or by any means, electronic, mechanical, photocopying, recording, or otherwise, except for the inclusion of brief quotations in a review, without prior permission in writing from the publisher.

Library of Congress Cataloging-in-Publication Data

Names: Olson, James Stuart, 1946– author. | Gumpert, Mariah, author.
Title: The Great Depression and the New Deal : key themes and documents / James S. Olson with Mariah Gumpert.
Description: Santa Barbara : ABC-CLIO, 2017. | Series: Unlocking American history | Includes bibliographical references and index.
Identifiers: LCCN 2017007596 (print) | LCCN 2017021568 (ebook) | ISBN 9781440834639 (ebook) | ISBN 9781440834622 (hardback)
Subjects: LCSH: Depressions—1929—United States. | New Deal, 1933–1939. | United States—Economic conditions—1918–1945. | United States—Social conditions—1933–1945. | United States—Politics and government—1929–1933. | United States—Politics and government—1933–1945. | BISAC: HISTORY / United States / 20th Century. | HISTORY / Modern / 20th Century. | HISTORY / Reference.
Classification: LCC HB3717 1929 (ebook) | LCC HB3717 1929 .O47 2017 (print) | DDC 330.973/0917—dc23
LC record available at https://lccn.loc.gov/2017007596

ISBN: 978-1-4408-3462-2
EISBN: 978-1-4408-3463-9

21 20 19 18 17   1 2 3 4 5

This book is also available as an eBook.

ABC-CLIO
An Imprint of ABC-CLIO, LLC

ABC-CLIO, LLC
130 Cremona Drive, P.O. Box 1911
Santa Barbara, California 93116-1911
www.abc-clio.com

This book is printed on acid-free paper ∞

Manufactured in the United States of America

Contents

Preface	vii
How to Use This Book	ix
Key Themes	xi
Introduction	xv
Alphabetical List of Entries	xxv
Topical List of Entries	xxix
List of Primary Documents	xxxiii
The Encyclopedia	**1**
Primary Documents	203
Sample Document-Based Essay Question (DBQ)	255
Top Tips for Answering Document-Based Essay Questions	259
Appendix A: Chronology of the Great Depression in America	261
Appendix B: Period Learning Objectives for Students	269
Appendix C: Listing of Biographical Entries	271
Appendix D: Listing of Entries Related to Supreme Court Cases and Acts of Congress	273
Bibliography	275
Index	285

PREFACE

Approximately one presidential administration removed from the Great Recession of 2008, an event still referred to as the worst economic crisis since the Great Depression, a study of that first economic crisis is not only timely but relevant, as the country still struggles to fully regain the economic footing that it lost with the burst of the housing bubble and the bankruptcy of Lehman Brothers. The Great Depression—the worst economic crisis the industrialized Western world has ever seen—permanently changed public policy, setting in motion many of the economic patterns, political templates, and government programs that still govern U.S. social and economic policies. Until the 1930s, most Americans believed that the economy regulated itself according to impersonal, natural economic laws, and they were comfortable leaving economic matters to those market forces. But President Franklin D. Roosevelt and the New Deal made the government a key player in the economy, and eventually Americans delegated to Washington, D.C., the responsibility of maintaining full employment and stable prices. The advent of Keynesian economics during the 1930s also gave the federal government unprecedented tools for controlling the economy.

This book is designed to support advanced high school and early undergraduate readers. It will support teachers and students in Advanced Placement U.S. History courses and provide a valuable supplement to any Common Core history curriculum that covers the era. In particular, the book's organization has been selected to align with primary- and secondary-source materials, in order to promote in-depth analysis and understanding of the specific details of the crisis and the patterns of change that it set in motion. The Advanced Placement curriculum framework for the period which encompasses the Great Depression (Period 7: 1890–1945) centers on key concepts such as economic cycles and market fluctuation, government responses to crises, the role of government and Americans' understanding of that role, mass media and culture, and political party ideals. A to Z entries provide the details needed for students to become fluent in these concepts. Finally, the AP Exam and the Common Core Standards for History and Social Studies for grades 11–12 focus on the incorporation of primary sources into analysis and presentation of course content along thematic lines.

How to Use This Book

The Great Depression and the New Deal: Key Themes and Documents is designed to provide students a ready reference for studying the course and impact of the Great Depression in the United States. The volume covers the period from the stock market crash of October 1929 to the beginning of World War II in 1939. Entries are categorized according to eleven key thematic categories: Agriculture, Arts and Culture, Banking and Economics, Business and Industry, Communication and Media, Environment, Government Programs, Organized Labor and Protest, Politics, Race Relations, and Work. The Introduction provides a summary of the causes leading up to the Great Depression and the New Deal response to the crisis. The body of the book consists of alphabetically arranged entries on important individuals, programs, pieces of legislation, government initiatives, and social responses. The book also includes a chronology of significant events, a range of primary-source documents from the period, a sample Document-Based Essay Question (DBQ) similar to those found on the Advanced Placement (AP) U.S. History Exam, together with a list of top tips for successfully answering DBQs, and a bibliography of suggested sources for further research. In addition, provided in the appendix of the book is a list of specific learning objectives students can use to gauge their working knowledge and understanding of the event. These objectives are similar to the thematic learning objectives presented in the AP U.S. History curriculum framework.

KEY THEMES

Agriculture—Much of the legislation passed in response to the Great Depression centered around farming, a field that employed almost one-fifth of the workforce. Farmers were already struggling to break even in a flooded international market after World War I, and worsening drought affected farmers across the Midwest, causing many families to uproot and migrate to California. Government initiatives like the Agricultural Adjustment Act offered mortgage assistance for farmers, promoted parity, and offered monetary compensation for reduced crop acreage to eliminate price-depressing surpluses.

Arts and Culture—Desperate to put people to work, President Roosevelt created a special arts component of the Works Progress Administration (WPA); the Federal Art Project, the Federal Music Project, the Federal Theatre Project, and the Federal Writers' Project generated initiatives and commissioned works in all areas of the arts. Farm Security Administration photographer Dorothea Lange captured now-famous images of farming families during the Dust Bowl. From the private sector, novelists like John Steinbeck and Erskine Caldwell captured the plight of migrant workers and families affected by poverty.

Banking and Economics—An unstable banking system and the stock market crash of 1929 catapulted the United States into the Great Depression. The Roosevelt administration addressed the crisis immediately by declaring a bank holiday, allowing only secure banks to reopen and offering aid to others. Subsequent economic reforms like the Glass-Steagall Act and the establishment of the Federal Deposit Insurance Corporation and the Securities and Exchange Commission helped stabilize the country's financial system, prevented future bank failures, and helped curb the unbridled speculation of the 1920s that had destabilized the economy. Roosevelt also took the United States off the gold standard, putting additional government monies into circulation and lowering interest rates.

Business and Industry—Many industries, like the railroad, steel, and textile industries, were showing signs of stagnation even before the crisis. By 1932, almost one-third of the country was unemployed. The Roosevelt administration passed legislation designed to help increase production, restore stability, and reduce corruption. Programs like the Tennessee Valley Authority brought low-cost hydroelectric power to areas in need. Production increased in the years leading up to U.S. involvement in World War II, revitalizing entire industries and helping to lift the country out of the Depression for good.

Communication and Media—Radio, the still-new and incredibly effective form of mass media, helped create a national response to the Depression. It became a steady source of entertainment and escape for people who increasingly could not afford other leisure activities. President Roosevelt's series of national radio addresses known as "fireside chats" helped reassure the nation and restore hope during the crisis.

Environment—Government programs like the Civilian Conservation Corps promoted environmental conservation while creating jobs. Later initiatives like the Shelterbelt Project and the Soil Conservation Act of 1935 were aimed at reducing erosion.

Government Programs—Franklin D. Roosevelt's New Deal set into motion a flurry of legislation and government initiatives designed to provide emergency relief, create jobs, reform unstable practices, and hasten the economy's recovery. Fifteen major pieces of legislation were passed in the first 100 days of his presidency alone. Roosevelt took a more active approach to governing than any previous president, carrying out what he saw as the government's duty to secure a better quality of life for its citizens.

Organized Labor and Protest—Unions made dramatic gains under New Deal legislation, organizing unskilled as well as skilled workers. New laws protected the right to bargain collectively, implemented fair practices in areas like maximum labor hours and minimum wage, and attempted to reduce unscrupulous practices by employers.

Politics—Franklin D. Roosevelt's response to the Great Depression has been criticized for both doing too much and not doing enough. Where previous presidents were content to allow the economy to take its natural course, the drastic nature of the crisis prompted "bold, persistent" action from the Roosevelt administration. In the end, Roosevelt's presidency reshaped both the role of the president and the responsibilities of government.

Race Relations—African Americans were among the hardest hit during the Great Depression, with almost half of all black Americans out of work by 1932. Hate crimes and lynchings increased. Roosevelt established the Fair Employment Practices Committee, though it lacked any real muscle. He also employed a group of African American advisers informally called the "black cabinet." With the New Deal's outreach to disenfranchised groups and people in need, many African Americans, traditionally Republican supporters, began to vote Democrat, a pattern that continues today.

Work—Upon taking office, one of Franklin D. Roosevelt's immediate goals was to put people back to work. Several initiatives, like the Federal Emergency Relief Administration, the Civil Works Administration, and the Works Progress Administration (WPA), were designed to create immediate, though often temporary, employment. FDR used government funds to put people to work repairing infrastructure and doing construction and conservation work. Later legislative efforts aimed to reform unstable practices and create permanent economic security in the United States.

Introduction

The Great Depression remains a seminal event in U.S. history, one of only a few historical occasions when the economy completely failed and Americans' legendary confidence went dormant. When the stock market crashed in October 1929 and the economy settled into the Great Depression, American optimism, for a short time at least, cratered as well. The event was the worst economic crisis ever to hit the industrialized Western world.

The roots of the Great Depression lie in the aftermath of World War I, which disrupted trade, exchange rates, and the flow of capital. Domestically, the laissez-faire economic model did little to address the unproductive climate. Farmers in the Midwest were also suffering from economic difficulties. European farmers had increased production after the war, flooding the international agricultural market and making it more difficult for farmers in the United States to break even. This was particularly damaging since agricultural production employed almost one-fifth of the American workforce. The Smoot-Hawley Tariff Act of 1930 raised tariffs on imported agricultural goods in an effort to create a more favorable economic climate for farmers but resulted in increased taxation on American products sold in Europe, further restricting trade. An outdated, inadequately regulated network of private banks and minimal government spending would offer little protection against the impending crisis.

Despite these factors, few could have predicted the suddenness and depth of the catastrophe. The stock market in the United States had undergone unprecedented, consistent growth in the 1920s, prompting increased investing, borrowing, and buying on credit. U.S. Treasury securities were removed from money market accounts and rerouted to Wall Street. Corporations invested more working capital in the stock market, as did middle-class Americans, who withdrew money from their bank accounts to buy stocks. When the Dow plummeted in October 1929, Wall Street was sent into a panic, wiping out thousands of investors. Billions of dollars were lost. Businesses failed. By November, the crash had wiped out 50 percent of all asset values.

The slide continued during the next three years as consumer confidence fell, buying and spending decreased, and industrial output slowed. Farmers had no resources to harvest crops, many of which were left to rot in fields. Bank failures and runs on banks became commonplace. By 1933 almost half of all U.S. banks had failed, and nearly 15 million Americans—over 25 percent of the workforce—were unemployed. The crisis was so devastating that some predicted a new Dark Ages, the end of not only capitalism but also the existing social order.

Contrary to popular myth, the Hoover administration did implement some relief initiatives, including the Reconstruction Finance Corporation Act of 1932, the Emergency Relief and Construction Act of 1932, and the Federal Home Loan Bank Act of 1932. But the American ideal of rugged individualism superseded any formal, comprehensive government action—especially on the part of Herbert Hoover who, upon his election in 1928, had promised such an era of prosperity as to guarantee "a chicken in every pot" and "a car in every garage." President Hoover believed that the economy would right itself through natural market forces and that the government should not directly intervene. It was difficult for the system to do that however, with such a dramatic lack of consumer purchasing power, despite the amounts of credit that banks did have.

The First 100 Days

By 1932, the nation was desperate, ready for a change in leadership. Herbert Hoover, the incumbent candidate, lost the presidential election to democrat Franklin Delano Roosevelt, who, as governor of New York, had already implemented a statewide relief system largely involving public works. Hoover suffered a humiliating defeat, winning only 59 electoral votes to FDR's 472. In his inauguration speech, Roosevelt took the first steps toward restoring the nation's hope and confidence when he famously asserted, "The only thing we have to fear is fear itself."

Roosevelt approached the Great Depression as if the nation were at war, taking full advantage of any executive powers that would have been available to a president during wartime. Where previous presidents had considered off limits anything not specifically allowed in the constitution, FDR assumed the right to do anything not explicitly prohibited in the document. His programs remained flexible—he would throw an idea against the wall, so to speak, to see if it stuck, even if he had previously tried its exact opposite. Further, with much of the initial New Deal legislation, Roosevelt was winging it; there was no precedent for such state-run programs. He was committed to what he felt was the "social duty" of government—to help those who could not help themselves.

The first 100 days of Roosevelt's presidency brought a flurry of revolutionary legislative action that became the New Deal. During this time more major legislation was passed than at any other time in U.S. history. The New Deal centered around the "Three R's": Relief, Recovery, and Reform. Relief, for an immediate halt to the economy's decline; Recovery, for temporary programs to restart the flow of consumer demand; and Reform, for permanent legislation to prevent such a crisis in the future. Several initiatives, like the Federal Emergency Relief Administration (FERA) and the Civil Works Administration (CWA), were launched purely to provide immediate, temporary jobs for the unemployed, even if many of those jobs were, as detractors accused, "wasted" on frivolous tasks. However, it was a clever component of New Deal programs that allowed people the dignity of being employed, rather than being passive recipients of the dole.

Roosevelt's first order of business was to address the banking crisis, declaring a four-day banking holiday so that the government could properly address the failing system. Congress passed the Emergency Banking Act, allowing all solvent banks to reopen and providing aid to banks in need. During the shutdown, Roosevelt delivered his first "fireside chat" radio address, explaining the banking crisis and his plans for its resolution to the American public. This was the first time a president had addressed the American public so intimately; the relatively new medium of radio made it possible for him to speak to the entire nation as one. By 1930, over 40 percent of American households owned at least one radio, even at the expense of other household items such as vacuums or cars. This early and effective form of mass media helped create a more cohesive national identity and response to the crisis. For its part, the first fireside chat helped restore the nation's confidence in the banks and, arguably, in the entire capitalist system.

Economic Reform

Once the banking crisis had been addressed, the Roosevelt administration passed a number of economic initiatives. The New Deal's economic and market reforms helped stabilize the country's financial system. They also prevented future bank failures and helped curb the unbridled speculation of the 1920s that had destabilized the economy. The Glass-Steagall Act (the Banking Act of 1933) prevented commercial banks from participating in investing. Through the Federal Deposit Insurance Corporation (FDIC), the government would ensure individual bank deposits of up to $5,000. The Securities and Exchange Commission was created to oversee and regulate the stock market. The Public Utility Holding Company Act of

1935 allowed the government to regulate interstate shipments of electrical power and natural gas, and restricted the freedom of public utility holding companies to exist simply for the purpose of issuing new securities. Roosevelt also took the United States off the gold standard, putting additional government monies into circulation and lowering interest rates. He encouraged the U.S. Treasury to purchase gold with paper money to achieve controlled inflation. He also urged Americans, who had been swapping out paper money for gold bars, to utilize paper money again and put their money back into the banks.

Public Works

The New Deal also involved, for the first time in U.S. history, the use of government money to create jobs, which initiated a controlled welfare state. In March 1933 Roosevelt created the Civilian Conservation Corps, employing almost 3 million young men in outdoor government camps and promoting conservation work. FERA allocated grant and loan money to states to create new, unskilled jobs in local and state governments. The CWA created temporary jobs, primarily in construction and municipal repairs, for the winter of 1933–1934.

One of the most ambitious New Deal programs was the Works Progress Administration (WPA), which put people to work building and repairing roads, bridges, and public buildings. It comprised the Federal Art Project, the Federal Music Project, the Federal Theatre Project, and the Federal Writers' Project, generating initiatives and commissioning works in all areas of the arts. The Public Works Administration likewise spent over $4 billion on over 34,000 longer-range projects, including dams, highways, bridges, hospitals, and schools.

Housing

One of the biggest threats to daily life was the threat of mortgage foreclosure. New Deal legislation offered mortgage assistance and refinancing, allowing for longer-term mortgages and helping to prevent foreclosures. To assist personal property owners and boost the construction industry, the government granted small loans to homeowners through the Federal Housing Administration (FHA). The Home Owners' Loan Corporation refinanced home mortgages. In 1937, the U.S. Housing Authority (USHA), began granting loans to states and communities to promote low-cost home construction. These programs essentially halted the spread of slums in the United States and dramatically increased the levels of home-ownership across the country.

Farming, Development, and the Expansion of the West

As it had done with personal property owners, New Deal legislation offered mortgage assistance and refinancing to farmers, allowing longer-term mortgages and helping to prevent foreclosures on farms. The Frazier-Lemke Farm Bankruptcy Act offered farmers a five-year postponement of mortgage foreclosures (though the Supreme Court eventually voted the act down). The Agricultural Adjustment Act (AAA) created parity for farmers and helped them pay their mortgages. Its agency, the Agricultural Adjustment Administration, essentially paid farmers not to farm, offering monetary compensation for reduced crop acreage in order to eliminate price-depressing surpluses. When the Supreme Court also voted down the AAA, Congress passed the Soil Conservation and Domestic Allotment Act of 1936, which likewise granted payments to farmers for reducing crop production—through letting fields lie fallow or planting soil-conserving plants like soybeans.

Despite the New Deal's many agricultural initiatives, however, farmers continued to struggle. They had grappled with drought and low food prices since the end of World War I. The AAA achieved mixed results, and the drought continued and worsened. Wind erosion combined with unsustainable farming methods resulted in a series of blackening dust storms, forcing many families from Missouri, Texas, Kansas, Arkansas, and Oklahoma to migrate west to California. In 1935, the government established the Resettlement Administration, helping struggling farmers relocate to better land.

In the meantime, the government began to recognize the potential for industrial development in the west. The Tennessee Valley Authority authorized the completion of federal hydroelectric power development projects, offering lower prices for power and promoting industrial and agricultural development throughout poor regions. The project, based in northern Alabama's Muscle Shoals region, was the government's most comprehensive economic development project to date.

It was clear that electrical power and available water sources could be the key to industrial development and the diversification of agriculture in the west. It was also clear that southern and western entrepreneurs needed more access to capital in order to make this happen. The Reconstruction Finance Corporation, originally created by President Hoover to grant business loans and provide financial support to local governments, was able to provide that capital. It funded infrastructure development in southern cities, as had been done earlier in major northern cities through private investment. This investment in infrastructure across the Sunbelt states paved the way for the development of the west in the 1940s, 1950s, and 1960s.

Organized Labor

The Roosevelt administration did more to expand and support organized labor than any administration before it. FDR's labor legislation was one of the long-term outcomes of the New Deal. The National Recovery Act guaranteed fair practices in the areas of maximum labor hours, minimum wage, and expanded allowances for collective bargaining. The National Recovery Administration (NRA) was established to promote the interests of industry, labor, and the unemployed. Once the Supreme Court voted down the NRA legislation, the National Labor Relations Act (also known as the Wagner Act) was passed, sparked by a series of walkouts in 1934. The act granted private sector employees the right to organize and to engage in collective bargaining with management. It also created the National Labor Relations Board to oversee the election of union leaders and their right to participate in collective bargaining with employers. It was the most comprehensive pro-labor legislation passed up to that point.

FDR's labor-friendly legislation allowed for a substantial increase in organized labor participation, most notably in the formation of the Committee for Industrial Organization (CIO). The CIO went up against General Motors and won. The strikers then took on U.S. Steel, though retaliation on the part of various, smaller steel companies resulted in violence—ten protesters were killed by Chicago police during the Memorial Day Massacre in 1927. In 1938, the Fair Labor Standards Act picked up where the NRA left off by establishing minimum wage and maximum hours standards, as well as child labor restrictions.

Critics and the Role of Government

The New Deal had its critics. There were liberals who believed that the legislation did not do enough to help the nation and conservatives who worried that it overstepped the boundaries of government. On the liberal side, Father Charles Coughlin, a Catholic priest with a popular radio show, initially supported Roosevelt but then accused him of unconstitutional monetary policies and supporting bankers over the common man. Huey Long, a senator from Louisiana, proposed a "Share the Wealth" program, which included limits on personal net worth and annual income, free college education, and an allowance of $5,000 for each family at the expense of the rich. Dr. Francis Townsend, a retiree, called for the creation of a government program whereby all senior citizens over the age of sixty would receive a monthly pension of $200.

From the other end, Republicans and conservative Democrats bitterly attacked initiatives like the Social Security Act for being communist-leaning and accused FDR's programs of penalizing the rich for their success. In 1936, Kansas governor Alf Landon ran against Roosevelt in the presidential election, criticizing the New Deal as wasteful and inefficient. Among Landon's backers was the American Liberty League, which had formed in 1932 to oppose what they believed to be FDR's socialist policies. Landon, though, was an ineffective campaigner, and in the end there were simply too many Americans still greatly in need of assistance. Roosevelt easily won the election with 523 electoral votes (Landon received 8).

FDR's approach to the economic crisis had raised critical questions about the role of government in society; the election of 1936 brought those issues to the forefront. How to achieve a balance between (a) individuals using capital to create industry while amassing wealth and (b) the government redistributing wealth among the general population through taxes and social programs still fuels political debates today.

FDR versus the Supreme Court

Although FDR was popular, his New Deal reforms were an unheard-of use of presidential power. Never in the history of the nation had a president interacted so directly with the economy or taken the responsibility of job creation so squarely onto the government's shoulders. With questions of constitutionality on the table, the Supreme Court took him to task. By 1937, the Court had declared seven New Deal programs unconstitutional, including the NRA, the AAA, and the Frazier-Lemke Farm Bankruptcy Act.

FDR had grown resentful of the Court and conceived of a scheme wherein he set out to appoint new judges; six of the court's nine members were over seventy and were becoming, Roosevelt argued, slow and "backlogged." Roosevelt proposed the Judicial Procedures Reform Bill (commonly known as the "court-packing plan"), which would allow him to add one additional justice to the court for each member over the age of seventy, for a maximum of fifteen justices. The bill was eventually defeated by Congress, and the plan drew many critics who accused even Roosevelt of having gone too far. Though the court did vote his way on many subsequent pieces of legislation, the court-packing plan showed that even Roosevelt was not infallible.

The Roosevelt Recession

For all its efforts, the New Deal still hadn't fully pulled the nation out of the Depression when Roosevelt began his second term in 1937. Unemployment, though nowhere near its high of almost one-third of the workforce, was still at 15 percent. Roosevelt had begun to move from the "relief" component of New Deal legislation toward more initiatives that supported reform and recovery, pulling back from spending in an effort to balance the budget. The country, however, was not yet ready for a decrease in relief efforts, and in 1937, these policies nudged the economy into temporary recession. In response, Roosevelt began implementing the principles of British economist John Maynard Keynes, who called for the government to use its own spending and taxation policies to supplement temporarily private investment, income, and spending. Keynes had argued that deficit spending—issuing government bonds to well-to-do investors—and then spending the proceeds on unemployment relief and public works construction would stimulate the economy and lift the country out of the Depression. By 1938, the economy had improved and the country was feeling the effects of expanded work-based initiatives like the WPA.

The Second New Deal

Legislation generated during the second half of the decade, referred to as the "Second New Deal," focused on antitrust activity, Keynesian deficit spending, and social reform initiatives. Several initiatives became permanent, such as the Social Security Act of 1935, which granted insurance and pensions to the elderly and the physically disabled. During this period Congress also passed the Reorganization Act of 1939, which created the Executive Office of the President, and the Hatch Act of 1939, which prevented unscrupulous methods in election campaigns. Also notable was the Fair Labor Standards Act of 1938, which established minimum wage and maximum hours standards.

Countdown to War

By the late 1930s things had improved greatly, but the Great Depression still had not fully abated. Unemployment still hovered around 14 percent. The country had been unable to extract itself from the need for regular infusions of government monies into the economy, in the form of relief, social programs, and job creation. Though millions were back at work with the worst years of the crisis behind them, what the country really needed—what it was still lacking—was an increase in consumer purchasing power. What eventually gave the economy its jump-start was its preparation for war. With World War II on the horizon, the demand for weapons, planes, ships, tanks, ammunition, and equipment increased spending, production, and employment. Factories operated around the clock, putting more Americans to work. Employment opportunities grew for women and minorities. The increase in manufacturing expanded existing industries, such as the auto industry, and created entirely new ones, such as the aerospace industry. Borrowing and spending increased. America emerged from the war as a global superpower, leaving, for the most part, the scourge of Depression behind.

Was the New Deal Successful?

This is the billion-dollar question, and it depends on who's answering it. FDR's approach to the Great Depression permanently changed U.S. economic and social policy, the role of government, the acceptable reach of governmental power, interpretation of the constitution, organized labor, political party affiliations, and the standard of living in the United States. Before the New Deal, the economy was left to operate according to natural market forces; since its implementation, the government has taken it upon itself to ensure employment and stabilize prices. On the conservative side, critics have called FDR a socialist, accused him of overreaching the limits of the federal government, of ruining the country's legacy of individual achievement. His works programs were dismissed as wasteful "boondoggling." He was accused of overspending through the expansion of the welfare state—the government providing national relief and wealth-redistribution programs, especially for its worst-off citizens—and of weakening the free enterprise system. Even as the economy bounced back during World War II, critics blamed Roosevelt's antibusiness policies for the recovery not happening *more* quickly.

Roosevelt also stretched the limits of the presidency further than anyone before him. With the country still in economic recovery as it prepared for war, FDR won an unprecedented third term in 1940 and a fourth in 1944, holding office for over twelve years (in 1951, the Twenty-Second Amendment limited all future presidents to two terms).

Roosevelt has also been blamed for not doing *enough*. For all its efforts, the New Deal did not actually end the Great Depression. FDR had continuously adjusted his economic policy, trying to raise prices and increase consumer spending, but he hadn't been able to accomplish it. Further, FDR himself *wanted* to do more. He had envisioned a "third New Deal" that would have guaranteed social housing, Social Security and health insurance, and jobs for all Americans—an end to "want," as he enumerated in his 1941 State of the Union address. That, too, was never achieved. The New Deal has also been criticized, largely in retrospect, for not doing enough for civil rights or minority groups.

While it is true that Roosevelt had not secured full recovery by the time of the recession in 1937–1938, it is also true that government spending, both before and after the recession, created jobs. Although the private sector was slower to recover, government jobs helped make up for the nation's severe unemployment in the meantime. In the short term, recovery efforts put people to work and put food on tables. In the long term, FDR may have saved the capitalist system. Not only was the nation united enough under the New Deal to survive its greatest crisis since the Civil War, but it emerged strong enough to fight in a world war and stand victorious.

In essence, New Deal legislation rewrote the American social contract. FDR's ultimate motive was to make the American way of life more secure. Although complete freedom from want may still—may always—be out of reach, the New Deal brought a new economic security to the United States. Initiatives such as unemployment relief, guarantees of bank deposits, mortgage assistance, infrastructure development, and insurance and pensions for the elderly helped protect Americans from many of the perils of its previously unstable markets. Further, programs like the Social Security Act, the National Labor Relations Act, the FDIC, the FHA, and the USHA became permanent components of U.S. domestic policy, removing some of the economic volatility from American daily life.

Alphabetical List of Entries

Agricultural Adjustment
  Administration 1
American Farm Bureau
  Federation 6
Arnold, Thurman 7
*Ashwander v. Tennessee Valley
  Authority* (1936) 8
Bankhead Cotton Control
  Act of 1934 9
Bankhead-Jones Farm Tenancy
  Act of 1937 10
Banking Act of 1935 11
Banking Crisis 13
Berle, Adolf 15
Black Cabinet 17
Bonus Army 18
Brains Trust 20
Bull Market 21
Business Advisory Council 22
Business Conferences of 1929 23
Caldwell, Erskine 25
Carter v. Carter Coal Company
  (1936) 26
Chandler Act of 1938 27
Citizens' Reconstruction
  Organization 27
Civilian Conservation Corps 28
Civil Works Administration 29
Cohen, Benjamin 30

Committee on Economic
  Security 30
Commodity Credit
  Corporation 31
Corcoran, Thomas 32
Coughlin, Charles Edward 33
Court-Packing Scheme 35
Dewson, Mary 37
Dos Passos, John 38
Dust Bowl and California
  Migration 39
Eccles, Marriner 41
Economy Act of 1933 42
Emergency Railroad
  Transportation Act
  of 1933 42
Emergency Relief and
  Construction Act of 1932 44
Evans, Walker 44
Export-Import Bank 45
Fair Employment Practices
  Committee 47
Fair Labor Standards Act
  of 1938 48
Farm Credit Administration 48
Farm Security
  Administration 49
Federal Anti-Price Discrimination
  Act of 1936 51

Federal Art Project   51
Federal Crop Insurance Act of 1938   52
Federal Dance Project   53
Federal Deposit Insurance Corporation   53
Federal Emergency Relief Administration   54
Federal Farm Bankruptcy Act of 1934   55
Federal Home Loan Bank Act of 1932   56
Federal Housing Administration   57
Federal Music Project   58
Federal Reserve Board   59
Federal Surplus Relief Corporation   60
Federal Theatre Project   61
Federal Works Agency   61
Federal Writers' Project   62
Film   63
Fireside Chats   65
First New Deal   66
First 100 Days   67
Fischer, Irving   68
Food, Drug, and Cosmetic Act of 1938   69
Glass-Steagall Act   71
Gold Standard   73
Hawley-Smoot Tariff of 1930   77
Helvering v. Davis (1937)   78
Henderson, Leon   79
Hickok, Lorena   80
Home Owners' Loan Corporation   81
Hoover, Herbert Clark   82
Hoover Moratorium   84
Hopkins, Harry Lloyd   85
Howe, Louis   86
Investment Company Act of 1940   87
Johnson, Hugh Samuel   89

Jones, Jesse   90
Kerr-Smith Tobacco Control Act of 1934   93
Keynes, John Maynard   93
Lange, Dorothea   95
Lemke, William   96
Lewis, John Llewellyn   97
The Literary Digest   98
Long, Huey P.   98
Lorentz, Pare   100
Morgan, John Pierpont, Jr.   101
Motor Carrier Act of 1935   102
Municipal Bankruptcy Act of 1934   102
National Association for the Advancement of Colored People   105
National Farmers' Union   106
National Housing Act of 1934   106
National Recovery Administration   107
National Resources Planning Board   110
National Youth Administration   110
New Deal   111
Organized Labor   113
Panama Refining Company v. Ryan (1935)   115
Parity   116
Pecora Committee   116
Peek, George Nelson   117
President's Organization on Unemployment Relief   118
Public Utility Holding Company Act of 1935   119
Public Works Administration   121
Radio   123
Railroad Retirement Board et al. v. Alton Railroad Company et al. (1935)   126
Recession of 1937–1938   127

Reciprocal Trade Agreements
   Act of 1934   128
Reconstruction Finance
   Corporation   129
Reno, Milo   131
Reorganization Act of 1939   132
Resettlement Administration   133
Revenue Act of 1932   135
Roosevelt, Anna Eleanor   136
Roosevelt, Franklin Delano   138
Rural Electrification
   Administration   141
*Schechter Poultry Corporation v.
   United States* (1935)   143
Scottsboro Boys   144
Second New Deal   146
Securities Act of 1933   147
Securities and Exchange
   Commission   148
Shahn, Benjamin   149
Shelterbelt Project   150
Silver Purchase Act of 1934   151
Simpson, John A.   152
Socialist Party   153
Social Security Act of 1935   154
Soil Conservation Act
   of 1935   155
Soil Conservation and
   Domestic Allotment Act
   of 1936   156
Southern Tenant Farmers'
   Union   157
Steinbeck, John Ernst   158
Stock Market Crash   159
Taylor Grazing Act of 1934   163
Technocracy   164

Temporary Emergency Relief
   Administration   164
Temporary National Economic
   Committee   165
Tennessee Valley Authority   166
Thomas, Elmer   169
Townsend, Francis Everett   169
Transportation Act of 1940   171
Tugwell, Rexford Guy   172
Unemployed Leagues   175
Unemployment   176
Union Party   177
United States v. Butler (1936)   178
Vann, Robert Lee   181
Wagner, Robert Ferdinand   183
Wagner-Peyser Act of 1933   184
Wagner-Steagall Housing
   Act of 1937   185
Wallace, Henry Agard   186
Walsh-Healey Public Contracts
   Act of 1936   187
Warburg, James   188
Warren, George Frederick   189
Warren Potato Control
   Act of 1935   190
Wealth Tax Act of 1935   190
Weaver, Robert Clifton   192
*West Coast Hotel Co. v.
   Parrish* (1937)   192
White, Walter Francis   193
Williams, Aubrey Willis   194
Willkie, Wendell Lewis   196
Winchell, Walter   197
Woodward, Ellen Sullivan   198
Works Progress
   Administration   199

Topical List of Entries

Agriculture
Agricultural Adjustment Administration
American Farm Bureau Federation
Bankhead Cotton Control Act of 1934
Bankhead-Jones Farm Tenancy Act of 1937
Commodity Credit Corporation
Dust Bowl and California Migration
Farm Credit Administration
Farm Security Administration
Federal Crop Insurance Act of 1938
Federal Farm Bankruptcy Act of 1934
Kerr-Smith Tobacco Control Act of 1934
National Farmers' Union
Parity
Peek, George Nelson
Reno, Milo
Resettlement Administration
Simpson, John A.
Soil Conservation and Domestic Allotment Act of 1936
Southern Tenant Farmers' Union
United States v. Butler (1936)
Wallace, Henry Agard
Warren, George Frederick
Warren Potato Control Act of 1935

Arts and Culture
Caldwell, Erskine
Dos Passos, John
Evans, Walker
Federal Art Project
Federal Dance Project
Federal Music Project
Federal Theatre Project
Federal Writers' Project
Film
Lange, Dorothea
The Literary Digest
Lorentz, Pare
Shahn, Benjamin
Steinbeck, John Ernst

Banking and Economics
Arnold, Thurman
Banking Act of 1935
Banking Crisis
Berle, Adolf

Bull Market
Chandler Act of 1938
Citizens' Reconstruction Organization
Commodity Credit Corporation
Eccles, Marriner
Economy Act of 1933
Export-Import Bank
Federal Deposit Insurance Corporation
Federal Home Loan Bank Act of 1932
Federal Housing Administration
Federal Reserve Board
Fischer, Irving
Glass-Steagall Act
Gold Standard
Hawley-Smoot Tariff of 1930
Home Owners' Loan Corporation
Hoover Moratorium
Investment Company Act of 1940
Jones, Jesse
Keynes, John Maynard
Morgan, John Pierpont, Jr.
Municipal Bankruptcy Act of 1934
National Housing Act of 1934
Pecora Committee
Public Utility Holding Company Act of 1935
Recession of 1937–1938
Reconstruction Finance Corporation
Revenue Act of 1932
Securities Act of 1933
Securities and Exchange Commission
Silver Purchase Act of 1934
Stock Market Crash
Temporary National Economic Committee
Thomas, Elmer
Tugwell, Rexford Guy
Warburg, James
Warren, George Frederick
Wealth Tax Act of 1935

Business and Industry

Ashwander v. Tennessee Valley Authority (1936)
Business Advisory Council
Business Conferences of 1929
Carter v. Carter Coal Company (1936)
Emergency Railroad Transportation Act of 1933
Federal Anti-Price Discrimination Act of 1936
Food, Drug, and Cosmetic Act of 1938
Hawley-Smoot Tariff of 1930
Investment Company Act of 1940
Motor Carrier Act of 1935
National Resources Planning Board
Panama Refining Company v. Ryan (1935)
Public Utility Holding Company Act of 1935
Railroad Retirement Board et al. v. Alton Railroad Company et al. (1935)
Reciprocal Trade Agreements Act of 1934
Rural Electrification Administration
Schechter Poultry Corporation v. United States (1935)
Tennessee Valley Authority
Transportation Act of 1940

Communication and Media

Coughlin, Charles Edward
Fireside Chats
Radio

Topical List of Entries | xxxi

Vann, Robert Lee
Winchell, Walter

Environment
Ashwander v. Tennessee Valley Authority (1936)
Civilian Conservation Corps
Resettlement Administration
Shelterbelt Project
Soil Conservation Act of 1935
Soil Conservation and Domestic Allotment Act of 1936
Taylor Grazing Act of 1934
Tennessee Valley Authority

Government Programs
Agricultural Adjustment Administration
Citizens' Reconstruction Organization
Civilian Conservation Corps
Civil Works Administration
Committee on Economic Security
Emergency Relief and Construction Act of 1932
Farm Security Administration
Federal Art Project
Federal Dance Project
Federal Emergency Relief Administration
Federal Housing Administration
Federal Music Project
Federal Surplus Relief Corporation
Federal Theatre Project
Federal Works Agency
Federal Writers' Project
First New Deal
First 100 Days
Helvering v. Davis (1937)
Hickok, Lorena
Hopkins, Harry Lloyd
Johnson, Hugh Samuel
Jones, Jesse
National Recovery Administration
National Youth Administration
New Deal
President's Organization on Unemployment Relief
Public Works Administration
Reorganization Act of 1939
Resettlement Administration
Second New Deal
Social Security Act of 1935
Temporary Emergency Relief Administration
Tennessee Valley Authority
Wagner-Peyser Act of 1933
Wagner-Steagall Housing Act of 1937
Woodward, Ellen Sullivan
Works Progress Administration

Organized Labor and Protest
American Farm Bureau Federation
Bonus Army
Lewis, John Llewellyn
National Farmers' Union
National Recovery Administration
Organized Labor
Reno, Milo
Simpson, John A.
Southern Tenant Farmers' Union

Politics
Black Cabinet
Brains Trust
Cohen, Benjamin
Corcoran, Thomas
Coughlin, Charles Edward
Court-Packing Scheme
Dewson, Mary
First 100 Days

Henderson, Leon
Hickok, Lorena
Hoover, Herbert Clark
Howe, Louis
Lemke, William
The Literary Digest
Long, Huey P.
Reorganization Act of 1939
Roosevelt, Anna Eleanor
Roosevelt, Franklin Delano
Second New Deal
Socialist Party
Technocracy
Townsend, Francis Everett
Unemployed Leagues
Union Party
Wagner, Robert Ferdinand
Weaver, Robert Clifton
Williams, Aubrey Willis
Willkie, Wendell Lewis
Woodward, Ellen Sullivan

Race Relations

Black Cabinet
Fair Employment Practices
    Committee
National Association for the
    Advancement of Colored
    People
Scottsboro Boys

Vann, Robert Lee
Weaver, Robert Clifton
White, Walter Francis
Williams, Aubrey Willis

Work

Civilian Conservation Corps
Civil Works Administration
Fair Employment Practices
    Committee
Fair Labor Standards Act of 1938
Federal Art Project
Federal Dance Project
Federal Music Project
Federal Theatre Project
Federal Works Agency
Federal Writers' Project
National Recovery Administration
National Youth Administration
Organized Labor
President's Organization on
    Unemployment Relief
Public Works Administration
Unemployment
Wagner-Peyser Act of 1933
Walsh-Healey Public Contracts
    Act of 1936
West Coast Hotel Co. v. Parrish
    (1937)
Works Progress Administration

List of Primary Documents

Rugged Individualism
Herbert Hoover's "Principles and Ideals of the United States Government,"
October 22, 1928

Muscle Shoals Veto Message
Herbert Hoover's Veto of the Muscle Shoals Resolution
March 3, 1931

Protest at the Bank of the United States
Image of a Bank Run
1931

The Philosophy of Government
Franklin D. Roosevelt's Speech to the Commonwealth Club of San Francisco
September 23, 1932

The Banking Crisis
Franklin D. Roosevelt's First Fireside Chat
March 12, 1933

Helping the American Farmer
Agricultural Adjustment Act
May 12, 1933

"The Teacher Faces the Depression"
Eunice Langdon, *Nation Magazine*
August 16, 1933

Legacy of the New Deal
The Social Security Act
August 14, 1935

WPA Workers in Alabama
Image of Honest Work Done through the Works Progress Administration
June 2, 1936

Moving toward Racial Equality
Executive Order 8802
June 25, 1941

A

Agricultural Adjustment Administration

Throughout the 1920s, a severe depression afflicted American agriculture. During World War I, to take advantage of high European demand for American commodities, farmers had gone deep into debt and expanded production. Enticed by unusually high prices, American farmers bought land and modern equipment and invested the capital necessary to make marginal land more productive. In the early years of the twentieth century, production boomed and farmers enjoyed an unprecedented era of prosperity. Although farmers had heavy debt burdens, income and cash flow were strong because of high commodity prices. They had little difficulty making debt payments.

But with the armistice in November 1918, European farmers went back into production. They planted their fields in the spring of 1919 and harvested them in the summer. By the fall of 1919, with so much new production on line around the world, overproduction had become a serious problem in American agriculture. Commodity prices began to fall, and American farmers sustained serious losses in income. Bankruptcy and foreclosures became all too common. Politicians and farm leaders came up with a variety of solutions—marketing cooperatives, foreign dumping of surpluses, and government-backed commodity storage programs—but nothing seemed to work. Discontent in rural America reached epidemic proportions.

A variety of solutions were proposed. In the McNary-Haugen Bill, which Congress passed twice and President Calvin Coolidge vetoed twice, the federal government would have purchased farm surpluses at domestic market prices and then sold them on the world market, with any losses being made up by a tax on farmers and consumers. Other proposals included federal assistance in establishing farm marketing cooperatives to assist farmers in selling products in a timely manner and shipping them at cheap, bulk prices. But nothing seemed to work. As commodity prices steadily declined during the 1920s, farmers simply produced more to generate the income necessary to cover their fixed costs, and the result was greater surpluses and lower prices.

This 1936 political cartoon depicts Chief Justice Charles Evans Hughes kicking the Agricultural Adjustment Administration (symbolized here by a Christmas tree) into pieces. The cartoon refers to the Supreme Court decision that declared the Agricultural Adjustment Act of 1933 unconstitutional. (Library of Congress)

In 1929, a new proposal began gaining converts. John Black, an economics professor at Harvard, wrote the book *Agricultural Reform in the United States*, which argued in favor of government-directed acreage reductions that would reduce crop surpluses and increase commodity prices. In other words, the federal government would pay farmers to reduce production, which would, Black claimed, lead to higher commodity prices. Black's ideas were first implemented by the secretary of agriculture, **Henry Wallace**, when Congress passed the Agricultural Adjustment Act (AAA) of 1933, which became the heart and soul of **New Deal** agricultural policy.

The AAA's long-range goal was to achieve **parity** for farmers—an economic equilibrium between the prices received for farm commodities and the prices paid for manufactured goods equivalent to the balance that had existed in the period of agricultural prosperity prior to 1914. Under the AAA, Henry Wallace, the secretary of agriculture, would negotiate "marketing agreements" in which individual farmers agreed to reduce production. The legislation defined wheat, cotton, hogs, corn, rice, tobacco, milk and others as "basic commodities" subject to the law. Parity would be achieved, New Dealers hoped, by raising the prices of basic commodities. The entire program would be financed by federal taxes on middlemen and food and fiber processors.

The Emergency Farm Mortgage Act, an amendment to the AAA, also reduced the frequency of farm foreclosures, authorizing Federal Land Banks to issue up to $2 billion in 4 percent, tax-exempt bonds guaranteed by the federal government. Proceeds from the bond sales would be used to refinance the mortgages.

The AAA was barely under way when it became embroiled in controversy. Cotton had been planted during the debates over the law, and sows had farrowed, which meant the legislation would have no impact on 1933 prices. Huge surpluses were anticipated in those commodities, so the AAA ordered the slaughter of 6 million little pigs and 200,000 sows and the plowing under of approximately 10 million acres of cotton. Although the decision made economic sense, given the AAA's objectives, it brought about a storm of protest. Since so many Americans were out of work and having trouble buying food and clothing, the destruction of those commodities gave Republican conservatives potent ammunition to criticize the **Roosevelt** administration.

The plight of poor sharecroppers and tenant farmers in the South also produced criticism. In the South, approximately 725,000 farms were managed by sharecroppers and tenant farmers who did not own the land. When landlords signed the marketing agreements, tens of thousands of tenant and sharecropping families were thrown off the land. The people who really benefited from the AAA checks were well-to-do landlords, not small, needy farmers.

The AAA also found itself the object of criticism from such farm groups as the National Farmers' Union and the National Farmers' Holiday Association, both of which represented the interests of small farmers. They were convinced that the AAA was actually a tool of the American Farm Bureau Federation, which represented large commercial farmers likely to reap the most from AAA policies. They accused the AAA of ignoring the needs of millions of small farmers. When AAA acreage reductions led to the layoffs of migrant farm laborers and sharecroppers, many of those criticisms gained credibility.

In spite of the criticism, the AAA aggressively recruited participating farmers, and by early 1934, more than 3 million farmers had signed the marketing agreements. With the Depression worsening in 1933, tens of thousands of farmers kept their economic heads above water in 1934 only because of the AAA checks they received. The AAA program then expanded in 1934 when the Jones-Connally Farm Relief Act made cattle a basic commodity; appropriated $200 million to assist ranchers in cutting production in order to raise beef prices; provided funds for the elimination of brucellosis among cattle; and awarded basic commodity status to barley, rye, peanuts, flax, and grain sorghum. That same year, The Jones-Costigan Sugar Act also defined sugarcane and sugar beets as basic commodities, and allowed for benefit payments to be paid from a processing tax on sugar.

But the AAA also encountered problems implementing the program because the farm economy remained plagued by huge surpluses. Farmers would often sign their marketing agreements, accept the government checks, and then try to squirm around the production limits of their contracts. Congress decided to tighten the program through more regulation. The **Bankhead Cotton Control Act of 1934** gave cotton farmers tax-exempt certificates for their contracted crop, with the total of all the tax-exempt certificates equaling a national crop quota of 10 million 500-pound bales. Stiff taxes were imposed on ginned cotton in excess of the quota. Subsequent legislation, such as the **Kerr-Smith Tobacco Control Act of 1934** and the **Warren Potato Control Act of 1935**, extended such regulations to other commodities.

Although conservative critics lambasted the AAA, calling it "**socialistic agriculture**," its greatest challenge came in the federal courts, where its constitutionality was questioned. The food and fiber processors claimed that the taxes they had to pay were unconstitutional. William Butler and several associates had purchased the bankrupt Hoosac Mills Corporation, and they refused to pay the AAA processing taxes on cotton. The federal government sued for recovery of the taxes, and the case of *United States v. Butler* went all the way to the Supreme Court. On January 6, 1936, the U.S. Supreme Court rendered its decision, declaring the AAA an unconstitutional violation of the Tenth Amendment to the Constitution. Farm problems, the Court ordered, were essentially state and local, not national, issues, and therefore the federal government had no jurisdiction; the AAA violated the Tenth Amendment to the Constitution. The Court also claimed that the AAA's voluntary marketing agreements were not voluntary at all and involved considerable coercion of farmers.

In the wake of the decision, farm production skyrocketed. In 1936 American farmers produced more than 18 million bales of cotton, and cotton prices fell. Similar gains occurred in wheat, corn, rice, and tobacco production. The Roosevelt administration responded almost immediately, and on February 29, 1936, Congress passed the **Soil Conservation and Domestic Allotment Act**, which allowed for government payments to farmers who would agree to practice soil conservation by taking acreage out of production. Participating farmers would lease the land not in production to the AAA, which would then make rent payments to them. It was, of course, little more than legal maneuvering to work around the Supreme Court's constitutional objections. Even then the program did not work well. In 1936, the nation's cotton crop exceeded 18 million bales, a record bumper crop, and cotton prices collapsed. Wheat, corn, and tobacco production was also up and prices similarly down.

In 1938, Congress passed a new Agricultural Adjustment Act, which eliminated all of the processing taxes and funded the program through general revenues. The new law allowed the AAA to establish compulsory production quotas once two-thirds of farmers raising a particular commodity had agreed to participate. Finally, the legislation allowed the **Commodity Credit Corporation** to make loans on surplus crops at prices just below parity levels and to allow farmers to store the crops at government expense until market prices hit or exceeded parity levels. The law also established the Federal Crop Insurance Corporation.

In 1939, the case of *Mulford v. Smith* posed a direct challenge to the Agricultural Adjustment Act of 1938. In the decision, the Supreme Court upheld the Agricultural Adjustment Act of 1938 and admitted that its 1936 decision in *United States v. Butler* had been a mistake. The Court readily admitted that the agricultural crisis was national in scope, well beyond the ability of state legislatures to solve, and that therefore Congress did enjoy jurisdiction.

Despite numerous pieces of legislation, the AAA never really solved the problem of commodity surpluses. Not until the outbreak of World War II, and the consequent huge increases in demand for food and fiber, did the surpluses disappear and commodity prices rise.

See also: Bankhead Cotton Control Act of 1934; Kerr-Smith Tobacco Control Act of 1934; Parity; Soil Conservation and Domestic Allotment Act of 1936; Warren Potato Control Act of 1935

Further Reading

Evans, Walker and James Agee. 2001 *Let Us Now Praise Famous Men: The American Classic, in Words and Photographs, of Three Tenant Families in the Deep*

South, New York: Mariner; Gilbert, Jess, 2015. *Planning Democracy: Agrarian Intellectuals and the Intended New Deal*, New Haven, CT: Yale University Press; White, Ann Folino. 2014. *Plowed Under: Food Policy Protests and Performance in New Deal America*, Bloomington: Indiana University Press; Woolley, John and Gerhard Peters. "FDR's Message to Congress on the Agricultural Adjustment Act, March 16, 1933," The American Presidency Project, http://www.presidency.ucsb.edu/ws/index.php?pid=14585&st=agricultural+adjustment+act.&st1=. Accessed September 1, 2016.

American Farm Bureau Federation

During the years of the Great Depression, the American Farm Bureau Federation (AFBF) became one of the strongest lobbies in the United States. Ever since the late nineteenth century, American agriculture had been plagued by the problem of chronic overproduction, which drove commodity prices down and sent millions of small farmers into bankruptcy. Farm advocates had promoted a series of ideas to raise prices, but none seemed to work. During the 1920s, the problem of overproduction became especially severe and the crisis on the farms especially acute.

The AFBF had its beginnings in 1911 when its first county bureau was opened, and in 1915, the first state federation of county bureau offices was organized. Other state federations soon appeared. At first, the local bureaus simply worked at disseminating new scientific information about farming, but when the Smith-Lever Act of 1914 created the Federal-State Agricultural Extension Service, with county agricultural extension agents, the AFBF offices found themselves working in close cooperation with the agents. In 1919, the formal organization of the American Farm Bureau Federation united all of the state federations.

By 1929, when the country slipped into the Great Depression, the AFBF had a membership of 163,000 people. But Americans suffering in rural areas were desperate for help, and many joined the AFBF because of its commitment to **parity**—having the federal government guarantee that farmer purchasing power would be restored to its 1909–1914 levels. Large commercial farmers became especially influential in the AFBF. In order to achieve this, the AFBF backed the voluntary domestic allotment program, in which farmers would be paid to reduce their production. During the 1930s the AFBF supported all federal programs designed to achieve parity through voluntary production controls, including the Agricultural Adjustment Act of 1933, the **Soil Conservation and Domestic Allotment Act of 1936**, and the Agricultural Adjustment Act of 1938. When World War II broke out in 1940, AFBF membership exceeded 1 million people.

See also: Organized Labor; Parity

Further Reading
Truelsen, Stewart R. 2009. *Forward Farm Bureau: Ninety Year History of the American Farm Bureau Federation*, Washington, DC: American Farm Bureau Federation; Voice of Agriculture. "Farm Bureau: Historical Highlights, 1919–1994," American Farm Bureau Federation, http://www.fb.org/about/history/. Accessed September 1, 2016; Voice of Agriculture, *Our History, Our Time: A Documentary on the History of American Farming and the American Farm Bureau from 1919 to the Present*, video, 22:05 min., American Farm Bureau Federation, http://fbvideos.org/about-us/our-history-our-time/2212092510001. Accessed September 1, 2016.

Arnold, Thurman

Although Thurman Arnold was relatively unknown outside government legal experts and academics, he wielded tremendous influence over public policy during the 1930s. As a member of the law faculty at Yale, he wrote *The Symbols of Government* (1935) and *The Folklore of Capitalism* (1937), both of which analyzed the influence of large corporations on the economy and the relationship between large business enterprises and the federal government. Arnold became convinced that mere size did not constitute a relevant issue in considering antitrust action. He instead wanted to apply the "rule of reason," which had been at the core of Theodore Roosevelt's New Nationalism and part of the later Woodrow Wilson administration, in dealing with potential and real restraints of trade. His books were well received in academic circles, giving Arnold a national legal reputation.

In 1938 Arnold left Yale to head up the Justice Department's antitrust division. In spite of his belief in the rule of reason and the need to discriminate between large corporations that behaved irresponsibly and those that competed with integrity, Arnold proved to be indefatigable in filing antitrust lawsuits. During his tenure at the Justice Department (1938–1943), he filed 230 antitrust suits and made liberal use of consent decrees, national investigations, and careful evaluations of prospective cases. In 1943 Arnold was appointed to the Court of Appeals for the District of Columbia, a post he held for two years. Arnold then began practicing law privately in Washington, D.C. He died on November 7, 1969.

Further Reading
Waller, Spencer Webber. 2005. *Thurman Arnold: A Biography*, New York: NYU Press.

Ashwander v. Tennessee Valley Authority (1936)

During the years of the Great Depression, Americans found themselves in the midst of a ferocious debate over the Constitution and the reach of the federal government.

The Supreme Court, tradition bound and dominated by conservative justices, was not prepared for the **New Deal** and its unprecedented expansion in the powers of Congress and the executive branch. One of the Court's most important decisions came in *Ashwander v. Tennessee Valley Authority*. The case was argued on December 1935 and decided on February 17, 1936.

Minority shareholders in a southern utility contested the company's decision to purchase electricity from the Tennessee Valley Authority (TVA), a large federal bureaucracy created by Congress in 1933 to provide hydroelectric power, flood control, and irrigation throughout the Tennessee River Valley. Many private utility companies resented the competition provided by TVA because they feared it would impose downward pressure on electricity rates. The minority stockholders argued that TVA was an unconstitutional expansion of governmental power.

In the end, the Court upheld the constitutionality of the Tennessee Valley Authority. Since the case was an internal matter within a company, it did not possess an adversarial context, nor had anybody been injured. As a result, the justices declined to interfere in the case. In their decision not to interfere, the Supreme Court helped legitimize a new role for the federal government in national economic affairs.

See also: Tennessee Valley Authority

Further Reading

Leuchtenburg, William E. 1995. *The Supreme Court Reborn: Constitutional Revolution in the Age of Roosevelt*, Oxford: Oxford University Press; Manganiello, Christopher J. 2015. *Southern Water, Southern Power: How the Politics of Cheap Energy and Water Scarcity Shaped a Region*, Chapel Hill: University of North Carolina Press.

B

Bankhead Cotton Control Act of 1934

Congress passed the Bankhead Cotton Control Act on April 21, 1934, to promote farmer participation in the **Agricultural Adjustment Administration**'s (AAA) programs, which were designed to reduce cotton production in the United States so that prices would rise and give farmers a living wage. Ever since the early 1920s, cotton prices had fluctuated widely on world markets, but the long-term trend was steadily lower, just as the long-term production trend had been higher and higher.

At first, the AAA required farmers to sign contracts agreeing to plow under from 25 to 50 percent of their 1933 crops. In return, the AAA would pay them in cash. In 1934–1935, a new series of contracts required farmers to plant only 45 to 55 percent of their usual acreage. The AAA cotton program, however, was voluntary, and many did not sign up; many of those who did sign up did not comply with their contracted acreage reductions, planting large crops anyway. Cotton production continued to climb, in spite of the AAA cotton program, and prices remained too low.

The Bankhead Cotton Control Act was designed to address the problems of enforcing AAA contracts and inducing more farmers into the program. Under the Bankhead law, individual farmers received tax-exempt certificates for their contracted crop. The total of all tax-exempt certificates would equal the predetermined crop quota of 10 million 500-pound bales. Such a total crop, the AAA had determined, would help raise cotton prices. A tax would be levied on "the ginning of cotton equal to 50 percent of the average price of the standard grade on the 10 principal spot markets, but not under 5 cents per pound." In doing so, the tax penalized any cotton ginned in excess of an individual farmer's allotment. It proved more successful in imposing limits on cotton production. When the Supreme Court declared the Agricultural Adjustment Act unconstitutional, the Bankhead Cotton Control Act had to be repealed, which Congress did on February 10, 1936.

See also: Agricultural Adjustment Administration

Further Reading

Gilbert, Jess. 2015. *Planning Democracy: Agrarian Intellectuals and the Intended New Deal*, New Haven, CT: Yale University Press; Volanto, Keith J. 2004. *Texas, Cotton, and the New Deal* (Sam Rayburn Series on Rural Life), College Station: Texas A&M University Press.

Bankhead-Jones Farm Tenancy Act of 1937

During the 1920s, the problems in the farm economy became acute. To finance acreage and production expansions during the World War I years, farmers went heavily into debt, and they put their farms up as collateral for the loans. Increasing numbers of farmers lost their land when they failed to make mortgage payments, and increasingly large numbers of American farms were run by tenants. Also contributing to the rise of farm tenancy were the high capital requirements needed to survive economically, especially in purchases of heavy equipment. By 1935, a total of 42 percent of American farms were operated by tenants. The cotton economy of the South was the region where farm tenancy increased the most dramatically.

To address the problem of farm tenancy, President **Franklin D. Roosevelt** in November 1935 established a Special Committee on Farm Tenancy. He also asked Senator John Bankhead of Alabama and Congressman Marvin Jones of Texas to begin work on federal legislation to ameliorate the suffering of farm tenants. Jones felt that the key to the problem involved the availability of credit. If local communities could use government funds to purchase available land, they could then resell the land at low interest rates to the tenants working the land. Jones's ideas became the Bankhead-Jones Farm Tenancy Act of 1937. The legislation authorized such rehabilitation loans, which tenants could also use for education and operating expenses, and appropriated $50 million for conservation programs on marginal lands. The Bankhead-Jones Farm Tenancy Act also established the **Farm Security Administration** to administer the legislation. The long-term consequences of the Bankhead-Jones Farm Tenancy Act were modest but real. Between 1937 and 1947, the Farm Security Administration made loans of $293 million to 47,104 farmers.

See also: Farm Security Administration

Further Reading

Gilbert, Jess. 2015. *Planning Democracy: Agrarian Intellectuals and the Intended New Deal*, New Haven, CT: Yale University Press; Grubbs, Donald H. 2000. *Cry from the Cotton: The Southern Tenant Farmers' Union and the New Deal*, Fayetteville: University of Arkansas Press.

Banking Act of 1933. *See* Glass-Steagall Act

Banking Act of 1935

By late 1934, a number of financial challenges faced the American banking system. First, the Banking Act of 1933 had required the officers of all national banks, by July 1, 1935, to divest themselves of all loans extended to them by their own banks. The logic, of course, was to make sure that bank officers made decisions consistent with the interests of all of their depositors and creditors and not just for their own individual interests. Many bank officers, however, felt that the July 1, 1935, deadline was approaching too quickly and that they would need more time to complete the divestiture. They wanted the federal government to give them a time extension. Second, the **Federal Deposit Insurance Corporation** (FDIC), also authorized by the Banking Act of 1933, was set to begin operation on January 1, 1935, but many bankers who wanted to participate in FDIC insurance felt that its proposed charges, or dues, were exorbitant and wanted them reduced. Finally, **Marriner Eccles**, newly appointed head of the **Federal Reserve Board** in Washington, D.C., felt that existing federal law relating to the Federal Reserve System was outdated and rendered the Federal Reserve Board largely ineffective in dealing with the Great Depression. Eccles was an early convert to the fiscal policy ideas of English economist **John Maynard Keynes**, who believed that the federal government, through its taxation and spending policies, could play a key role in stimulating the economy. Eccles wanted to shift the base of power in the Federal Reserve System from the regional Federal Reserve Banks to the Federal Reserve Board in Washington, D.C. In a national economy, the idea of twelve regional banks pursuing contradictory monetary policies seemed ludicrous to Eccles. He wanted the Federal Reserve Banks raising or lowering interest unitedly or engaging in the same open market operations, buying or selling government securities on the open market, at the same time and in the same volumes. Only then could the Federal Reserve System truly engage in national economic policymaking.

President **Franklin D. Roosevelt** and his economic staff put together an omnibus bill that addressed all these concerns. He realized that private commercial bankers would resist the centralization of Federal Reserve powers, but he suspected that he could get them to swallow the proposal in return for reducing FDIC membership charges and giving national bank officers a time extension in divesting themselves of loans for their own banks. The legislation made its way through the House and the Senate and then through a conference committee in the summer of 1935, and on August 23, 1935, President Roosevelt signed the legislation into law.

The Banking Act of 1935 was divided into three separate titles. Title I pleased private commercial bankers by substantially reducing annual membership fees in the **Federal Deposit Insurance Corporation** and allowed the FDIC to begin formal operations as scheduled. Title II implemented many of Eccles's proposals. It dismantled the Federal Reserve Board and replaced it with a board of governors of the Federal Reserve System. The board would consist of seven members, each appointed by the president and confirmed by the U.S. Senate. The first appointments to the board were for terms ranging from two to fourteen years, so that board members would be rotated off on a steady schedule and the board would be more able to maintain policy continuity. At each regional Federal Reserve Bank, the office of governor was replaced by a president who served a five-year term. Each president was selected by the board of directors of the regional bank. The president's nomination had to be confirmed by the board of governors in Washington, D.C. Title II scrapped the old Federal Open Market Committee, which had consisted of the twelve governors of the regional Federal Reserve Banks, and replaced it with a new Federal Open Market Committee that was composed of the board of governors of the Federal Reserve System and five presidents from the regional Federal Reserve Banks. The legislation gave complete control of open market operations to the new Federal Open Market Committee. Finally, Title II liberalized Federal Reserve discount policies by allowing local Federal Reserve Banks, with the permission of the board of governors, to advance cash to local commercial banks on a broader range of collateral. Title III of the Banking Act of 1935 extended the deadline for national bank officers to refinance loans from their own banks with loans from other national banks.

Historians look back on the Banking Act of 1935 as a turning point in U.S. financial and economic history. The Federal Reserve System now had dramatically increased powers for controlling the flow of credit to banks, businesses, and consumers, and it had at its head a man—Marriner Eccles—who was a confirmed Keynesian. For the first time in U.S. history, commercial banks had become part of a coordinated banking system. Since the Banking Act of 1935, the federal government has played a key role in the functioning of the money markets.

See also: Federal Deposit Insurance Corporation; Federal Reserve Board

Further Reading

Bagehot, Alexander. "Episode 1: Show No Signs of Panic," The Bankster Podcast, April 18, 2016, http://www.thebanksterpodcast.com/home/2016/4/18/episode-1-show-no-signs-of-panic. Accessed September 1, 2016; Bagehot, Alexander. "Episode 3: The Committee, Part I," The Bankster Podcast, May 6, 2016, http://www.thebanksterpodcast.com/home/2016/5/6/episode-3-the-committee-part-i. Accessed September 1, 2016; Ganzel, Bill. 2003. "New Financial Laws," Ganzel Group, http://www.livinghistoryfarm.org/farminginthe30s/money_15.html. Accessed September 1, 2016; Meltzer, Allan H. 2004. *A History of the Federal Reserve, Volume 1: 1913–1951*, Chicago: University of Chicago Press; Richardson, Gary, Alejandro Komai, and Michael Gou. 2013. "Banking Act of 1935: August 23, 1935," Federal Reserve History, http://www.federalreservehistory.org/Events/DetailView/26. Accessed September 1, 2016.

Banking Crisis

During the Great Depression, the money markets constituted the weakest sector of the economy, and within the money markets, the banking system was the most fragile. During the 1920s, a catastrophe had stricken the money markets. At the beginning of the decade, there were more than 30,000 commercial banks as well as thousands of savings banks, building and loan associations, investment companies, private banks, industrial banks, credit unions, and finance companies, for a total of more than 50,000 financial institutions. Most of the banks were undercapitalized, and in rural areas, there were simply too many banks and not enough business. It was not unusual for a community with only 500 people to be served by two banks, neither one of which could produce sufficient profits. To put it simply, America was badly overbanked.

Rural banks also suffered from the decline of the farm economy. Overproduction and low commodity prices had long plagued American agriculture, and during the 1920s, both problems intensified. Many rural banks had loaned heavily to expand agricultural production during World War I, and bankruptcies increased during the 1920s. When banks had to foreclose on bankrupt property, they lost assets, and the number of bank failures increased. Between 1921 and 1929, more than 5,400 rural banks went out of business in the United States. Another 4,100 had to merge with other banks in order to survive.

The **stock market crash** of 1929 then sent banks into a tailspin. Those banks that had invested in or loaned heavily to brokers to buy stocks discovered that their assets were badly eroded, and a tidal wave of panic-stricken depositors showed up demanding their cash. When bankers had to liquidate assets to generate the cash, stock prices fell further, only making matters worse. In 1929, 641 American banks closed their doors, and in 1930, the number jumped to 1,350. In 1931 a total of 1,700 banks went belly up. Bad agricultural loans, collapsing stock values, and defaults on business loans had made life all but impossible for bankers.

Dealing with the banking crisis became a preoccupation of the **Hoover** administration. In 1932 Congress passed and President Hoover signed legislation creating the **Reconstruction Finance Corporation** (RFC) to loan money to troubled banks, but loans proved insufficient. During the last weeks of February 1933, as the Hoover administration was winding down and **Franklin D. Roosevelt** was preparing to take the oath of office as president, the banking system collapsed. With 95 percent of the nation's banks threatening to shut down amid a huge wave of panic-stricken depositors, President Herbert Hoover and his advisers considered a banking holiday, but they could get little cooperation from the incoming **New Deal**ers and decided not to act. On March 6, 1933, President Franklin D. Roosevelt signed a proclamation declaring a moratorium on all banking operations in the United States. This was perhaps the most dramatic economic and political event of the Great Depression. The proclamation was later confirmed by the Emergency Banking Act, which Congress passed on March 9.

Congress and the general public were desperate for action, and the Emergency Banking Act passed within a matter of hours. Title I of the law legalized Roosevelt's extraordinary action of declaring a bank holiday. Title II authorized the office of the comptroller of the currency to name a conservator to subordinate certain depositor and stockholder interests so that those banks could then be legally reorganized. Title III permitted the RFC to invest in the preferred stock or capital notes of banks and trust companies. Such a provision, the administration believed, would provide banks with long-term capital and relieve them of short-term debt repayments to the RFC. Title IV permitted the Federal Reserve Banks to discount previously ineligible assets and to issue new Federal Reserve notes on the basis of those assets as a means of ending the currency shortages in certain regions of the country. Title V provided $2 million to implement the legislation. The Emergency Banking Act then provided the legal initiative for the reconstruction of the banking system during the rest of the decade.

Although the Roosevelt administration had only the vaguest notions of what to do about the crisis, they did know that when the holiday ended, only sound banks should reopen. Even a few failures could trigger another panic and liquidity crisis. The administration decided to make sure that each reopened bank was safe and secure and to inform the public of its safety. Bank examiners from the RFC, the Treasury Department, the comptroller of the currency, and the Federal Reserve System launched a crash program to examine the basic solvency of every national bank in the country. Healthy banks were licensed to reopen. Weaker banks could receive investment capital and loans from the RFC and then reopen. The weakest banks were not allowed to reopen at all but were forced into bankruptcy or into consolidation with stronger institutions. State banking officials used similar procedures to examine state banks.

On March 14, 1933, the night before the first banks were to reopen, President Roosevelt addressed the nation by **radio** in what was labeled a "fireside chat." He explained that Americans could rest assured that the banks reopening the next day were safe and could be trusted and that money deposited in any of those reopened banks would be safe. On March 15, 1933, federal and state officials allowed 12,756 banks to reopen, compared to the 18,390 banks in operation before the holiday. The bank holiday was a success, and the crisis eased. With investment capital instead of loans, bankers had time to deal with depositors and did not have to engage in panic sales of stocks or loan calls that so damaged the money markets. Throughout the rest of the 1930s, the annual number of bank failures registered in dozens, not the hundreds or thousands as before.

See also: Fireside Chats; Stock Market Crash

Further Reading

Kennedy, Susan Estabrook. 2014. *The Banking Crisis of 1933*, reprint ed., Lexington: University Press of Kentucky; Kiewe, Amos. 2007. *FDR's First Fireside Chat: Public Confidence and the Banking Crisis* (Library of Presidential Rhetoric), College Station: Texas A&M University Press; Lumley, Darwyn H. 2009. *Breaking the Banks in Motor City: The Auto Industry, the 1933 Detroit Banking Crisis, and the Start of the New Deal*, Jefferson, NC: McFarland; Richardson, Gary. 2013. "Banking Panics of 1930 and 1931: November 1930–August 1931," Federal Reserve History, http://www.federalreservehistory.org/Events/Detail View/20. Accessed September 1, 2016.

Berle, Adolf

Adolf Augustus Berle was one of the least well-known but most influential Americans during the Great Depression.

During the 1920s, he carefully studied the operation of the economy and began writing about it. In 1932, with his coauthor Gardiner Means, Berle published *The Modern Corporation and Private Property*, which many economists credit as being one of the most influential books of the 1930s. In the book, Means and Berle described an economy in which the 200 largest corporations were becoming increasingly influential as more and more economic power became concentrated in them. At the same time, these corporations were becoming increasingly divorced from stockholder or public control. The onset of the Great Depression made *The Modern Corporation* influential especially among economists and public policymakers because much of America was holding the large corporations responsible for the economic debacle. When **Franklin D. Roosevelt** and the Democrats took control of Congress and the White House in 1932, Berle's star in America rose commensurately. He served as a member of Roosevelt's so-called **Brains Trust**, which had great influence on early **New Deal** policies, and Berle wrote FDR's Commonwealth Club speech, which set out a progressive, activist agenda for the New Deal.

Except for a brief role with the **Reconstruction Finance Corporation** in 1933, Berle never held an official position in Washington, D.C. He remained in New York City and at Columbia University. Between 1934 and 1937, Berle served as chamberlain of New York City under Mayor Fiorello La Guardia. He also played a key role in 1934–1935 formulating the plan to refinance New York City's bonded indebtedness to stave off bankruptcy. Throughout the 1930s, Berle kept up a chatty but intellectual correspondence with President Franklin D. Roosevelt, always beginning his letters with "Dear Caesar." In 1938, Roosevelt finally brought him to Washington, D.C., as an assistant secretary of state, but the president primarily used him as an adviser concerning the federal government's approach to the recession of 1937–1938.

Two of Berle's ideas played key roles in the New Deal. During the first Roosevelt administration, Berle insisted that the nation's money markets needed to be stabilized so that credit could flow to worthy business borrowers; otherwise, the economy would never get out of the Depression. Berle's ideas could be found in the Reconstruction Finance Corporation, the Emergency Banking Act of 1933, the Banking Acts of 1933 and 1935, and such New Deal agencies as the **Federal Deposit Insurance Corporation** and the **Commodity Credit Corporation**. Second, Berle always voiced opposition to the antitrust movement, especially when it gained momentum in the late 1930s. He believed that the rise of large corporations was inevitable and that antitrust policy per se made little economic sense. Instead, Berle argued, the federal government should regulate and direct larger economy through planning.

Berle remained at his post as assistant secretary of state until 1944, when FDR appointed him U.S. ambassador to Brazil. In 1946, Berle returned to the United States. He continued to advise the Harry Truman administration in hemispheric affairs, and between 1949 and 1971, Berle also served as president of the Twentieth Century Fund.

Further Reading
Berle, Adolf A., and Gardiner C. Means. 1991. *The Modern Corporation and Private Property*, reprint ed., Livingston, NJ: Transaction Publishers. Spartacus Educational. 2016. "Adolf Berle," http://spartacus-educational.com/SPYberle.htm. Accessed September 1, 2016.

Black Cabinet

Journalists first coined the term "black cabinet" to refer to a small circle of black people centered around Frederick Douglass, who had some influence in the Republican Party during the 1870s and 1880s. The term was revived during the 1930s and sometimes referred to as the "black **Brains Trust**," a group of African Americans influential in the **New Deal**. President **Franklin D. Roosevelt** was interested in completing the shift of black voters away from the Republican Party and to the Democratic Party. In order to do that, he needed to develop policies that would benefit black people, and he needed to raise his profile among them.

Secretary of the Interior Harold Ickes played a key role in assembling the so-called black cabinet. Ickes had once served as head of the Chicago chapter of the **National Association for the Advancement of Colored People**, and because of that experience, he became the president's liaison between the administration and the black community. As a first step, Ickes ended segregation in the Department of the Interior. He next hired a contingent of black engineers, accountants, architects, and attorneys. He named William Hastie, a black lawyer, as assistant solicitor in the department, and he appointed **Robert C. Weaver** as his adviser on black problems. Mary McLeod Bethune was appointed as director of minority affairs in the **National Youth Administration**, and **Robert L. Vann**, editor of the *Pittsburgh Courier*, worked as a special assistant in the Justice Department.

All of these individuals met informally and periodically to discuss the challenges of the black community, and they exerted all the pressure they could to make sure that African Americans received their fair share of government jobs and their fair share of government grants and loans. First

Lady **Eleanor Roosevelt** also cultivated a close relationship with members of the black cabinet, and in doing so she helped elevate the New Deal in the minds of most black people. In the end, the New Deal's initiatives for the black community were not much more than symbolic gestures, but it was enough to accelerate the conversion of most African Americans to the Democratic Party.

See also: National Association for the Advancement of Colored People; Vann, Robert Lee; Weaver, Robert Clifton

Further Reading

McCluskey, Audrey Thomas, and Elaine M. Smith. 2001. *Mary McLeod Bethune: Building a Better World, Essays and Selected Documents*, reprint ed., Bloomington: Indiana University Press; Sklaroff, Lauren Rebecca. 2009. *Black Culture and the New Deal: The Quest for Civil Rights in the Roosevelt Era*, Chapel Hill: University of North Carolina Press; Woolner, David. 2010. "African Americans and the New Deal: A Look Back in History," Roosevelt Institute, http://rooseveltinstitute.org/african-americans-and-new-deal-look-back-history/. Accessed September 1, 2016.

 Bonus Army

As a payment for their loyal service to the nation during World War I, veterans learned in 1924 that Congress had issued to them compensation, or bonus, certificates. The certificates were due to mature in 1945, at which time the veterans could trade them in for cash or convert them into a pension. But the onset of the Great Depression threw millions of veterans out of work, and many of them demanded early payment of the bonuses. Veterans groups like the American Legion lobbied Congress for enabling legislation, and in February 1931, Congress complied, allowing the veterans to borrow up to 50 percent of the amount of their certificates. But President Herbert **Hoover** vetoed the bill for fiscal reasons, claiming that it would bust the federal budget. Congress overrode the veto. Later in the year, sensing a popular political issue, Democrats in Congress began preparing legislation for a complete payout of the bonus.

In May and June 1932, more than 17,000 veterans arrived in Washington, D.C., to demonstrate their support for the legislation. The Hoover administration opposed the law. The veterans, dubbed the "Bonus Expeditionary Force" or the "Bonus Army" by the press, camped out at Anacostia Flats on the outskirts of Washington, D.C. Some of them also took up residence in abandoned government buildings. President Hoover supported, and

A Bonus Army family in the Anacostia mud flats in Washington, D.C., ca. 1932. (Library of Congress)

Congress passed, legislation providing $100,000 for the protestors to use in going home. By early July 1932, all but 2,000 protestors had departed the city. But those left behind were militant about the issue and refused to leave without action of cash redemptions of the bonus certificates. A small, anti-Semitic remnant calling themselves the Khaki Shirts demanded payment of veterans' bonuses, the abolition of Congress, the expansion of the money supply through silver currency, and large increases in the defense budget.

Near the end of the month, District of Columbia police tried to evict the protestors from government buildings, and a riot ensued in which two policemen and two rioters were killed. The president asked General Douglas MacArthur to use army troops to evict the protestors, and MacArthur accepted the assignment with excessive zeal. On July 29, using tanks, tear gas, sabers, rifle fire, and torches, the troops attacked the veterans and drove them from the buildings and from Anacostia Flats. It was a political nightmare for Hoover, since headlines and photographs of the maneuver found their way into the next day's newspapers. Americans were horrified at the sight of army troops attacking poor veterans. Hoover was appalled at what had happened, and it cost him dearly politically, convincing most Americans that he was an uncaring man detached from the problems of everyday people. **Franklin D. Roosevelt**, the Democratic candidate for president in the upcoming November elections, remarked on hearing the news of the attack, "Well, this will elect me."

In 1935 Congressman Wright Patman of Texas, a supporter of veterans' groups, sponsored a new bonus bill, but it did not see the light of day until 1936, when the upcoming congressional elections gave it a great deal of political currency. In January 1936, Congress passed the Adjusted Compensation Act, which provided for full payment of the bonuses by allowing the Treasury to issue nine-year, interest-bearing bonds redeemable in cash at any time. President Roosevelt vetoed the measure, but Congress overrode the veto. On June 15, 1936, more than $1.5 billion in bonus bonds were distributed to more than 3 million World War I veterans.

See also: Hoover, Herbert Clark

Further Reading

Dickson, Paul, and Thomas B. Allen. 2006. *The Bonus Army: An American Epic*, New York: Walker & Co.; Kast, Sheilah. February 13, 2005. "Soldier against Soldier: The Story of the Bonus Army," *Weekend Edition Sunday*, NPR, http://www.npr.org/templates/story/story.php?storyId=4494446. Accessed September 1, 2016; Library of Congress. "The Bonus Army March," American Treasures of the Library of Congress, http://www.loc.gov/exhibits/treasures/trm203.html.

Brains Trust

During his tenure as governor of New York (1929–1933), **Franklin D. Roosevelt** had displayed a willingness, even enthusiasm, to seek out the counsel of academics in trying to formulate public policy. He did not always take their counsel because he had a shrewd sense of what was politically possible, but more than any other political figure in the United States, he sought to generate programs to solve social and economic problems. That continued during his run for the presidency in 1932 and during the transition months before his inauguration.

In 1932, Governor Roosevelt, like most other Americans, was baffled by the tenacity of the Great Depression. He needed campaign suggestions that would allow him to criticize the **Herbert Hoover** administration and to offer policy alternatives of his own. In March 1932, Samuel Rosenman, Roosevelt's general counsel, suggested that a team of academics and intellectuals be formed to develop campaign themes and programs to stimulate an economic recovery. He turned first to Raymond Moley, a political scientist at Columbia University who had written speeches occasionally for Governor Roosevelt. As a specialist on agriculture policy, Rosenman tabbed Professor **Rexford Tugwell**, also of Columbia. Professor Adolf Berle of the Columbia University Law School was recruited for his expertise on corporate and economic issues. Roosevelt's longtime law partner, Basil O'Conner, also joined the group. Moley served as the de facto head of the group, and they met weekly throughout 1932 to discuss issues and formulate policy. Periodically, the governor sat in on the meetings.

In September 1932, *New York Times* columnist James Kieran dubbed the group the "Brains Trust." The Brains Trust possessed a definite philosophical bias. They rejected completely the Woodrow Wilson–Louis Brandeis version of progressivism that defined bigness in business as inherently bad. Instead, Berle, Tugwell, and Moley accepted large corporations as a modern economic reality. The government should not try to break up big business but merely prevent abuse of the public by concentrated corporate power. Regulation, not antitrust, should be the focus of government activity. They recognized that bigness could bring economies of scale to the market and drive down prices. Tugwell went even farther than Berle or Moley in calling for national economic planning, with the federal government, not the market, acting as the arbiter.

During the campaign, Governor Roosevelt had the good sense *not* to let the Brains Trust go public with their proposals. Conservatives would have been up in arms over the proposals, and Roosevelt knew that the election was his to lose. Avoiding controversy was the key to victory since public disillusionment with Hoover ran so deep. But when Roosevelt won the election in November 1932, the Brains Trust played the central role in formulating the administration's policies, and during the **first 100 days**, they found expression in such proposals as the **National Recovery Administration**, the bank holiday, and the **Agricultural Adjustment Administration**.

Further Reading

Armstrong Economics. "Roosevelt's Brains Trust," https://www.armstrongeconomics.com/research/economic-thought/economics/roosevelts-brains-trust/. Accessed September 1, 2016; The Eleanor Roosevelt Papers Project. "FDR's Brains Trust," Teaching Eleanor Roosevelt Glossary, https://www.gwu.edu/~erpapers/teachinger/glossary/brains-trust.cfm. Accessed September 1, 2016; Leuchtenburg, William E. 2009. *Franklin D. Roosevelt and the New Deal: 1932–1940*, New York: Harper Perennial.

Bull Market

During the 1920s, the stock market underwent unprecedented growth in a mania of speculation. In 1921, the New York Stock Exchange composite index stood at 54. It then increased to 65 in 1923, 106 in 1924, 245 in 1927, and 449 in 1929. These extraordinary gains were not tied, however, to improving dividends and corporate profits. American investors had dumped World War I profits into the stock market, and because the war had brought about an enormous transfer of wealth from Europe to the United States, those funds were huge. Republican policies during the 1920s—tax cuts on the wealthy and reductions in the federal debt—directed even more money into the securities markets. Corporations began directing profits into the market, as did small investors who pumped money from savings accounts into Wall Street. The result of such an infusion of cash was the greatest bull market in history. When the crash came in October 1929, it was an abrupt drop that became a free fall. The greatest bull market in history became the greatest bear market in history. By 1931 the New York Stock Exchange composite index stood at only 51, and it fell to 37 in 1932, more than wiping out the gains of the previous decade and sending the country into the Great Depression.

See also: Stock Market Crash

Further Reading
Galbraith, John Kenneth. 2009. *The Great Crash 1929*, reprint ed., New York: Mariner Books; Payne, Phillip G. 2015. *Crash! How the Economic Boom and Bust of the 1920s Worked* (How Things Worked series), Baltimore, MD: Johns Hopkins University Press.

Business Advisory Council

In June 1933 Secretary of Commerce Daniel Roper established the Business Advisory and Planning Council, later known as the Business Advisory Council (BAC), to provide President **Franklin D. Roosevelt** with input from the business community on how to best stimulate the economy. The BAC included forty-one of the most powerful businessmen in the country, including Arthur Sloan of General Motors, Robert Wood of Sears Roebuck, Walter Gifford of American Telephone and Telegraph, and Pierre du Pont. Gerard Swope of General Motors chaired the BAC.

There was a brief political honeymoon between the BAC and the Roosevelt administration, but the direction of the **New Deal** soon troubled them. Such laws as the **Securities Act of 1933** and the Securities Exchange Act of 1934 alienated most big businessmen, who believed that the New Deal had brought about a dangerous accumulation of power in the federal government. Many BAC members resigned in 1934 and 1935, and in 1935 and 1937, the BAC called for fiscal retrenchment and a balanced federal budget. By that time, of course, Roosevelt considered them completely irrelevant. The rise of **Keynes**ian economics, in which the federal government used tax and spending techniques to stimulate the economy, alienated the remaining members of the BAC. At the same time, however, the BAC did not represent any ideological, laissez-faire point of view. They supported the Banking Acts of 1933 and 1935 and the **Social Security Act of 1935** and were not averse to the idea of national economic planning.

Further Reading
Roosevelt, Franklin D. May 2, 1935. "Statement on Resolutions of the Business Advisory Council of the Department of Commerce," Gerhard Peters and John T. Woolley, The American Presidency Project, http://www.presidency.ucsb.edu/ws/?pid=15050. Accessed September 1, 2016.

Business Conferences of 1929

When the **stock market** crashed in October 1929, President **Herbert Hoover** was convinced that the economic pain would be short term. In fact, he believed that the crash might actually be good in the long term for the economy because it would pop the speculative bubble and redirect investment capital back into more productive enterprises, which he was convinced would stimulate the economy. For Hoover, the key to economic recovery was the restoration and preservation of confidence. To convince major corporations not to cut jobs and spending in a panicky mode, the president convened a series of conferences for executives in manufacturing, finance, railroads, construction, and public utilities. The conferences were held during November 19–23, 1929, and when they were concluded, three initiatives had been launched. The National Business Survey Conference consisted of 170 trade associations that, through the national Chamber of Commerce, would work to maintain wages and stimulate new investment. The National Building Survey Conference would work to stimulate new construction. Finally, a new division of public construction in the Department of Commerce would try to accelerate federal public works construction projects.

The long-term achievements of the business conferences were paltry, to say the least. Individual corporate leaders did not have Hoover's vision, or at least they could not afford his vision. They had to meet the needs of stockholders and could not afford to maintain wages or increase investment spending in the face of declining sales. In 1930, terrible quarterly earnings reports forced them into massive retrenchment and downsizing, cutting the workforce and new spending. It was exactly what President Hoover had hoped to avoid, and it strengthened the assumptions of some that only the federal government would have the authority and the resources to have a significant impact on the economy.

Further Reading

Herbert Hoover Presidential Library and Museum. "Gallery Six: The Great Depression," http://hoover.archives.gov/exhibits/Hooverstory/gallery06/. Accessed September 1, 2016.

C

Caldwell, Erskine

Erskine Caldwell, an American author, was born in White Oak, Georgia, in 1903. He studied at Erskine College in South Carolina and the University of Virginia and then went to work as a reporter for *The Atlanta Journal*. Caldwell wrote short stories on the side and in 1926 moved to Maine, where he could spend more time writing fiction. *Scribner's Magazine* began publishing some of his work, and then *Scribner's* published Caldwell's two most important works— *American Earth* (1930) and *Tobacco Road* (1932). Both novels—as well as his third, *God's Little Acre* (1933) – dealt with poverty-stricken Georgia sharecropping families. In 1933 *Tobacco Road* became a successful Broadway play, guaranteeing that the term "Tobacco Road" would become a euphemism for rural poverty and squalor. With his wife Margaret Bourke-White, the renowned photographer, Caldwell wrote *You Have Seen Their Faces* (1937), which depicted the

Erskine Caldwell wrote vivid fictional chronicles of the lives of the poor in the rural South during and after the Great Depression. His *Tobacco Road* shocked sensibilities in the 1930s with its unflinching portrayal of a family brought low by grinding poverty. (Library of Congress)

poverty-stricken misery of poor black and white southern farmers. The body of Caldwell's work during the 1930s brought to the attention of millions of Americans the depth of southern poverty and helped lead to the **Resettlement Administration** and the **Farm Security Administration**. Although Caldwell continued to write until his death on April 11, 1987, his post-1940 work did not have nearly the influence.

Further Reading

Stevens, C. J. 2000. *Storyteller: A Life of Erskine Caldwell*, Phillips, ME: John Wade; Walter J. Brown Media Archives and Peabody Awards Collection. *Erskine Caldwell Says as a Novelist He Emphasizes Content of Living*, video, 0:54 min., wsbn31652, WSB Newsfilm Collection, reel WSBN0709, Athens: The University of Georgia Libraries, http://dlg.galileo.usg.edu/news/id:wsbn31652. Accessed September 9, 2016.

Carter v. Carter Coal Company (1936)

During the Great Depression of the 1930s, wages and working conditions in the bituminous coal industry were scandalously low. To stem overproduction and cutthroat competition in the industry, Congress passed the Bituminous Coal Conservation Act of 1935 as part of President **Franklin D. Roosevelt**'s **New Deal**. The legislation empowered the federal government to establish local boards that could set the price of coal above market levels. It also mandated collective bargaining arrangements to raise wages and improve working conditions. Several coal companies filed lawsuits against the measure, arguing that it was an unconstitutional increase in the power of the federal government in what would normally be a state matter. The Bituminous Coal Conservation Act of 1935, so their legal argument went, violated the Tenth Amendment to the Constitution. In a decision handed down on March 18, 1936, by a narrow 5 to 4 vote, the U.S. Supreme Court ruled against the New Deal, agreeing that the legislation violated the Tenth Amendment. Outrage in Congress and the White House over the decision was so intense that it helped inspire President Roosevelt's infamous **court-packing scheme** in 1937.

Further Reading

Lawnix. "Carter v. Carter Coal Co.—Case Brief Summary," http://www.lawnix.com/cases/carter-coal.html. Accessed September 1, 2016; Legal Information Institute (LII). "Carter v. Carter Coal Co.," text of the opinion, Cornell University Law School, https://www.law.cornell.edu/supremecourt/text/298/238. Accessed September 1, 2016.

Chandler Act of 1938

During the 1930s, the unprecedented number of corporate bankruptcies wreaked havoc in the corporate bond markets and weakened the portfolios of thousands of banks. In addition, the bankruptcy proceedings often discriminated against small investors who held limited amounts of corporate debt. The Chandler Act of 1938 amended existing federal bankruptcy law and gave the **Securities and Exchange Commission** power to participate in corporate reorganizations in order to protect the interests of small and inarticulate investors. The bill also allowed wage earners to extend debt payments over longer periods of time.

See also: Securities and Exchange Commission

Further Reading
Skeel, David. 2006. *Icarus in the Boardroom: The Fundamental Flaws in Corporate America and Where They Came From*, New York: Oxford University Press.

Citizens' Reconstruction Organization

During the late 1920s and early 1930s, the nation's banking system entered a period of instability and collapse. Millions of depositors lost faith in the system and began converting their deposits into cash, a phenomenon that created serious liquidity problems for bankers and a credit crunch for borrowers. In January 1932, President **Herbert Hoover** and Congress created the **Reconstruction Finance Corporation** to make loans to troubled banks, and in February 1932, the president established the Citizens' Reconstruction Organization (CRO) as a voluntary group to launch and sustain an anti-currency hoarding publicity campaign. Frank Knox, owner of the *Chicago Daily News*, headed the CRO, and a conference of more than forty public relations and journalist groups was convened in Washington, D.C., to promote the campaign. Local CRO groups were established at the state and local levels, and the publicity campaign continued throughout 1932.

But the CRO proved to be too little, too late. As more and more banks failed in 1932, bank depositors discounted CRO propaganda and continued to withdraw their money, exacerbating the banking system's liquidity problems. The absolute collapse of the banking system late in 1932 and early in 1933 made the CRO a symbol of the impotency of the Hoover administration.

See also: Hoover, Herbert Clark; Stock Market Crash

Further Reading

Rappleye, Charles. 2016. *Herbert Hoover in the White House: The Ordeal of the Presidency*, New York: Simon and Schuster; Rothbard, Murray N. 2002. *A History of Money and Banking in the United States: The Colonial Era to World War II*, Auburn, AL: Mises Institute.

Civilian Conservation Corps

One of the real problems facing the country in the early 1930s was **unemployment** among urban young men. Early in 1933 more than 50 percent of all men between the ages of fifteen and twenty-four were unemployed or had only part-time jobs. To deal with that problem as well as to promote some conservation work, President **Franklin D. Roosevelt** asked Congress to establish the Civilian Conservation Corps (CCC). Congress created the CCC on March 31, 1933. Robert Fechner was named director of the CCC. It offered jobs at $30 a month to young men between the ages of seventeen and twenty-four. They were placed under the authority of U.S. Army supervisors, and the CCC had all the trappings of military authority. Organized into companies of approximately 200 men, CCC workers constructed

Members of a Civilian Conservation Corps crew work on a reforestation project during the Great Depression. (National Archives)

national park facilities, fought forest fires, built roads in national forests, and worked intensively in reforestation projects, planting more than 200 million trees. During the 1930s, the CCC employed more than 2.5 million men, with more than 500,000 employed at the same time during the peak year of 1935. In 1942, with World War II well under way, Congress stopped funding the CCC.

Further Reading

Cornebise, Alfred Emile. 2004. *The CCC Chronicles: Camp Newspapers of the Civilian Conservation Corps, 1933–1942*, Jefferson, NC: McFarland; Maher, Neil M. 2009. *Nature's New Deal: The Civilian Conservation Corps and the Roots of the American Environmental Movement*, New York: Oxford University Press; Stone, Robert, dir. 2010. *American Experience: Civilian Conservation Corps*, 60 min., DVD, PBS.

Civil Works Administration

The Civil Works Administration (CWA) was created by an executive order of President **Franklin D. Roosevelt** on November 9, 1933. He appointed **Harry Hopkins**, head of the **Federal Emergency Relief Administration**, to head the CWA. Instead of just handing out checks to the unemployed, Hopkins believed in work relief. By February 1934 the CWA was employing 4.2 million workers, paying them minimum wage, and putting them to work on a variety of public construction projects, disaster relief, and historic preservation. Those individuals then spent their wages, and their purchasing power helped stimulate the economy. CWA workers constructed more than 40,000 schools, 469 airports, and 255,000 miles of streets and roads. Eventually, the CWA was absorbed into the much larger and more comprehensive **Works Progress Administration**.

See also: Unemployment; Works Progress Administration

Further Reading

Roosevelt, Franklin D. November 8, 1933. "Remarks on Signing Executive Order Creating Civil Works Administration," Gerhard Peters and John T. Woolley, The American Presidency Project, http://www.presidency.ucsb.edu/ws/?pid=14547. Accessed September 1, 2016; University of Washington University Libraries Digital Collections. "Civil Works Administration Photographs," http://content.lib.washington.edu/civilworksweb/index.html. Accessed September 1, 2016.

Cohen, Benjamin

Benjamin Victor Cohen was one of the most influential, if unseen, figures in the **New Deal**. In 1933, Cohen came to Washington, D.C., to assist James Landis in drafting the **Securities Act of 1933**. When he met **Thomas Corcoran**, a counsel for the **Reconstruction Finance Corporation**, the two became fast friends and formed one of the most important legal partnerships in the history of American public policy.

During the next several years, Cohen and Corcoran drafted the legislation that eventually became the Securities Exchange Act of 1934, the **Federal Housing Administration**, the **Tennessee Valley Authority**, and the **Public Utility Holding Company Act of 1935**. They earned sterling reputations for the tightness of the legal language they employed in drafting complex legislation, and they then played central roles in shepherding the legislation through Congress. He spent most of the rest of his life in public service. Cohen died on September 4, 1983.

Further Reading
Lasser, William. 2002. *Benjamin V. Cohen: Architect of the New Deal*, New Haven, CT: Yale University Press.

Committee on Economic Security

Ever since the early 1900s, social welfare advocates in the United States had promoted the idea of federal pensions for senior citizens, and in the early 1930s, the idea gained momentum from labor unions and especially from the increasing popularity of **Francis Townsend**'s Old-Age Revolving Pensions, Ltd. To satisfy liberals in his own party and to steal some thunder from Townsend, President **Franklin D. Roosevelt** in June 1934 established the Committee on Economic Security. The committee was chaired by Secretary of Labor Frances Perkins and charged with developing a federal insurance plan before the end of the year. Proposals for national health insurance, federal **unemployment** insurance, and old-age pensions were all considered.

The committee had two difficult issues to resolve. First, it had to decide whether a system of unemployment compensation should be a single, federal government program or a state-based plan. The committee decided to promote the state-based plan, with the federal government setting certain minimum standards. The second issue to be resolved was how to finance old-age pensions. Liberals wanted the federal government simply to finance it out of general revenues, which would have the effect of redistributing national income. Conservatives wanted a financing system based on payroll deductions from employees and employers. The committee recommended the more conservative proposal. The committee also recommended supplemental benefits for the indigent elderly, for the blind, and for dependent children. Committee members decided not to make any proposals concerning national health insurance. The committee handed its report over to President Roosevelt on January 15, 1935, and the president quickly turned it over to Congress. Senator **Robert Wagner** of New York and Congressmen David J. Lewis and Robert Doughton sponsored the legislation. The **Social Security Act** became law on August 14, 1935.

See also: Social Security Act of 1935; Townsend, Francis Everett

Further Reading

Beland, Daniel. 2005. *Social Security: History and Politics from the New Deal to the Privatization Debate* (Studies in Government and Public Policy). Lawrence: University Press of Kansas.

Commodity Credit Corporation

One of the great challenges facing farmers in the 1920s and 1930s revolved around their difficulties in marketing their commodities. Overproduction and depressed prices had become chronic problems, and it was an even worse problem during harvest time, when cash-poor farmers all dumped certain commodities on the market at the same time, depressing prices even more. On a seasonal basis, prices were artificially low because crops hit the market at the same time. Farmers asked the **Roosevelt** administration for federal assistance in creating more stable marketing conditions.

On October 18, 1933, President Franklin D. Roosevelt by executive order created the Commodity Credit Corporation (CCC), which had its origins in three subtreasury schemes of the Populists. The CCC assumed control of a **Reconstruction Finance Corporation** (RFC) loan program established during the **Herbert Hoover** administration. The RFC loaned money to banks and agricultural credit corporations for the orderly marketing of commodities. Such loans allowed farmers to hold their crops off the market until more favorable marketing conditions had materialized. In order to avoid making too many loans directly and undermining local financial institutions, the CCC agreed to buy up all such loans private bankers made. When banks refused to make such loans, the CCC made them directly.

Between 1933 and 1935 the CCC was a subsidiary of the RFC. It then became an independent agency. The CCC made loans on cotton, corn, wheat, turpentine, rosin, figs, peanuts, raisins, butter, dates, cowhides, wool, and tobacco. By 1936 CCC loans—the vast majority of them made originally through private banks—totaled $628 million. By 1939 they had reached $900 million and helped stabilize commodity prices. The outbreak of World War II, with its huge demand for farm products, brought about a dramatic increase in commodity prices and farm profits.

See also: Reconstruction Finance Corporation

Further Reading

Folsom, Burton W. November 30, 2011. "The First Government Bailouts: The Story of the RFC," Foundation for Economic Education (FEE), https://fee.org/articles/the-first-government-bailouts-the-story-of-the-rfc/. Accessed September 1, 2016; Gou, Michael, Gary Richardson, Alejandro Komai, and Daniel Park. "Banking Acts of 1932," Federal Reserve History, http://www.federalreservehistory.org/Events/DetailView/12. Accessed September 1, 2016.

Commodity Dollar. *See* Gold Standard

Corcoran, Thomas

Thomas Gardiner Corcoran, nicknamed "The Cork," was one of President **Roosevelt**'s advisers and a member of his **Brains Trust**. In 1932 he joined the staff of the **Reconstruction Finance Corporation** (RFC), and in 1933, at Felix Frankfurter's suggestion, Franklin D. Roosevelt hired Corcoran as an assistant to Secretary of the Treasury William Woodin. One year later, Corcoran returned to the RFC as special counsel and remained there until 1941.

During his stay in Washington, D.C., Corcoran formed an informal partnership with **Benjamin Cohen**, and together they drafted and shepherded through Congress some of the **New Deal**'s most important legislation, including the Securities Exchange Act of 1934, the **Public Utility Holding Company Act of 1935**, and the legislation creating the **Tennessee Valley Authority** and the **Federal Housing Administration**. Corcoran and Cohen shared an apartment in Georgetown and worked ninety-hour weeks for years, earning the nickname "the gold dust twins" or "Frankfurter's two chief little hot dogs." Although Corcoran's job was special counsel to the RFC, he actually ranged very widely throughout Washington,

D.C., and was known by everyone to enjoy the ear of the president. In 1941, Corcoran resigned and launched a highly lucrative legal career in Washington. By that time, he was probably the most well-connected lawyer in the country and remained so for the rest of his life. Corcoran died on December 6, 1981.

See also: Brains Trust; Cohen, Benjamin

Further Reading

McKean, David. *Peddling Influence: Thomas "Tommy the Cork" Corcoran and the Birth of Modern Lobbying*, Hanover, NH: Steerforth Press; *The New York Times*. December 7, 1981. "Thomas G. Corcoran, Aide to Roosevelt, Dies," Obituaries, http://www.nytimes.com/1981/12/07/obituaries/thomas-g-corcoran-aide-to-roosevelt-dies.html. Accessed September 1, 2016.

Coughlin, Charles Edward

Charles Coughlin was born on October 25, 1891, and raised in Hamilton, Ontario, Canada. After studying theology at the University of Toronto, Coughlin became a Roman Catholic priest. After teaching for ten years at Assumption College in Windsor, Ontario, he was transferred in 1926 to a parish in Royal Oaks, Michigan. Coughlin had only been at his new assignment for two weeks when a local Ku Klux Klan group burned a cross in front of the parish church. In reaction, Coughlin started a radio broadcast from his "Shrine of the Little Flower," which quickly became very popular in the local area. Coughlin soon figured out that his warnings about the dangers of communism resonated especially well, and by 1930, his weekly radio show began reaching a national audience.

Soon, however, Coughlin began peddling hate and hyperbole. He blamed the depression on international bankers, Jews, and communists. Because he had invested all of his own money in silver mines, he began advocating the remonetization of silver. Coughlin also praised the early accomplishments of Benito Mussolini in Italy and Adolf Hitler in Germany. He was an early supporter of **Franklin D. Roosevelt** and the **New Deal**, telling his millions of listeners that the "New Deal is Christ's Deal."

But in 1934 Coughlin broke with the Roosevelt administration, criticizing the large bureaucracies created by the **National Recovery Administration** and the **Agricultural Adjustment Administration**, labeling the "New Deal the Jew Deal," and even suggesting the need for Franklin D. Roosevelt to be assassinated. In November 1934, Coughlin formed the

Through his radio broadcasts, Father Coughlin began promoting hatred of such targets as the New Deal, Jews, union labor, and communism. He was eventually silenced by the Catholic Church. (Library of Congress)

National Union for Social Justice to promote his commitment to inflationary monetary policies and redistribution of the national income. By early 1935, the National Union for Social Justice had a membership of more than 500,000 people.

In the summer of 1935, Coughlin threw in his lot with Senator **Huey P. Long** and **Francis Townsend**, and together they planned the formation of the **Union Party**. They hoped to run Long as a Union Party presidential candidate in the presidential election of 1936, but after Long's assassination, the Union Party nominated **William Lemke**. Lemke proved to be not only anti-Semitic but anti-Catholic, splitting the coalition. Coughlin became increasingly hostile to Roosevelt, so much so that Roman Catholic prelates intervened to suppress Coughlin's broadcasts. Lemke ended up with only 2 percent of the vote in 1936.

Coughlin's vitriol only worsened. He became so blatantly anti-Roosevelt, anti-Semitic, and pro-Hitler that the Vatican formally condemned him. In 1942, when he described World War II as a "Roosevelt-Jewish-British" conspiracy, the Church ended his radio broadcasts. The National Union for Social Justice disbanded in 1944. Father Coughlin died on October 27, 1979.

See also: Long, Huey P.

Further Reading

Brinkley, Alan. 1983. *Voices of Protest: Huey Long, Father Coughlin, and the Great Depression*, New York: Vintage; Charles River Editors. 2016. *Father Charles Coughlin: The Life of the Controversial Catholic Priest Who Revolutionized Radio.*

Court-Packing Scheme

As soon as President **Franklin D. Roosevelt** took the oath of office on March 4, 1933, the federal government aggressively attacked the economic problems associated with the Great Depression. With **unemployment** skyrocketing and prices plunging, with the money markets frozen into paralysis, and with the industrial and farm economies in a state of meltdown, the **New Deal** embarked on a remarkable expansion in the power and scope of the federal government.

But the U.S. Supreme Court, dominated by conservative justices appointed in the 1910s and 1920s, could not tolerate the New Deal. It seemed to crush states' rights in the name of federal power and ran roughshod over the property rights of corporations. In a series of highly controversial decisions, the Court systematically dismantled much of the early New Deal. The Court declared unconstitutional, in *Louisville Joint Stock Bank Radford* (1935), a law providing mortgage relief to farmers. In *Schechter Poultry Corporation v. United States* (**1935**), the justices destroyed the **National Recovery Administration**. The **Agricultural Adjustment Administration** was declared unconstitutional in the Supreme Court's *United States v. Butler* (1936) decision.

Enraged that the Supreme Court seemed bent on thwarting the will of Congress, the president, and the people, Franklin D. Roosevelt decided to redesign the Court. He waited until after his landslide victory in the election of 1936. The president asked Attorney General Homer Cummings to come up with a plan that would reduce the Court's conservative majority to a minority. At first Cummings proposed a constitutional amendment increasing the number of justices on the Court, but New Dealers felt the amendment process would be too time-consuming. Roosevelt wanted more immediate action. Instead, the administration proposed to Congress a measure that would add one justice to the Supreme Court for every other justice who had reached the age of seventy, up to a maximum of six new appointments. The plan also called for forty-four new justices at the district and court of appeals levels.

The proposal, when it was made public on February 7, 1937, generated a storm of protest. Republicans denounced the measure, but so did moderate and conservative Democrats, newspapers, and bar associations. Although he had badly miscalculated the political fallout of the proposal, Roosevelt refused to back down, and a constitutional crisis loomed. Congress refused to approve the measure. But the standoff dissipated when the Court upheld the constitutionality of a minimum wage law and of the National Labor Relations Act of 1935, legal battles that New Dealers had expected to lose.

A series of resignations during the next two years also gave the president the opportunity to replace conservatives with liberals. The president had lost a battle but won the war. One year later, however, when voters went to the polls in the congressional elections of 1938, the court-packing scheme cost Roosevelt badly. Republicans staged huge gains in Congress, dramatically reducing Roosevelt's Democratic majorities in the House and the Senate.

Further Reading

Leuchtenburg, William E. May 2005. "When Franklin Roosevelt Clashed with the Supreme Court and Lost," *Smithsonian* Magazine, http://www.smithsonianmag.com/history/when-franklin-roosevelt-clashed-with-the-supreme-court-and-lost-78497994/?no-ist. Accessed September 9, 2016; Shesol, Jeff. 2011. *Supreme Power: Franklin Roosevelt vs. the Supreme Court,* New York: W. W. Norton & Company; Solomon, Burt. 2009. *FDR v. The Constitution: The Court-Packing Fight and the Triumph of Democracy,* New York: Walker & Co.

D

Dewson, Mary

Mary Williams Dewson was a major female figure in the Democratic Party during the 1930s. A liberal Democrat interested in social welfare legislation, Dewson worked in Europe for the American Red Cross, then returned to the United States, and went to work in New York for the National Consumers' League. In 1925, she became president of the Consumers' League of New York, where she earned a national reputation for her advocacy of women's rights, national health insurance, a national minimum wage, and federal old-age pension programs. Her profile earned her the attention of prominent Democrats, and Dewson became a close friend of **Eleanor Roosevelt**, wife of Governor **Franklin D. Roosevelt** of New York. Dewson played a key role in organizing women's groups within the Democratic Party.

When Franklin D. Roosevelt won the presidential election of 1932, Dewson inherited real political power. In 1933 she was named head of the women's division of the Democratic National Committee. As political momentum accelerated for Social Security legislation, Dewson's expertise positioned her for a key role. In 1934, Roosevelt named her to the **Committee on Economic Security**, which was charged with studying and then drafting Social Security legislation. When the **Social Security Act of 1935** was passed, Roosevelt credited Dewson for making a major contribution to the law. She was appointed a member of the Social Security Board in 1937. Poor health, however, forced her resignation in 1938. Mary Dewson retired that year and died on October 24, 1962.

Further Reading

Social Welfare History Project. "Mary Dewson," Virginia Commonwealth University Libraries, http://socialwelfare.library.vcu.edu/people/dewson-mary-2/. Accessed September 1, 2016.

Dos Passos, John

John Dos Passos, one of the country's leading novelists and literary critics during the 1920s and 1930s, was born in Chicago, Illinois, on January 14, 1896. In 1916, he graduated from Harvard with all of the romantic illusions of the era, but World War I soon revolutionized his politics. The sheer brutality of the war and loss of tens of millions of lives stunned Dos Passos, leaving him depressed and without faith, completely convinced that human nature was inherently mean and brutal, and his first novels reflected that pessimism. In *One Man's Initiation* (1919) and *Three Soldiers* (1921) he argued for the absolute absurdity of war and how World War I had completely destroyed liberal illusions.

American culture during the 1920s only reinforced Dos Passos's pessimism. The rise of a consumer culture disgusted Dos Passos. The idea of an entire society existing only to make money and purchase commodities seemed pathetically empty to him, and having the federal government dominated by big business further alienated him. He worked diligently to prevent the execution of Nicola Sacco and Bartolomeo Vanzetti, who had been convicted of murder during a robbery in Braintree, Massachusetts, because he felt they were the victims of ethnic and political persecution. After their executions in 1927, Dos Passos began work on his famous literary trilogy: *The 42nd Parallel* (1930), *1919* (1932), and *The Big Money* (1936). In the novels, Dos Passos held up to ridicule the materialism, violence, and paranoia in American culture and society.

For John Dos Passos, the onset of the Great Depression proved his critique. A society devoted to consumerism found itself mired in an economic decline of unprecedented proportions. Massive **unemployment**, poverty, and pessimism had bankrupted the consumer culture, at least in Dos Passos's mind. For a time he became a **socialist** convinced that turning the economy over to the federal government was the only answer to the Great Depression. His second trilogy—*Adventures of a Young Man* (1939), *Number One* (1943), and *The Grand Design* (1948)—reflected that. Eventually, Dos Passos abandoned his belief in socialism. He became too skeptical of human nature to believe that government could rationally restructure society. Instead, he spent his last years as a confirmed Jeffersonian liberal. Dos Passos died on September 28, 1970.

Further Reading

Carr, Virginia Spencer. 2004. *Dos Passos: A Life*, Evanston, IL: Northwestern University Press; Spartacus Educational. "John Dos Passos," http://spartacus-educational.com/Jpassos.htm. Accessed September 1, 2016.

Dust Bowl and California Migration

The term "Dust Bowl" became prominent in the mid-1930s to describe the huge dust storms blowing out of the Midwest. During World War I and the 1920s, when the economy boomed, farmers dramatically increased the number of acres in production, plowing up huge amounts of soil that for tens of thousands of years had been held in place by prairie grasses. When a drought hit the Great Plains in the 1930s, the exposed soil dried out and winds lifted clouds of dirt into the skies. More than 150,000 square miles of farmland in the Midwest and Southwest were affected—especially in Kansas, Colorado, Oklahoma, Texas, Arkansas, Missouri, and New Mexico. The huge dust storms blackened the skies, dirtied homes, exacerbated respiratory diseases, and in some cases caused death. Farmers could not plant crops, and small-town economies throughout the affected areas suffered. In 1935, the dust storms, which tended to blow from west to east, darkened the skies of Baltimore, Washington, D.C., and Philadelphia. Tens of thousands of families pulled up stakes and hit the road, hoping to find work, land, or both. These families were often called "Okies," since so many of them had come from Oklahoma (or, less commonly, "Arkies," in reference to migrants from Arkansas). Historians estimate that between 300,000 and 400,000 people lost their land in Texas, Arkansas, Missouri, and Oklahoma

A sharecropper family from Oklahoma arrives in California, 1935. Photo by Dorothea Lange. (Library of Congress)

alone and that perhaps 100,000 of those arriving in California were from Oklahoma. The migrants generally traveled west via Route 66, carrying everything they owned in their trucks or automobiles. Many came to California based on highly exaggerated rumors of abundant jobs; when they arrived, they were sorely disappointed. They often ended up unemployed in what became known as "ditch bank" settlements near irrigation ditches, in "**Hoover**villes" near large city landfills, or in urban slums.

Native Californians resented the migrants, who imposed increased demands on public schools, city shelters, and public hospitals, and increased competition for limited jobs. When migrant workers joined the United Cannery, Agricultural, Packing, and Allied Workers of America Union, resentment increased even more. Though the federal government tried to assist the migrants through such agencies as the **Resettlement Administration** and the **Farm Security Administration**, the California state legislature made it a misdemeanor to assist indigent people migrating to the state. In 1941, in *Edwards v. People of the State of California*, the Supreme Court ruled against the state law because it placed "an unconstitutional burden on interstate commerce." Justice William O. Douglas added that U.S. citizenship guaranteed the right of an individual to move freely from state to state.

The plight of families migrating west during the Dust Bowl was immortalized in 1939 by **John Steinbeck**'s novel *The Grapes of Wrath* and by John Ford's 1940 film of the same name. The novel traces the plight of the Joads, a farm family from southern Oklahoma that loses land to the banks during the Depression. After seeing their property foreclosed upon and auctioned off, the Joads head west to California with tens of thousands of other migrants, but the "promised land" turns out to be a life of misery and exploitation as migrant farmworkers. The novel presents capitalism as the culprit imposing poverty and suffering on the disadvantaged farmers, and the federal government as an agent in their redemption. The novel remained on the best-seller lists for more than a year.

See also: Resettlement Administration; Steinbeck, John Ernst

Further Reading

Agee, James, and Walker Evans. Reprint. 2001. *Let Us Now Praise Famous Men*. New York: Mariner; Burns, Ken. 2012. *The Dust Bowl: A Film by Ken Burns*, DVD, 240 min., PBS; Egan, Timothy. 2006. *The Worst Hard Time: The Untold Story of Those Who Survived the Great American Dust Bowl*, New York: Mariner.

E

Eccles, Marriner

Marriner S. Eccles was born in Logan, Utah, on September 9, 1890. His family was wealthy, with their money rooted in lumber, sugar, railroads, food processing, cattle, and mining. After a three-year tour as a Mormon missionary in Scotland, Eccles returned to manage the family businesses, which he built into a multimillion-dollar enterprise. In 1929, he took the family into the banking business when he founded the First Security Corporation. Up until the onset of the Great Depression, Eccles had maintained a traditionally conservative Republican approach to questions of political economy.

By 1933, Eccles was convinced that the real cause of the Great Depression was underconsumption and that the federal government needed to stimulate the economy through deficit spending if necessary. In that sense, Eccles anticipated some of the economic views of English economist **John Maynard Keynes**. In October 1933 he came to Washington, D.C., as an economic adviser to the **Roosevelt** administration. He continually urged more spending programs upon the Roosevelt administration as a means of reducing the suffering of the unemployed and to boost consumer purchasing power and revive the economy. In June 1934, Eccles was appointed to head the **Federal Reserve Board**.

Eccles presided there when the Banking Act of 1935 invested the Federal Reserve Board in Washington, D.C., with enhanced power. The legislation gave the Federal Reserve's open market operations more direct authority over monetary policy. Eccles became a leading member of the group of **New Deal** advisers urging President Franklin D. Roosevelt to stimulate the economy through relaxed monetary policies, deficit spending, and tax cuts. It was not until the recession of 1937–1938, however, that Eccles's ideas finally prevailed. Eccles remained at the helm of the Federal Reserve Board until 1948. He spent three more years as a member of the board before returning to the family business. Eccles died on December 18, 1977.

See also: Federal Reserve Board

Further Reading

Board of Governors of the Federal Reserve System. "Marriner S. Eccles," Federal Reserve History, http://www.federalreservehistory.org/People/DetailView/75. Accessed September 3, 2016; Fraser Federal Reserve Archive. "Statements and Speeches of Marriner S. Eccles, 1934–1951." Federal Reserve Bank of St. Louis. https://fraser.stlouisfed.org/title/446. Accessed September 3, 2016; Meltzer, Allan H. 2004. *A History of the Federal Reserve, Volume 1: 1913–1951*, Chicago: University of Chicago Press.

Economy Act of 1933

When President **Franklin D. Roosevelt** assumed office in March 1933, he faced a range of suggestions from Democrats about how to handle the Depression. Many conservative Democrats were as committed as President **Herbert Hoover** had been to fiscal caution and urged a balanced budget and cuts in federal spending. Their logic was that such policies would restore business confidence and lead to increases in business investment and industrial production. The Economy Act was designed to satisfy these conservatives. Signed by Roosevelt on March 20, 1933, the Economy Act cut $100 million from the federal budget by reducing government salaries and veterans' allowances and cutting departmental spending budgets. Eventually, the Economy Act saved a total of $243 million. Of course, at the same time, Congress was passing a series of relief and recovery measures that drove the federal budget through the roof and rendered the Economy Act meaningless in terms of the total economy.

Further Reading

Northrup, Cynthia Clark. 2003. *The American Economy: A Historical Encyclopedia*, Santa Barbara, CA: ABC-CLIO; Rauchway, Eric. 2015. *The Money Makers: How Roosevelt and Keynes Ended the Depression, Defeated Fascism and Secured a Prosperous Peace*, New York: Basic Books.

Emergency Railroad Transportation Act of 1933

During the late nineteenth and early twentieth centuries, most American railroads took upon themselves long-term debts in order to finance construction. But they badly overbuilt, laying more miles of track than the economy could absorb. Competition for freight became cutthroat, and freight revenues declined. Early in the 1900s, the advent of the internal combustion engine and the appearance of the trucking industry brought even more competition. But because of their debt structures, the railroads had fixed payments on long-term bonds that had to be paid. The onset of the Great Depression only exacerbated railroad financial problems. By 1933, the American railroad industry teetered on collapse. Decades of overbuilding, duplication of services, and onerous debts left many railroads unable to meet their short-term or even long-term obligations. It was also a critical problem for the financial system because so many banks and other financial institutions had purchased long-term railroad bonds. If the roads went bankrupt, bank assets would decline even further.

The Emergency Railroad Transportation Act was designed to restore financial stability to the industry. It created a federal coordinator of transportation to divide the nation's railroad network into three subgroups: eastern, southern, and western. Each group would then establish a coordinating committee of railroad managers, who would then eliminate duplication, promote cost-saving joint use of tracks and terminals, and encourage financial reorganization to cut fixed costs. The federal coordinator had the administrative power to force recalcitrant managers to cooperate, although all decisions could be appealed to the Interstate Commerce Commission.

President **Franklin D. Roosevelt** appointed Joseph B. Eastman as federal coordinator, but he could achieve very little in his position. At every turn, he encountered pitched opposition. Railroad managers resisted consolidation attempts because they feared the loss of corporate independence. Railroad labor unions opposed consolidation because it would cut costs and jobs. Many communities opposed consolidation because they feared losing railroad service. Finally, large, powerful industries shipping freight by railroad feared that consolidation would lead to higher freight rates. What saved the railroads from financial collapse during the 1930s were billions of dollars in loans from the **Reconstruction Finance Corporation**.

Further Reading

Huibregtse, Jon R. 2010. *American Railroad Labor and the Genesis of the New Deal, 1919–1935* (Working in the Americas), Gainesville: University Press of Florida; Richardson, Gary. April 2, 2014. "The Great Depression: 1919–1941," Federal Reserve History, http://www.federalreservehistory.org/Period/Essay/10. Accessed September 3, 2016; Wolmar, Christian. 2012. *The Great Railroad Revolution: The History of Trains in America*, London: Atlantic Books.

Emergency Relief and Construction Act of 1932

When the economy slipped into the Great Depression in 1929 and 1930, President **Herbert Hoover** was slow to implement any significant federal efforts to provide relief to the unemployed. He feared that federal relief would become a dole that would undermine the American character. But as the Depression worsened in 1931 and 1932, Hoover had no choice. With the presidential election of 1932 approaching, political reality dictated some type of federal relief effort. The Emergency Relief and Construction Act, Hoover's answer to the problem, was passed in July 1932. The legislation was actually quite modest, too modest to address the massive **unemployment** problem. The bill authorized the **Reconstruction Finance Corporation** to issue up to $1.5 billion in bonds to state and local governments, with the money targeted at self-amortizing public construction projects, such as toll roads, toll bridges, hydroelectric power projects, water systems, and sewage systems. The RFC also received authorization to loan up to $300 million to state and local government relief commissions for emergency distribution to the poor and the unemployed.

In the end, the money proved to be too little, too late. The public works construction projects had a long developmental lead time, and none of the money was spent during Hoover's administration. Also, the $300 million in relief loans was pitifully inadequate. Local relief commissions could have easily distributed $3 billion to the worthy poor. The Emergency Relief and Construction Act of 1932 eventually only reinforced the public impression of President Hoover as a stingy, heartless leader and all but doomed his chances for reelection.

See also: Hoover, Herbert Clark; Reconstruction Finance Corporation

Further Reading

Herbert Hoover Presidential Library and Museum. "Gallery Six: The Great Depression," http://hoover.archives.gov/exhibits/Hooverstory/gallery06/. Accessed September 1, 2016; Rappleye, Charles. 2016. *Herbert Hoover in the White House: The Ordeal of the Presidency*, New York: Simon and Schuster.

Evans, Walker

Walker Evans was born in 1903 in St. Louis, Missouri. The child of a wealthy family, Evans enjoyed private education and attended Williams College.

He then studied art and literature in Paris, where he acquired an interest in photography, which eventually became his passion. In the 1930s, he joined the **Farm Security Administration**'s program to chronicle the suffering of poor people caught in an economic depression. He worked with such leading lights in American photography as Roy Stryker, **Dorothea Lange**, Carl Mydans, and Arthur Rothstein, and they took more than 75,000 photographs. Evans worked in the slums of New York City; the coal mines of Ohio, West Virginia, and Pennsylvania; and the hard scrabble world of tenant farmers in the Southeast.

Evans is best remembered for his partnership with writer James Agee. He left the Farm Security Administration temporarily in 1938 and traveled in Alabama with Agee. They lived for two months with the families of sharecroppers Bud Fields, Frank Tengle, and Floyd Burroughs. Agee and Evans also traveled throughout Alabama, Georgia, and Mississippi. Their book *Let Us Now Praise Famous Men*, which revealed the lives of poor sharecroppers, became an American classic. Evans went on to become a contributing photographic editor at *Time* and then *Fortune*. From 1965 until his death in April 1975, Evans was a professor of design at Yale.

See also: Farm Security Administration; Lange, Dorothea

Further Reading

Agee, James, and Walker Evans. Reprint. 2001. *Let Us Now Praise Famous Men*, New York: Mariner; Ganzel, Bill. 2003. "Farming in the 1930s: FSA Photographers," Wessels Living History Farm, http://livinghistoryfarm.org/farmingin the30s/water_14.html. Accessed September 3, 2016; Thompson, Jerry L. 2012. *The Story of a Photograph: Walker Evans, Ellie Mae Burroughs, and the Great Depression* (Kindle Singles), Kindle ed., Now and Then Reader.

Export-Import Bank

Early in the **New Deal**, President **Franklin D. Roosevelt** decided to stimulate foreign trade and American exports in order to stimulate an economic recovery. The **Reciprocal Trade Agreements Act of 1934** was designed to lower global tariff rates, and the Export-Import Bank was intended to provide loans to companies wishing to expand overseas operations. In February 1934, as part of extending diplomatic recognition to the Soviet Union, Roosevelt established the Export-Import Bank as a subsidiary of the **Reconstruction Finance Corporation**. In March 1934, when Cuba requested U.S. assistance to purchase and mint silver coins, the president established the Second Export-Import Bank to handle the transactions. Roosevelt soon expanded the Second Export-Import Bank's operations to include trade with other nations. The original Export-Import Bank remained confined to trade with the Soviet Union. The Second Export-Import made many direct loans, primarily for the export of railway and heavy equipment, and created a secondary market for commercial banks financing companies in the export business. By 1937, the bank had made $37 million worth of loans, a paltry amount given its grandiose goals. After 1937 its operations greatly expanded because it made loans directly to foreign governments. By 1940, the bank was more of a diplomatic than an economic institution.

See also: Reconstruction Finance Corporation

Further Reading

Export-Import Bank of the United States. "History of the Export-Import Bank of the U.S.," http://www.exim.gov/about/history-0. Accessed September 3, 2016; Peters, Gerhard, and John T. Wooley. "Executive Orders in the APP Collection," The American Presidency Project, http://www.presidency.ucsb.edu/executive_orders.php?year=1933. Accessed September 3, 2016.

F

Fair Employment Practices Committee

In 1941, as the economy continued its shift toward increased defense spending, African American leaders expressed increasing concern about employment discrimination against black workers. A. Philip Randolph, head of the Brotherhood of Sleeping Car Porters, emerged as a black spokesman on the issue, especially after he threatened to stage a march on Washington, D.C., to protest racial discrimination. President **Franklin D. Roosevelt** wanted to avoid such a march, which he was convinced would distract Americans from "more important" **New Deal** issues and make the United States look bad abroad. After meeting with Randolph and other black leaders, Roosevelt asked New York City mayor Fiorello La Guardia to head a commission to study the issue, and La Guardia soon called for a presidential executive order banning such discrimination. Roosevelt agreed, and on June 25, 1941, by executive order, he established the Fair Employment Practices Committee (FEPC). The FEPC proved to be more symbolic than real. Roosevelt could not give the FEPC any real power or money for fear of alienating southern Democrats, who controlled most congressional committees. Therefore, the FEPC held hearings and made proposals but had no powers of enforcement.

Further Reading

Amistad Digital Resource. "Plantation to Ghetto, Years 1919–1953: Section 08— The Great Depression," 2009, http://www.amistadresource.org/plantation_to_ghetto/the_great_depression.html. Accessed September 3, 2016; Greenberg, Cheryl. 2009. *To Ask for an Equal Chance: African Americans in the Great Depression* (The African American History Series), Lanham, MD: Rowman and Littlefield; Gale: *U.S. History in Context*. http://ic.galegroup.com/ic/uhic/ReferenceDetailsPage/DocumentToolsPortletWindow?displayGroupName=Reference&jsid=7812016b5ea4d6684ea4837e2c6ef921&action=2&catId=&documentId=GALE%7CCX3404500017&u=sand55832&zid=b57acc008e359910d5c

24de390bb447b. Accessed September 3, 2016; Trotter, Joe W. 2004. "African Americans, Impact of the Great Depression on." *Encyclopedia of the Great Depression*. Vol. 1. Robert S. McElvaine, ed. New York: Macmillan Reference USA.

Fair Labor Standards Act of 1938

In 1935, when the Supreme Court in its **Schechter** decision declared unconstitutional the National Industrial Recovery Act of 1933 (NIRA), it also overturned the only significant federal labor standards laws on the books. The NIRA had mandated minimum wage and maximum hours standards and had declared yellow-dog contracts illegal, and when the law was declared unconstitutional, labor leaders began to lobby for new legislation. The **Walsh-Healey Public Contracts Act of 1936** mandated minimum wage and maximum hours for all federal contractors (requiring overtime for work in excess of eight hours a day or forty hours a week), but comprehensive legislation did not emerge until 1938. The Fair Labor Standards Act became law on June 25, 1938.

The legislation established a wage and hour division in the Department of Labor to enforce its provisions. For all workers engaged in interstate commerce or producing goods destined for interstate shipment, the law mandated a minimum wage of twenty-five cents an hour for 1938 and thirty cents an hour for 1939. The minimum wage would rise to forty cents an hour in 1946. The law also set the maximum workweek at forty-four hours for 1938 and forty hours for 1939 and after. It outlawed child labor and defined a child worker as anyone under the age of sixteen. More than 13 million workers fell under the jurisdiction of the Fair Labor Standards Act of 1938; the most conspicuous workers excluded were agricultural laborers, intrastate retail employees, seamen, street railway operators, and fishermen.

See also: Unemployment; Walsh-Healey Public Contracts Act of 1936

Further Reading

Grossman, Jonathan. June 1978. "Fair Labor Standards Act of 1938: Maximum Struggle for a Minimum Wage," *Monthly Labor Review*. Accessed via U.S. Department of Labor. https://www.dol.gov/oasam/programs/history/flsa1938.htm. Accessed September 3, 2016.

Farm Credit Administration

A dramatically expanded role for the federal government in agricultural affairs was central to the **New Deal**, and in March 1933, by executive order,

President **Franklin D. Roosevelt** established the Farm Credit Administration (FCA) to coordinate the activities of the Federal Farm Board, the Federal Farm Loan Board, Federal Land Banks, Federal Intermediate Credit Banks, **Reconstruction Finance Corporation** regional agricultural corporations, and Department of Agriculture farm loans. The president named Henry Morgenthau as the first governor of the FCA.

Legislative authorization for the executive order was provided by the 1933 Farm Credit Act, which authorized the establishment of local credit institutions for farmers to ease their working capital and marketing problems. The act was intended to help relieve the massive debt faced by farmers who were having difficulty securing normal production loans from cautious rural bankers.

By early 1935, the FCA had refinanced more than 20 percent of the farm loans in the United States, rescuing millions of farmers from the threat of foreclosure. Also, Congress passed the Crop Loan Act in February 1934, which authorized the FCA to make direct production and harvest loans to farmers. In January 1934, Congress passed the Farm Mortgage Refinancing Act, which established the Federal Farm Mortgage Corporation with $2 billion to refinance farm debts. By the end of 1940, FCA loans totaled $6.87 billion.

Further Reading

Gilbert, Jess. 2015. *Planning Democracy: Agrarian Intellectuals and the Intended New Deal*, New Haven, CT: Yale University Press; Roosevelt, Franklin D. Roosevelt. March 27, 1933. "Executive Order 6084 Consolidating Federal Farm Credit Agencies," Gerhard Peters and John T. Woolley, The American Presidency Project, http://www.presidency.ucsb.edu/ws/?pid=14599. Accessed September 4, 2016.

Farm Security Administration

During the mid-1930s, the activities of the **Southern Tenant Farmers' Union** publicized the plight of poor sharecroppers and farm laborers. In January 1937, President **Franklin D. Roosevelt** established the Special Committee on Farm Tenancy to study the problem, and several months later the committee recommended a comprehensive federal program of landownership, rehabilitation, and the use of farm cooperatives by poor farmers. Late in 1937, Secretary of Agriculture **Henry Wallace** Jr. established the Farm Security Administration (FSA) to implement some of those objectives and to assume control over the activities of the **Resettlement Administration**. The FSA also supervised the provisions of the **Bankhead-Jones Farm Tenancy Act of 1937**, which authorized low-interest loans to

A Farm Security Administration (FSA) supervisor talks to a client at the FSA office in Taos County, New Mexico, in December 1941. (National Archives)

tenants, farm laborers, and sharecroppers to purchase their own land. Will W. Alexander was appointed head of the FSA.

The FSA invited the wrath of large commercial farmers, especially in the South, who feared losing their source of cheap labor. The FSA's resettlement programs helped only 15,000 farm families to relocate. Its loan programs supplied $300 million to help farmers purchase their own farms. Large commercial farmers hated the FSA's ninety-five camps for migrant laborers, which housed 75,000 people. The existence of the camps made migrant farmworkers more likely to demand higher wages from growers. The **American Farm Bureau Federation** called for the dissolution of the FSA, and the American Medical Association hated the FSA's health cooperatives. Conservatives in Congress accused the FSA of trying to redistribute wealth in the United States. Beginning in 1941, Congress steadily slashed the FSA budget, and in 1946 the Farmers Home Administration assumed its duties.

See also: American Farm Bureau Federation; Bankhead-Jones Farm Tenancy Act of 1937; Southern Tenant Farmers' Union; Wallace, Henry Agard

Further Reading

Agee, James, and Walker Evans. Reprint. 2001. *Let Us Now Praise Famous Men*, New York: Mariner; Cohen, Stu. 2008. *The Likes of Us: Photography and the Farm Security Administration*, Boston: David R. Godine; Grubbs, Donald H. 2000.

Cry from the Cotton: The Southern Tenant Farmers' Union and the New Deal, Fayetteville: University of Arkansas Press; Roberts, Charles Kenneth. 2015. *The Farm Security Administration and Rural Rehabilitation in the South*, Knoxville: University of Tennessee Press.

Federal Anti-Price Discrimination Act of 1936

A great advantage large chain stores had over smaller retailers was an ability to purchase in bulk, at low costs, from wholesalers and manufacturers. The retail prices large chain stores charged were often lower than the wholesale prices small businessmen and wholesalers had to charge to cover margins and make a profit. Under the codes of the **National Recovery Administration**, independent retailers and wholesalers had enjoyed protection from chain store buying power, but the *Schechter* decision in 1935, which overturned the National Industrial Recovery Act, dislodged those protections.

Senator Joseph Robinson of Arkansas and Congressman Wright Patman of Texas decided to push legislation that would restore those protections and give them statutory authority. Congress responded, and on June 20, 1936, President **Franklin D. Roosevelt** signed the Federal Anti-Price Discrimination Act. The law prohibited price discrimination by manufacturers in favor of large chain stores. Discounts, rebates, and high selling allowances were also prohibited. Under the legislation, the Federal Trade Commission was empowered to investigate and abolish all forms of price discrimination that had the effect of reducing competition.

Further Reading
Howard, Vicki. 2015. *From Main Street to Mall: The Rise and Fall of the American Department Store*, Philadelphia: University of Pennsylvania Press.

Federal Art Project

As part of the **Works Progress Administration**'s mission to relieve **unemployment**, the **Franklin D. Roosevelt** administration established the Federal Art Project to provide work for unemployed artists. Holger Cahill was named director of the program. Because the Federal Art Project was decentralized and tried to accommodate itself to local tastes, it was an immediate hit. At its peak in March 1936, the Federal Art Project employed more than 6,000 people, who produced paintings, mosaics, and sculptures, taught art classes, and conducted art research, the most important of which was the Index of American Design. The Index of American Design completed more than 20,000 reproductions of American art, paintings, sculptures, handicrafts, and folk art. As part of its art education projects, the Federal Art Project also established hundreds of community art centers and staged hundreds of exhibitions. The Federal Art Project continued well into World War II before it was terminated.

See also: Works Progress Administration

Further Reading

Carter, Ennis. 2008. *Posters for the People: Art of the WPA*, Philadelphia: Quirk Books; Grieve, Victoria. 2009. *The Federal Art Project and the Creation of Middlebrow Culture*, Champaign: University of Illinois Press; Hapke, Laura. 2008. *Labor's Canvas: American Working-Class History and the WPA Art of the 1930s*, Newcastle, UK: Cambridge Scholars Publishing.

Federal Crop Insurance Act of 1938

As early as the 1890s, farm advocates had proposed the idea of federal crop insurance to protect farmers from natural disasters. Widespread drought during the 1930s increased demands for some federal insurance program. Severe drought in 1936 prompted both presidential candidates—President **Franklin D. Roosevelt** for the Democrats and Alf Landon for the Republicans—to endorse the idea. Roosevelt established the President's Committee on Crop Insurance to study the issue, which early in 1937 recommended crop insurance for wheat. Senator James Pope of Idaho then introduced legislation into Congress, which was passed as Title V of the Agricultural Adjustment Act of 1938. The legislation established a Federal Crop Insurance Corporation, with capital of $100 million, in the Department of Agriculture. Congress also provided $6 million in annual operating costs. It provided insurance of 50 to 75 percent of the losses on wheat crops. By 1941 more than 371,392 farmers were participating in the program. In 1941, President Franklin D. Roosevelt signed legislation adding cotton to the program.

Further Reading

Glass, Andrew. February 26, 2012. "Congress Created the Federal Crop Insurance Corp, February 16, 1938," *Politico*, http://www.politico.com/story/2012/02/this-day-in-politics-072923. Accessed September 5, 2016; USDA Risk Management

Agency. "History of the Crop Insurance Program," United States Department of Agriculture, http://www.rma.usda.gov/aboutrma/what/history.html. Accessed September 5, 2016.

Federal Dance Project

As part of the **Works Progress Administration**'s effort to relieve **unemployment**, the **Roosevelt** administration established the **Federal Theatre Project** to provide work for unemployed professional actors, dancers, and theater technicians. Hallie Flanaghan became the first director of the Federal Theatre Project (FTP), but feuding erupted immediately between dancers and theater types in the FTP, and in March 1936, an independent Federal Dance Project (FDP) was established with Don Becque as director. Even then, internecine warfare characterized the FDP, especially between modern dancers and ballet enthusiasts. And when the FDP offered free dance classes to Americans, private dance teachers erupted in protest, worried that the FDP would destroy their businesses. Late in the 1930s, conservatives accused the FDP of being too liberal. Although the FDP put on hundreds of dance productions throughout the country, it became a victim of political infighting and external political hostility. The Emergency Relief Appropriation Act of 1939 cut funding to the FDP.

See also: Works Progress Administration

Further Reading
Franko, Mark. 2002. *The Work of Dance: Labor, Movement, and Identity in the 1930s*, Middletown, CT: Wesleyan University Press; Graff, Ellen. 1997. *Stepping Left: Dance and Politics in New York City, 1928–1942*, Durham, NC: Duke University Press.

Federal Deposit Insurance Corporation

Between 1921 and 1933, more than 9,000 banks failed in the United States, creating a monetary crisis of unprecedented proportions. During the presidency of **Herbert Hoover**, Congressman Henry Steagall of Alabama proposed creation of a federal corporation that would insure individual bank accounts. Steagall's logic was simple: if individual depositors knew that they would be able to get their money from a troubled bank or from the federal government, they would be less likely to make a "run" on the bank.

During such runs, panic-stricken depositors demanded their money in cash, forcing banks to liquidate their assets, which only further eroded bank capital reserves. But President Hoover opposed such an expansion of federal authority, and private bankers were almost unanimous in their opposition.

But the virtual meltdown of the financial markets in 1932–1933, the bank holiday, and the Emergency Banking Act of 1933 created a powerful political momentum in favor of bank deposit insurance. Early into the **New Deal**, Steagall's proposal was included in the Banking Act of 1933, which President **Franklin D. Roosevelt** signed on June 16, 1933. It provided for creation of a Federal Deposit Insurance Corporation (FDIC). All national banks had to join the FDIC, and state banks wanting to join had to agree to join the Federal Reserve System as well. The insurance program went into effect on January 1, 1934, insuring bank deposits up to a maximum of $5,000. By the end of 1935, more than 14,400 banks had joined the FDIC, and bank failures that year totaled only thirty-two. The FDIC proved to be one of the most enduring and successful of the New Deal agencies, ending the era of depositor panic, epidemics of bank failures, and catastrophic fluctuations in the money supply.

See also: Banking Crisis

Further Reading

Bradshaw, Gilbert J. October 25, 2015. "The History of the Federal Deposit Insurance Corporation," Bradshaw Law Group, http://bradshawlawgroup.com/the-history-of-the-federal-deposit-insurance-corporation/. Accessed September 9, 2016; FDIC. "The First Fifty Years—Chapter 3: Establishment of the FDIC," July 24, 2006, https://www.fdic.gov/bank/analytical/firstfifty/chapter3.html. Accessed September 9, 2016.

Federal Emergency Relief Administration

When **Franklin D. Roosevelt** took office in March 1933, more than 25 percent of Americans were unemployed, and the need for government relief and work relief was enormous. In July 1932, Congress had passed the **Emergency Relief and Construction Act**, which among other things provided $300 million in loans to states for relief programs. The money was exhausted in a few months. Social workers and such leading politicians as senators **Robert Wagner** of New York, Edward Costigan of Colorado, and Robert La Follette of Wisconsin demanded new federal appropriations, and on May 12, 1933, Congress responded with the

Federal Emergency Relief Act, creating the Federal Emergency Relief Administration (FERA) and endowing it with $500 million in grants, not loans, to the states.

President Franklin D. Roosevelt appointed **Harry Hopkins** to head the FERA. The president charged Hopkins to put the money to work as quickly as possible, even if it meant ignoring local Democratic politicians who wanted to use the money as patronage. The FERA focused on small work projects—such as sidewalks, curbs, bridges, and parks—that could be implemented without expensive, time-consuming engineering and architectural planning. Eventually, the FERA completed 235,000 projects and employed nearly 2.5 million workers. The FERA was extremely popular among working-class people and helped cement FDR's reputation among the poor.

See also: Emergency Relief and Construction Act of 1932

Further Reading
Leuchtenburg, William E. 2009. *Franklin D. Roosevelt and the New Deal: 1932–1940*, New York: Harper Perennial; University of Washington Digital Libraries. "Essay: The Federal Emergency Relief Administration," FERA Collection, http://content.lib.washington.edu/feraweb/essay.html. Accessed September 9, 2016.

Federal Farm Bankruptcy Act of 1934

The Federal Farm Bankruptcy Act of 1934, also known as the Frazier-Lemke Farm Bankruptcy Act, was designed to assist those farmers whose debts so exceeded the value of their property that their financial outlook was hopeless. Congressman **William Lemke** of North Dakota sponsored legislation that was supported by the National Farmers' Holiday Association and the Non-Partisan League. The law allowed a debt-ridden farmer to declare bankruptcy; federal courts would then scale down a farmer's debts until they were roughly equal to the value of his or her property. Once the farmer succeeded in retiring his debts at the scaled-down figure, he would gain permanent title to the property. The law allowed farmers to repurchase their properties at the newly appraised value. They were charged 1 percent annual interest and had six years to pay the debt off. If creditors opposed such an arrangement, the farmer could retain possession of the property for five years with no foreclosure occurring.

Creditors, especially rural bankers, bitterly opposed the Federal Farm Bankruptcy Act of 1934 and sued in federal courts. The case of *Louisville Joint Stock Land Bank v. Radford* represented creditor interests, and in

1935 the U.S. Supreme Court declared the law unconstitutional because it denied creditors due process of law. William Lemke returned quickly with new legislation that Congress soon passed—the Farm Mortgage Moratorium Act of 1935, also known as the Frazier-Lemke Act of 1935. The law provided for a three-year moratorium on foreclosures against farmers who had defaulted on their debt payments.

See also: Lemke, William

Further Reading
Gilbert, Jess. 2015. *Planning Democracy: Agrarian Intellectuals and the Intended New Deal*, New Haven, CT: Yale University Press.

Federal Home Loan Bank Act of 1932

By early 1932, the nation's money markets were in an advanced state of meltdown. A liquidity crisis tied up tens of billions of dollars, and most financial institutions had grown quite cautious about lending. In fact, the economy was caught in a credit crisis. Economic confidence was at an all-time low and **unemployment** at an all-time high. President **Herbert Hoover** was anxious to find new ways to stimulate the economy. The Federal Home Loan Bank Act of 1932 was one of his initiatives to do so. The president signed the bill into law on July 22, 1932. It established a five-person Home Loan Bank Board and a system of government banks empowered to discount home mortgages. Each Federal Home Loan Bank received $125 million in capital to discount the home mortgages issued by building and loan associations, savings banks, and insurance companies. As the logic of the legislation went, financial institutions would be more willing to make home mortgage loans if they knew they could get cash for the mortgages from the federal government. Hoover was convinced the Federal Home Loan Banks would help liquefy the money markets and stimulate a revival in the home construction industry.

What Hoover did not anticipate, however, was the reality of the liquidity trap. Interest rates were at all-time lows, but the number of credit-worthy borrowers applying for loans and the number of financial institutions willing to put their capital at risk were at an all-time low. Home construction throughout 1932 continued to decline, as did the number of new mortgages issued. Any hopes the president had of reviving the construction industry before the presidential election of 1932 were dashed.

See also: Hoover, Herbert Clark; Reconstruction Finance Corporation

Further Reading
Gou, Michael, Gary Richardson, Alejandro Komai, and Daniel Park. "Banking Acts of 1932," Federal Reserve History, http://www.federalreservehistory.org/Events/DetailView/12. Accessed September 9, 2016; Meltzer, Allan. 2003. *A History of the Federal Reserve: Volume 1, 1913 to 1951*, Chicago: University of Chicago Press.

Federal Housing Administration

In 1933, nearly one-third of all unemployed men in the United States were construction workers, and President **Franklin D. Roosevelt** and the **New Deal** became committed to reviving the home construction market. He appointed the President's Emergency Commission on Housing to study the issue, and among the commission's recommendations was the establishment of a Federal Housing Administration (FHA) to insure bank housing loans, for home repair or new construction, made to middle-income families. The commission felt that if banks and savings and loans had guarantees that the federal government would purchase any delinquent loans they made, they would be more willing to extend credit and revive the construction industry. In June 1934 Congress passed the **National Housing Act**, which provided for establishment of the FHA. The measure attracted considerable opposition from building and loan associations. The law also established a Federal Savings and Loan Insurance Corporation to insure deposits in building and loan and savings and loan associations. Between 1934 and 1940, the FHA provided credit to 1,544,217 homeowners to repair or modernize their houses. The FHA also helped finance construction of nearly 500,000 new homes. By 1940, FHA loans totaled nearly $4.1 billion.

See also: National Housing Act of 1934

Further Reading
Griffith, John. October 11, 2012. "The Federal Housing Administration Saved the Housing Market," Center for American Progress, https://www.americanprogress.org/issues/housing/report/2012/10/11/40824/the-federal-housing-administration-saved-the-housing-market/. Accessed September 9, 2016; Smith, Jason Scott. 2014. *A Concise History of the New Deal* (Cambridge Essential Histories), Cambridge: Cambridge University Press.

Federal Music Project

The Federal Music Project (FMP) was one of the **Works Progress Administration**'s (WPA) programs for unemployed artists and professionals. Headed by former Boston Symphony Orchestra violinist Nikolai Sokoloff from 1935 to 1939, the FMP became the most successful of the WPA's art programs.

By 1933, the **unemployment** rate among professional musicians had exceeded 65 percent, primarily because music and entertainment were perceived as luxuries, not necessities. The FMP had two missions: educational and performance. FMP teachers directed bands, choruses, and orchestras and conducted classes in vocal and instrumental music. They also directed amateur community productions and local singing groups. On the performance side, the FMP staged public performances in schools, hospitals, nursing homes, parks, community centers, settlement houses, prisons, and orphanages. The FMP also produced **radio** programs. The FMP employed 15,000 musicians at its peak, and by March 1940, they had conducted 1.5 million music classes with 17.7 million students. Its performance groups had put on more than 14,000 performances to a combined audience of 159 million people, not including more than 14,000 radio broadcasts.

Poster of *Carmen*, an opera and ballet performed by the Cuyahoga County Opera Association and the Federal Music Project. (Library of Congress)

See also: Works Progress Administration

Further Reading

Gough, Peter. 2015. *Sounds of the New Deal: The Federal Music Project in the West* (Music in American Life), Champaign: University of Illinois Press.

Federal Reserve Board

Economic historians today credit Federal Reserve Board policies with aggravating the speculative boom of the 1920s and contributing to the **stock market crash** of 1929. Federal Reserve officials found themselves caught on the horns of two dilemmas. First, they erroneously believed that in the wake of World War I, European nations would not be able to stimulate their damaged economies until they could return to the **gold standard**, but at the time, the strength of the American economy and its positive trade balance attracted gold away from Europe and to the United States. Only a credit rate differential between New York and London, with interests low in New York and high in London, could attract cash reserves to Europe. That reality made it difficult to inhibit the speculative stock market boom in the United States. If the Federal Reserve Board raised interest rates in the United States to discourage the stock market, it would only stimulate the flow of more gold from Europe to America. On the other hand, an easy money policy that reduced domestic interest rates would please foreign leaders but only stimulate the stock market. Either choice left Federal Reserve officials with potential consequences they did not want to face.

The second dilemma revolved around how to discourage securities speculation without at the same time inhibiting legitimate business expansion. High interest rates might stem the Wall Street tide but also make it more difficult for legitimate businessmen to acquire needed capital. Low interest rates would please businessmen but stimulate securities speculation. Throughout the 1920s, because of such impossible choices, Federal Reserve Board officials pursued contradictory and dilatory policies.

What the Federal Reserve Board decided was to peg discount rates at high levels while purchasing larger volumes of banker acceptances. They erroneously concluded that the funds banks received for the sale of the acceptances would only be used for legitimate business needs and not for speculation. They assumed that the method of increasing the money supply determined the uses to which the funds would be put; they failed to appreciate that the purchase of acceptances would increase the volume of excess reserves that could then be invested into the securities markets. The board actually expected that its high discount rates would discourage speculation, while its purchases of bankers' acceptances would stimulate a credit expansion and business growth. It was a pipe dream. With the fresh infusion of Federal Reserve funds, bankers increased their reserve balances and reduced their Federal Reserve Bank indebtedness, which negated the impact of the discount rate.

In the end, Federal Reserve policies attracted more money into the stock markets. Many corporations diverted surplus funds into the securities markets, which only drove prices higher. At the time, the Federal Reserve Board did not assume responsibility for managing the flow and destination of nonbank investment funds, and that oversight would prove critical to the speculative boom and to the ultimate crash of the stock market in 1929.

See also: Gold Standard; Stock Market Crash

Further Reading

Bernanke, Ben. 2013. *The Federal Reserve and the Financial Crisis*, Princeton, NJ: Princeton University Press; Hetzel, Robert. 2008. *The Monetary Policy of the Federal Reserve: A History*, Cambridge: Cambridge University Press; Meltzer, Allan. 2003. *A History of the Federal Reserve: Volume 1, 1913 to 1951*, Chicago: University of Chicago Press; Richardson, Gary, Alejandro Komai, and Michael Gou. "Roosevelt's Gold Program," Federal Reserve History, http://www.federalreservehistory.org/Events/DetailView/24. Accessed September 9, 2016.

Federal Surplus Relief Corporation

One of the real ironies of the Great Depression was the existence of huge agricultural surpluses, along with tens of millions of poor, unemployed people, many of whom did not have enough to eat. To deal with that irony, President **Franklin D. Roosevelt** had the **Agricultural Adjustment Administration** in October 1933 establish the Federal Surplus Relief Corporation (FSRC). The FSRC was designed to collect surplus agricultural production and distribute the commodities to **New Deal** relief agencies, which would then get the food in the hands of the poor. **Harry Hopkins**, head of the **Federal Emergency Relief Administration**, was named president of the FSRC. The problem, of course, was that perishable commodities often did not survive bureaucratic complexities. The FSRC did see to the distribution of such commodities as pork, butter, flour, syrup, and cotton, but it did prove inefficient and unable to fulfill the vision of its creators. When its programs were discontinued in November 1935, the FSRC's significance was more symbolic than real, but it did at least convey an image that the federal government was trying to deal with a chronic problem.

See also: Agricultural Adjustment Administration

Further Reading

Gilbert, Jess. 2015. *Planning Democracy: Agrarian Intellectuals and the Intended New Deal*, New Haven, CT: Yale University Press; Gunderson, Gordon W.

June 17, 2014. "National School Lunch Program (NSLA): USDA," http://www.fns.usda.gov/nslp/history_4. Accessed September 9, 2016; Ziegelman, Jane, and Andrew Coe. 2016. *A Square Meal: A Culinary History of the Great Depression*, New York: HarperCollins.

Federal Theatre Project

As part of its diverse programs to assist the unemployed, the **Works Progress Administration** tried to put unemployed artists and professionals to work. The Federal Theatre Project (FTP) was designed to assist unemployed actors, directors, playwrights, and theater technicians. By the end of 1935, with headquarters in New York City, the FTP had hired 3,500 people and established five distinct units, which included the Living Newspaper, the Popular Price Theatre, the Experimental Theatre, the Negro Theatre, and the Tryout Theatre, as well as a classical repertory theater, a unit for poetic drama, a vaudeville unit that performed in Yiddish, an Anglo-Jewish theater, a children's unit, and a one-act play group. The FTP was headed by Hallie Flanagan. During the years of its existence, FTP groups played to a total audience of several million people. But it also found itself in constant political trouble, primarily because many conservatives perceived its plays as too liberal and too socially conscious. In 1939, Congressman Martin Dies and the House Committee to Investigate Un-American Activities Committee targeted the FTP, and Congress severely cut its funding.

See also: Works Progress Administration

Further Reading
Library of Congress. "The New Deal Stage: Selections from the Federal Theatre Project," American Memory, January 25, 2012, http://memory.loc.gov/ammem/fedtp/fthome.html. Accessed September 3, 2016; Witham, Larry. 2003. *The Federal Theatre Project: A Case Study*, Cambridge, UK: Cambridge University Press.

Federal Works Agency

The Federal Works Agency (FWA) was created by the **Reorganization Act of 1939** to consolidate and coordinate all of the federal government's relief and work relief agencies. The FWA assumed control of the **Works Progress Administration**, the **Public Works Administration**, the Bureau of Public Roads, and the U.S. Housing Agency. Congress abolished the FWA in 1949 and transferred its responsibilities to the General Services Administration.

See also: Public Works Administration; Reorganization Act of 1939; Works Progress Administration

Further Reading
National Archives. "General Records of the Federal Works Agency (FWA)," August 15, 2016, http://www.archives.gov/research/guide-fed-records/groups/162.html. Accessed September 5, 2016.

Federal Writers' Project

The Federal Writers' Project (FWP) was one of the **Works Progress Administration**'s programs for unemployed professionals and artists. It primarily hired lawyers, teachers, social workers, librarians, journalists, and ministers, putting them to work as researchers and writers. Henry Alsberg was appointed head of the FWP. FWP writers wrote local history, travel guides, nature studies, ethnographies, and black studies. Eventually, the FWP spent more than $27 million and produced hundreds of books and monographs, including 378 books that were commercially published. The FWP's most memorable product was the American Guide Series, a state-by-state and city-by-city description of regional America as it existed in the mid-1930s. The books, one for each state as well as Puerto Rico, Alaska, and Hawaii, received almost universal praise.

The WPA also commissioned interviews with African Americans who were former slaves. Between 1936 and 1938, writers and researchers met with more than 2,300 ex-slaves in seventeen states, compiling first-person accounts about life in bondage, including twenty-six audio recordings. This body of work still stands as one of the most important records of slavery ever compiled.

Late in the 1930s, like the **Federal Theatre Project** and the **Federal Music Project**, the FWP encountered serious criticism from conservative Republicans, who believed the program was too liberal politically. Congress became more and more stingy with funds, and on June 30, 1943, the FWP went out of business.

See also: Works Progress Administration

Further Reading
Hirsch, Jerrold. 2003. *Portrait of America: A Cultural History of the Federal Writers' Project*, Chapel Hill: University of North Carolina Press; Library of Congress.

"American Life Histories: Manuscripts from the Federal Writers' Project, 1936–1940," American Memory, http://memory.loc.gov/ammem/wpaintro/wpahome.html. Accessed September 3, 2016; Stewart, Catherine A. 2016. *Long Past Slavery: Representing Race in the Federal Writers' Project*, Chapel Hill: University of North Carolina Press; Taylor, David A. 2009. *Soul of a People: The WPA Writers' Project Discovers Depression America*, Hoboken, NJ: Wiley.

Film

The 1930s marked the beginning of what is known as Hollywood's "golden age"—from 1930 through the end of the 1940s. The decade saw numerous advances in filmmaking, particularly the increased use of sound and technicolor. With the transition to sound, which began in the late 1920s, dialogue became more developed and character-driven style more prevalent, in contrast to the slapstick-heavy films of the silent movie era. This allowed for the development of more defined genres in film, such as screwball comedies, westerns, gangster films, musicals, and horror. It also helped create a new crop of major stars, such as Clark Gable, Mae West, Greta Garbo, the Marx Brothers, Errol Flynn, and Shirley Temple, the highest-grossing star of the era.

The film industry was not unaffected by the Depression—the major studios took a hit as theater attendance decreased by almost one-third—but movies never lost their popularity; between 60 and 80 million people still went to a movie each week. Depression-era films tended to offer escapism, heroes, idealism, and feel-good entertainment—but also cynical, gritty realism like James Cagney in *Public Enemy* (1931) or the war film *All Quiet on the Western Front* (1930).

The highest-grossing film of the decade was the sprawling epic *Gone with the Wind* (1939), based on Margaret Mitchell's best-selling novel of the same name. The film reflected the prevailing false sentiment toward the Reconstruction-era South: dashing cavaliers, corseted belles, genteel plantation owners, and contented slaves, all maintaining their dignity in the face of an exploitive, greedy, aggressive North. Actress Hattie McDaniel won an Academy Award for Best Supporting Actress for her portrayal of Mammy—the first African American ever to win an Oscar. The film also helped skyrocket Clark Gable and Vivian Leigh, already major celebrities, to superstardom.

The movie musical also increased in popularity during the Depression. After the genre briefly fell out of favor in the early 1930s, it was revived partly by the inclusion of better dance numbers, especially those staged by director Busby Berkeley in movies like *42nd Street* (1933). Audiences flocked to see Fred Astaire and Ginger Rogers, who danced their way through ten films, including *The Gay Divorcee* (1934), *Top Hat* (1935), and *Swing Time* (1936). Most beloved of all was child star Shirley Temple, the most popular movie actress of the decade. Between 1934 and 1937, the curly-haired, dimpled Temple became Hollywood's top box-office draw, grossing $5 million a year in films like *Bright Eyes* (1934), *The Little Colonel* (1935), *Heidi* (1937), and *Rebecca of Sunnybrook Farm* (1938). Other notable musical actors included Bing Crosby, Mickey Rooney, Judy Garland, and Alice Faye.

In 1939, Walt Disney released the first full-length animated film: *Snow White and the Seven Dwarfs*. Adapted from the Grimms' fairy tale, *Snow White* was also the first Disney cartoon to feature people as the protagonists, rather than animal characters, like Mickey Mouse. The story was a classic tale of a virtuous young woman, a wicked queen, and a happy ending with a noble prince. The film received rave reviews and was a box-office smash.

Perhaps the most important genre to come into its own during the Great Depression was the horror film. The inclusion of sound in film added new levels to the terror a movie monster could evoke. Early horror films found their inspiration in gothic literature, and tended to explore the conflict between science and religion, in contrast to the "slasher" films of the 1970s and 1980s, or the supernatural themes in later films like *The Exorcist* (1973) and *Poltergeist* (1982). *Frankenstein* (1931), based on Mary Shelley's 1818 novel, and *Dracula*, based on Bram Stoker's 1897 book, are credited by many film historians as the formal birth of the horror film genre. The monster played by Boris Karloff in *Frankenstein* was made thoroughly believable to Depression-era audiences through some of the most advanced special-effects makeup to date. Bela Lugosi in *Dracula* was the prototypical movie monster, with his sinister, slow-paced delivery and forbidding, silent close-ups. Both actors went on to star in several similar roles, and their movies helped define approaches to horror filmmaking for decades to come.

Due to the release of certain risqué films and the prevalence of off-screen Hollywood scandals, the Motion Picture Producers and Distributors of America began enforcing the Motion Picture Production Code in 1934 (though it was actually created in 1930). Also known as the Hays Code, the code was a set of moral and aesthetic standards for all movies released in the United States. It prohibited things like nudity and profanity onscreen, but also dealt with items like criminals being portrayed in a sympathetic light and improper depiction of the American flag. The censorship began to loosen in the 1950s with the advent of television and less-restrained foreign films. By the late 1960s, the code was abandoned in favor of the Motion Picture Association of America rating system still in use today.

Further Reading

Dickstein, Morris. 2010. *Dancing in the Dark: A Cultural History of the Great Depression*, New York: W. W. Norton & Company; Jewell, Richard. 2007. *The Golden Age of Cinema: Hollywood, 1929–1945*, Oxford, UK: Blackwell Publishing; Whitington, Paul. April 10, 2008. "How the Great Depression Inspired Hollywood's Golden Age," Entertainment: Movies page, *Independent* (Ireland), http://www.independent.ie/entertainment/movies/how-the-great-depression-inspired-hollywoods-golden-age-26481978.html. Accessed September 5, 2016.

Fireside Chats

The term "fireside chats" referred to the informal **radio** talks **Franklin D. Roosevelt** delivered during his governorship of New York (1929–1933) and his presidency. On March 12, 1933, just eight days into his administration,

President Franklin D. Roosevelt delivers one of his popular fireside chats, a series of evening radio talks to the American public. Roosevelt used these chats to explain New Deal programs during the Great Depression and war policies during World War II. (Library of Congress)

FDR delivered his first radio address, a soothing discussion of the banking crisis and his reassurances that all would be well. He had an innate ability to address millions of people as if he were talking to a single family. More than 17 million families tuned into the address, and many historians believed that with that radio address FDR cemented his enduring political relationship with the American public. On June 24, 1933, before another FDR radio address, Harry C. Butcher of CBS Radio advertised the program as a "fireside chat." He eventually delivered twenty-eight fireside chats. In doing so, Roosevelt gave birth to the age of media politics.

See also: Banking Crisis; Radio

Further Reading

Kiewe, Amos. 2007. *FDR's First Fireside Chat: Public Confidence and the Banking Crisis* (Library of Presidential Rhetoric), College Station: Texas A&M University Press; Latson, Jennifer. March 12, 2015. "How FDR's Radio Voice Solved a Banking Crisis," *Time*, http://time.com/3731744/fdr-fireside-chat-banking/. Accessed September 5, 2016; Roosevelt, Franklin Delano. 2015. *The Fireside Chats of Franklin Delano Roosevelt*, CreateSpace Independent Publishing Platform.

First New Deal

Historians have used the term "First New Deal" to describe the legislation passed by Congress in 1933 and 1934 to deal with the Great Depression. The key concerns of the First New Deal were relief and recovery and a commitment to using the federal government to coordinate diverse interest groups to boost production and employment. The First New Deal had no faith in the ability of the market economy to allocate resources and dictate production and prices and envisioned the federal government playing a new role in national economic planning. The First New Deal included the **National Recovery Administration (NRA)**, the **Agricultural Adjustment Administration (AAA)**, the **Tennessee Valley Authority**, the **Civilian Conservation Corps**, the **Federal Emergency Relief Administration**, and the **Civil Works Administration.**

But the First New Deal began to disintegrate late in 1934 and early in 1935. It became obvious to most Americans that large corporations had seized control of the NRA and that the AAA had been captured by large commercial farmers. In 1935 and 1936, the Supreme Court declared the NRA and AAA unconstitutional. At this point, the First New Deal began to give way to what became known as the "Second New Deal," an emphasis on social reform, antitrust, and **Keynes**ian economics.

See also: First 100 Days

Further Reading
Alter, Jonathan. 2007. *The Defining Moment: FDR's Hundred Days and the Triumph of Hope*, New York: Simon & Schuster; Cohen, Adam. 2010. *Nothing to Fear: FDR's Inner Circle and the Hundred Days That Created Modern America*, New York: Penguin Books; Kiewe, Amos. 2007. *FDR's First Fireside Chat: Public Confidence and the Banking Crisis*, College Station: Texas A&M University Press.

First 100 Days

The first 100 days of **Franklin Delano Roosevelt**'s presidency comprised the special session of the 73rd Congress that launched the **New Deal**. Immediately on taking office, President Roosevelt wasted no time in addressing a nation in crisis. In direct response to former president **Herbert Hoover**'s emphasis on private charity, small government, and the untouched operation of the free market, the Roosevelt administration passed more major legislation than at any other time in U.S. history, as part of what Roosevelt felt was the "social duty" of government—to help those who could not help themselves.

The most pressing issue was the banking crisis. During the 1920s, thousands of banks had failed, eroding assets, weakening depositors' confidence, and sparking runs on banks. In late February 1933, just before Roosevelt took office, 95 percent of the nation's banks were threatening to shut down. On March 6, Roosevelt declared a bank holiday—a moratorium on all banking operations in the United States. The Emergency Banking Act was passed on March 9, allowing the government to reopen all banks that were solvent and provide aid to banks in need. Before the banks reopened, Roosevelt gave a **radio** address, the first of his **fireside chats**, to the nation. He clearly outlined what the government had done and why, explaining that money—and banks—would be safe when the banks reopened. The first fireside chat is credited with restoring the nation's confidence in the banking system; in a matter of weeks, Americans had deposited over $1 billion into the banks.

Between March 9 and June 16, 1933, Congress passed fifteen major bills, including the Emergency Banking Act, the Economy Act, the Civilian Conservation Corps, the Reforestation Relief Act, the Federal Emergency Relief Act, the Agricultural Adjustment Act, the **Securities Act**, the National

Employment System Act, the Home Owners' Refinancing Act, the Banking Act, the Farm Credit Act, the **Emergency Railroad Transportation Act**, and the National Industrial Recovery Act, and established the **Tennessee Valley Authority**. The legislation also, for the first time, federally regulated the stock market and set a precedent for what became known as the welfare state—the government providing national relief and wealth-redistribution programs, especially for its worst-off citizens.

Historians today consider the first 100 days of the Roosevelt administration the most dramatic period in the history of American public policy. Since then, symbolic attention has been paid to each subsequent president's first 100 days, as a potential measure of that presidency's success.

See also: Banking Crisis; New Deal; Roosevelt, Franklin Delano

Further Reading

Alter, Jonathan. 2007. *The Defining Moment: FDR's Hundred Days and the Triumph of Hope*, New York: Simon & Schuster; Cohen, Adam. 2010. *Nothing to Fear: FDR's Inner Circle and the Hundred Days That Created Modern America*, New York: Penguin Books; Kiewe, Amos. 2007. *FDR's First Fireside Chat: Public Confidence and the Banking Crisis*, College Station: Texas A&M University Press; Walsh, Kenneth T. February 12, 2009. "The First 100 Days: Franklin Roosevelt Pioneered the 100-Day Concept," *U.S. News & World Report*, http://www.usnews.com/news/history/articles/2009/02/12/the-first-100-days-franklin-roosevelt-pioneered-the-100-day-concept. Accessed September 3, 2016.

Fischer, Irving

Irving Fischer was one of the Great Depression's most popular and most misguided economists. He was born on February 27, 1867, in Saugerties, New York. Fischer earned his undergraduate and doctoral degrees at Yale, where he specialized in mathematical economics. In 1890, he joined the Yale faculty and published widely on bimetallism, prices, capital, and interest rates. At the same time, he became a health food fanatic, an advocate of the League of Nations, and a prohibitionist. His 1928 book *The Money Illusion* enjoyed wide popularity.

But Fischer's popularity and his personal fortune were wiped out with the **stock market crash** of 1929. He also lost much of his reputation as one of the country's leading economists. Things only became worse for him. In 1930, his book *The Stock Market Crash and After* predicted that the nation's economic downturn would be shorter and superficial. When those predictions went unfulfilled, Fischer began touting currency manipulation as the way out of the Great Depression. He urged President **Franklin D. Roosevelt** to scuttle the **gold standard** to try to restore currency values to 1926 levels. Fischer had come to agree with silver advocates that bimetallism would end the Depression. The president's ill-fated gold-buying program of 1933–1934 tried to manipulate prices and stem deflation by buying and selling gold. Of course, the scheme was poorly conceived and of no effect.

Fischer eventually became one of the **New Deal**'s most vociferous critics, blaming Franklin Roosevelt for leading the country down the road to socialism and big government. In the process, his own stature among economists fell steadily, particularly as **Keynes**ian economics gained more and more acceptance. Irving Fischer died on April 29, 1947.

Further Reading

Atack, Jeremy, and Peter Passell. *A New Economic View of America History: From Colonial Times to 1940*, 2nd ed., New York: W. W. Norton & Company.

Fletcher-Rayburn Bill. *See* Securities Act of 1933

Food, Drug, and Cosmetic Act of 1938

Historians consider the Food, Drug, and Cosmetic Act of 1938 to be the last legislative achievement of the **New Deal**. Consumer advocates had long been calling for a strengthening of the Pure Food and Drug Act of 1906, and major pharmaceutical companies joined the chorus in the 1930s because of the proliferation of inconsistent regulatory legislation at the state level. In October 1937, the push for new legislation accelerated when more than one hundred Americans died after taking the drug sulfanilamide to treat venereal disease and strep infections. The drug was produced by S. E. Massengill Company, a manufacturer of veterinary medicines. Senator Royal Copeland of New York and Congressman Clarence Lea of California sponsored the Food, Drug, and Cosmetic Act, which President **Franklin D. Roosevelt** signed into law on June 25, 1938. The law greatly expanded on the 1906 legislation, giving the Food and Drug Administration (FDA) the power of injunction to seize commodities and impose criminal sanctions on drug manufacturers guilty of mislabeling products or making unsubstantiated claims of drug effectiveness. The law also required food manufacturers to list ingredients on visible labels and to adhere to government standards on the quality and fill of containers. The FDA could also inspect factories to ensure compliance.

Further Reading

Martin, Barbara J. 2014. *Elixir: The American Tragedy of a Deadly Drug*, Barkerry Press; U.S. Food and Drug Administration. "FDA History—Part II: The 1938 Food, Drug, and Cosmetic Act," September 24, 2012, http://www.fda.gov/AboutFDA/WhatWeDo/History/Origin/ucm054826.htm. Accessed September 5, 2016.

Frazier-Lemke Farm Bankruptcy Act. *See* Federal Farm Bankruptcy Act of 1934

G

Glass-Steagall Act

During the 1920s, as tens of thousands of banks failed in the United States, critics and economists began proposing major reforms to protect depositors and to stabilize the money markets. Some actually called for creation of a single federal banking system and scrapping of the decentralized Federal Reserve System, with its twelve regional banks and weak central board in Washington, D.C. Radicals even demanded federal nationalization of the entire banking system. Some state banking authorities argued that state regulation of their individual banking systems would be sufficient and that all forms of federal regulation should be scrapped.

In 1931, the investigation into banking practices by Congressman Ferdinand Pecora (**Pecora Committee**) exposed serious problems in the banking system, none more important than the fact that the lines between commercial banking and investment banking had become hopelessly blurred, with bankers siphoning money from commercial bank depositors and channeling them into speculative new securities offerings. When the **stock market** crashed in 1929–1930, millions of depositors saw their savings wiped out. Small bankers were also concerned about the trend for large commercial banks to establish small branches in smaller cities and towns. Such an invasion of local markets, they were convinced, would send small, independent banks toward bankruptcy. Many economists worried that the failure of more than 5,600 banks during the 1920s had ominous implications for the future and that the federal government needed to provide a system of guaranteeing bank deposits so that panic-stricken depositors would not make runs on troubled financial institutions. When several thousand more banks failed during the financial meltdown of 1931–1932, demands for some type of federal deposit insurance escalated.

Throughout 1932, several bills surfaced in Congress to address these problems, and the most influential among them was sponsored by Senator Carter Glass of Virginia and Congressman Henry Steagall of Alabama. The bill called for a liberalization of Federal Reserve rediscounting regulations but said nothing about other problems in the money markets, and the **Hoover** administration was paralyzed anyway, unable to achieve anything politically because of its complete loss of credibility. When the banking system virtually collapsed in 1932–1933, the administration of the newly elected president **Franklin D. Roosevelt** enjoyed, or faced, overwhelming support and overwhelming pressure to do something about the banking system.

In March and April 1933, **New Deal** officials carefully studied the problem, and in mid-May, Carter and Glass submitted new legislation to Congress. It was an omnibus measure that made the nation's banking system stronger and less vulnerable to foreign manipulation and domestic panic. The bill called for an increase in Federal Reserve control over bank credit and more careful coordination of Federal Reserve open market operations, and it awarded official legal recognition to the Federal Open Market Committee. The bill gave control to the **Federal Reserve Board** of all the foreign operations of its member banks. To prevent future speculative manias and protect depositors' savings, the bill separated investment banking from commercial banking and outlawed a mixing of the two functions within the same bank. Banks would have to define themselves as commercial banks or investment banks. Commercial banks could underwrite the securities only of state and local governments and had one year to divest themselves of their securities affiliates. Officers of national banks could no longer accept loans from their own banks. Also, national banks could establish branch banks but only in states that had authorized them to do so by law. To regulate chain and group banking, the comptroller of the currency had power to regulate the stock voting rights of the holding company affiliate of national banks. The legislation also raised the capital requirements of national banks to give them more power and resiliency during times of financial crisis. Finally, the law established a **Federal Deposit Insurance Corporation** (FDIC) to insure bank deposits. The FDIC received $150 million in capital from the federal government and operating funds from each member bank participating in the insurance program. The FDIC would begin operations on July 1, 1936. In mid-June, the Glass-Steagall Banking Act, or Banking Act, of 1933 passed in both houses of Congress, and President Franklin D. Roosevelt signed it into law.

See also: Federal Deposit Insurance Corporation; Federal Reserve Board; Pecora Committee

Further Reading

Irwin, Neil. October 14, 2015. "What Is Glass-Steagall? The 82-Year-Old Banking Law That Stirred the Debate," The Upshot, *New York Times*, http://www.nytimes.com/2015/10/15/upshot/what-is-glass-steagall-the-82-year-old-bank

ing-law-that-stirred-the-debate.html?rref=collection%2Ftimestopic%2FGlass-Steagall%20Act%20(1933)&action=click&contentCollection=timestopics&region=stream&module=stream_unit&version=latest&contentPlacement=10&pgtype=collection. Accessed September 5, 2016; Long, Heather. October 14, 2015. "What the Heck Is the Controversial Glass-Steagall Act?" Money. CNN, http://money.cnn.com/2015/10/14/investing/democratic-debate-what-is-glass-steagall-act/. Accessed September 5, 2016.

Gold Standard

For centuries, the world's developed economies had taken pride in the fact that their currencies were backed by gold. The "gold standard," political leaders and economists were convinced, was a prerequisite to price stability and confidence in the world's money markets. But the onset of the Great Depression undermined the gold standard. A great concern to the **Franklin D. Roosevelt** administration and to the business community during the early years of the Great Depression was the deflationary spiral in prices. Deflation made it difficult for businessmen to plan ahead and therefore made them reluctant to invest capital in their enterprises. At the same time, Roosevelt faced pressure from western farmers and western mining interests to inflate the currency.

Panic-stricken bank depositors and investors, worried about bankruptcies in financial institutions and imploding security prices, launched a "flight to gold," or hard currency, which they believed had inherent value. But in London, Paris, New York, Berlin, and Vienna, there was not enough gold to fill the demand. In 1931, the bankruptcy of Austria's largest bank, the Credit Anstalt, triggered a run for cash that led Great Britain to abandon the gold standard. Convinced that adherence to the gold standard only made deflation more intense, President Roosevelt took the United States off the gold standard on April 19, 1933, refusing any longer to convert paper currency into gold. This extremely unpopular decision among America's richest investors was called by budget director Lewis Douglas "the end of Western civilization."

Several months later, the president implemented a gold-buying program to satisfy the demands of economists like **Irving Fischer** and **George Warren**, who believed in the so-called commodity dollar. Their notion was that if the federal government bought gold at steadily rising prices, the value of the dollar would go down and prices would rise. In the process, the United States would also capture a larger share of world trade. Business confidence would rise, as would production and employment. From October 1933 to January 1934, Roosevelt met daily with economic advisers to set the price at which the government would purchase gold. To keep speculators off balance, they set the price above the world price for gold and changed it each day.

But the scheme made no economic sense. The price of commodities was not directly connected to the relative price of gold versus the dollar, and the administration's daily manipulation of gold prices only added chaos to the money markets. Also, farm prices continued to fall. In January 1934, President Roosevelt decided to abandon the scheme, and on January 30, he signed the Gold Reserve Act, which empowered him to fix the price of gold in the United States. The next day, he set the price of gold at $35 an ounce, which fixed the value of the dollar at 59 percent of its pre-1933 level. Wall Street could not have been happier, but inflationists out west kept up the pressure to inflate the currency. Their demands soon led to the **Silver Purchase Act of 1934**.

On February 18, 1935, by a narrow 5 to 4 vote, the U.S. Supreme Court decided four cases known as the "Gold Clause Cases"—*Norman v. Baltimore & Ohio Railroad Company*, *United States et al. v. Bankers' Trust Company*, *Nortz v. United States*, and *Perry v. United States*. All four cases revolved around Congress's decision in 1933 to nullify the clauses in public and private contracts requiring debt repayments in gold. At the time, President Roosevelt, through **New Deal** legislation, was trying to prevent the drain and ultimate exhaustion of the country's gold reserves, and by suspending redemption in gold of U.S. government bonds, the government conserved national gold reserves. Bondholders, however, argued that Congress had violated legal contracts in passing such legislation and, in doing so, had violated Fifth Amendment rights to due process and private property.

When the cases reached the Supreme Court, a bitter debate ensued behind the Court's closed doors. In the end, the Supreme Court upheld the New Deal's abrogation of gold clauses in contracts on the grounds that the federal government in general and Congress in particular exercised primary control over the monetary system. Although admitting that the legislation impaired existing contracts, the Court argued that congressional authority over monetary policy justified the action.

See also: Federal Reserve Board

Further Reading

Bernake, Ben. 2012. "Chairman Ben S. Bernanke Lecture Series Part I," USTREAM, Internet Archive Wayback Machine, https://web.archive.org/web/20120327042254/http://www.ustream.tv/recorded/21242022. Accessed

September 5, 2016; Eichengreen, Barry. 1996. *Golden Fetters: The Gold Standard and the Great Depression, 1919–1939*, New York: Oxford University Press; Scranton, Philip. December 12, 2011. "The Gold Standard and the Great Depression: Echoes," BloombergView, https://www.bloomberg.com/view/articles/2011-12-12/the-gold-standard-and-the-great-depression-echoes. Accessed September 5, 2016.

H

Hawley-Smoot Tariff of 1930

During the 1920s, strong protectionist sentiments infected Republican Party leaders, who were convinced that keeping foreign goods out of American markets would stimulate American manufacturing and insulate American jobs from competition. But economic theorists argue that protectionism in the long run stunts economic growth, and that would prove all too true. During the 1920s, American exports far exceeded American imports, and when foreign countries retaliated against high U.S. tariffs by passing high tariffs of their own, the United States found itself losing valuable export markets. Two tariffs in particular brought about the decline: the Fordner-McCumber Tariff Act of 1921 and the Hawley-Smoot Tariff of 1930.

President **Herbert Hoover**, when he came into office in March 1929, was unusual among Republicans because he wanted tariff reform and

Smoot and Hawley tax petitions at the Capitol, December 7, 1929. (Library of Congress)

understood economic theory. But as the legislation made its way through Congress, the "logrolling" effect took over, in which individual congressmen added tariff after tariff to those products needing protection within their own district. Congressman Willis C. Hawley of Oregon, a tariff reformer, shepherded it through the House, but Senator Reed Smoot of Utah, an avowed protectionist, was in charge of the bill in the Senate. When it finally passed, the Hawley-Smoot Tariff raised tariffs on raw materials between 50 and 100 percent and upped ad valorem rates from 33 to 40 percent. President Hoover criticized the measure but eventually signed it into law.

The Hawley-Smoot Tariff received universal criticism from economists and international trade experts who knew that it would reduce exports and imports, increase prices, subsidize wasteful and inefficient production, and generate retaliatory tariffs from other countries. That is exactly what happened, and economic historians today identify the Hawley-Smoot Tariff as one of the causes of the Great Depression. Just as the stock market was collapsing, international trade went into a tailspin, forcing American manufacturing enterprises to lay off workers. Between 1929 and 1933, the total annual volume of world trade fell from nearly $35 billion to less than $12 billion, exacerbating what was already a serious worldwide depression.

See also: Agricultural Adjustment Administration; Hoover, Herbert Clark

Further Reading

Economist. December 18, 2008. "The Battle of Smoot-Hawley," http://www.econ omist.com/node/12798595. Accessed September 5, 2016; Irwin, Douglas A. 2011. *Peddling Protectionism: Smoot-Hawley and the Great Depression*, Princeton, NJ: Princeton University Press.

Helvering v. Davis (1937)

The case of *Helvering v. Davis* was one of the first to indicate that the conservative majority on the U.S. Supreme Court was beginning to disintegrate. In 1935 and 1936, the Supreme Court had overthrown the **National Recovery Administration** and the **Agricultural Adjustment Administration**, two linchpins of the **New Deal**, and in response, President **Franklin D. Roosevelt** had launched his ill-conceived attempt to "pack" the Supreme Court. But in *Helvering v. Davis*, Justice Owen Roberts, once part of the conservative majority, switched sides, indicating a drift for the Court toward more liberal decisions.

The case revolved around the constitutionality of the **Social Security Act of 1935**. Opponents sued, arguing that old-age pensions were properly the domain of state governments, not Congress, and that, therefore, the legislation violated the Tenth Amendment to the Constitution. The Court disagreed and on May 24, 1937, by a 7 to 2 vote, upheld the constitutionality of the Social Security Act. The justices claimed that the Great Depression had posed a national crisis far beyond the ability of forty-eight state legislatures to address independently.

See also: Court-Packing Scheme; Social Security Act of 1935

Further Reading

Hall, Kermit L., and James W. Ely Jr. 2009. *The Oxford Guide to United States Supreme Court Decisions*, 2nd ed., New York: Oxford University Press.

Henderson, Leon

Leon Henderson was born on May 26, 1895, in Millville, New Jersey, and educated at Swarthmore and the University of Pennsylvania. A gifted economist, Henderson taught at the Wharton School of the University of Pennsylvania and then at the Carnegie Institute of Technology. Between 1925 and 1934 he served as director of consumer credit for the Russell Sage Foundation. He was working there when he became director of research and planning at the **National Recovery Administration** (NRA). When the NRA was declared unconstitutional, Henderson went to work for the Senate Committee on Manufactures. He then worked for a time for the Democratic National Committee and then for **Harry Hopkins** in the **Works Progress Administration**. Inside the **Roosevelt** administration, Henderson joined people like Lauchlin Currie, **Marriner Eccles**, William Douglas, and Harry Hopkins, who had converted to **Keynes**ian economics and called for the federal government to spend the country out of the Depression. As executive secretary of the **Temporary National Economic Committee** in 1938–1939, Henderson also called on the federal government to engage in antitrust activities in order to maintain a competitive economy. Between 1939 and 1941, Henderson served on the board of the **Securities and Exchange Commission**. During World War II, he worked for the Office of Price Administration and then the War Production Board. After the war, Henderson was president of the International Hudson Corporation. He died on October 19, 1986.

Leon Henderson takes a test ride on a new bicycle. Henderson worked as director of research and planning for the NRA before it was struck down by the Supreme Court. He later lobbied for a Keynesian approach to government spending to combat the "Roosevelt Recession" of 1937. (Library of Congress)

Further Reading

Ennis, Thomas W. October 21, 1986. "Leon Henderson, A Leading New Deal Economist," Obituaries, *New York Times*, http://www.nytimes.com/1986/10/21/obituaries/leon-henderson-a-leading-new-deal-economist.html. Accessed September 5, 2016.

Hickok, Lorena

Lorena Hickok was born on March 7, 1893, in East Troy, Wisconsin. Just a few years out of high school, she went to work as a reporter for the Associated Press, specializing in politics and election campaigns. During the 1932 presidential campaign, she became acquainted with **Eleanor Roosevelt**, and their ensuing friendship lasted for the rest of their lives.

When **Franklin D. Roosevelt** was inaugurated in March 1933, Hickok left the Associated Press and went to work for the administration, traveling widely throughout the country, serving as the eyes and ears of the **New Deal**. She regularly reported back to **Harry Hopkins** on how New Deal legislation was being implemented and how the public was reacting to government initiatives. Hickok's reports were read by the most powerful people in the Roosevelt administration, including the president, and gave her tremendous influence. Her gifted prose described the suffering of poor, unemployed people throughout the country and led to increased federal relief and welfare efforts. Hickok left Washington, D.C., in 1936 and worked for several years in public relations, but in 1940 she returned to Washington, D.C., lived in the White House with the Roosevelts, and worked for the Democratic National Committee. She returned to private life in 1945 and spent the rest of her life writing. Included in her later work are *The Story of Franklin D. Roosevelt* (1959), *The Story of Eleanor Roosevelt* (1959), and *Reluctant First Lady* (1962). Hickok died on May 1, 1968.

See also: Roosevelt, Anna Eleanor

Further Reading

Golay, Michael. 2016. *America 1933: The Great Depression, Lorena Hickok, Eleanor Roosevelt, and the Shaping of the New Deal*, New York: Simon & Schuster Paperbacks; Scutts, Joanna. April 5, 2016. "The Journalist Who Lived at the White House," *Time*, http://time.com/4276317/lorena-hickok/. Accessed September 1, 2016.

Home Owners' Loan Corporation

Because of the collapse of the economy and the disintegration of the banking system in 1932–1933, millions of home owners faced the loss of their homes through foreclosure. By 1933, a total of 41 percent of all home mortgages, worth more than $20 billion, were in default. Not only did home owners face the loss of their houses, but thousands of lending institutions confronted serious erosions of their capital. To deal with the problem, Senator Joseph Robinson of Arkansas sponsored the Home Owners' Refinancing Act, which President **Franklin D. Roosevelt** signed on June 13, 1933. A Home Owners' Loan Corporation (HOLC) was established with $200 million in capital from the **Reconstruction Finance Corporation**. The HOLC was authorized to issue up to $2 billion in its own bonds, and that amount was increased to $3 billion in June 1934 and $4.75 billion in

May 1935. The Home Owners' Loan Act of April 1934 then provided federal guarantees of the principal and interest on HOLC bonds.

The law allowed investors or home owners to trade up to $14,000 in HOLC bonds for mortgages and their conversion into a single new mortgage. In addition, the HOLC could make cash advances for payment of taxes and repairs up to 50 percent of the value of the home. The HOLC also had the authority to redeem properties lost by foreclosure after January 1, 1930. Mortgagees had to repay the HOLC at 5 percent interest over a period of fifteen years. By 1936, after it had stopped accepting loan applications, the HOLC had made 992,531 loans for a total of more than $3 billion. The HOLC went out of business in 1951 after it had collected its outstanding debts.

See also: Reconstruction Finance Corporation

Further Reading

Blinder, Alan S. February 24, 2008. "From the New Deal, A Way Out of a Mess," *New York Times*, http://www.nytimes.com/2008/02/24/business/24view.html?_r=0. Accessed September 5, 2016; Roosevelt Institute. August 31, 2010. "Time to Bring Back the Home Owners Loan Corporation?" http://rooseveltinstitute.org/time-bring-back-home-owners-loan-corporation/. Accessed September 5, 2016.

Hoover, Herbert Clark

Herbert Hoover, the 31st president of the United States, was elected in 1928, less than eight months before the 1929 **stock market crash** that plunged the country into the Great Depression. In 1928, as the Republican Party nominee, Hoover easily defeated Democratic candidate Al Smith for president. It was an auspicious beginning for a presidential administration full of great promise, and at his inaugural, Hoover promised "two chickens in every pot and a car in every garage," as well as an end to poverty in America. But just months later, the stock market crashed and the economy nosedived into the most severe depression in U.S. history. Afraid of creating a huge federal bureaucracy, he postponed establishing government relief programs, and his name soon became synonymous with wealth, apathy, and arrogance.

Actually, Hoover had not relied on laissez-faire indifference and market forces to correct the economy. At first he tried to marshal private, voluntary resources to stimulate the economy and provide relief to the unemployed and to use the federal government to coordinate the effort. When those initiatives failed, he tried other programs, including the Agricultural Marketing Act of 1929, the **Reconstruction Finance Corporation** Act of 1932, the **Emergency Relief and Construction Act of 1932**, and the **Federal Home Loan Bank Act of 1932**.

Nothing worked. Hoover was still wedded to classical economic notions and believed that massive infusions of credit into the economy would automatically lead to increases in consumer purchasing power, production, and employment. But the Great Depression had its roots not in credit shortages but in a lack of consumer purchasing power, and Hoover never realized that. The economy got steadily worse during his administration, with the **unemployment** rate hitting 25 percent by the end of 1932. When Hoover ran for reelection in November 1932, he did not have a chance of victory. He lost to **Franklin D. Roosevelt** by the greatest margin in American history. Hoover's name had become synonymous with poverty, homelessness, and hunger, creating a new lexicon: garbage dumps were "Hoovervilles," because so many hungry people scavenged them for food; newspapers were "Hoover blankets," because people used them in lieu of blankets to keep warm; and park benches became known as "Hoover homes," because so many homeless Americans slept on them at night. In Arkansas, Texas, Louisiana, and Mississippi, armadillos became known as "Hoover hogs" because so many hungry people had resorted to eating them.

Ironically, prior to the Wall Street crash, Hoover had carried a reputation as a humanitarian and a brilliant administrator. During World War I he organized relief efforts to provide food and clothing for European civilians and soldiers stationed overseas. After the war, as part of the Harding and Coolidge administrations, he went on to become one of the most successful secretaries of commerce in American history, working to develop organized interest groups—trade associations, labor unions, farm cooperatives, and so on—which he believed would increase rational competition and improve professional standards and productivity in the economy.

After the 1932 election Hoover retired to private life and during the 1930s offered a mild critique of the **New Deal**. He worried that the unprecedented expansion in the size and power of the federal government would, in the long term, damage the American economy and American society. He came out of retirement late in the 1940s to preside over a government commission designed to streamline the operation of the federal government. For the rest of his life, Hoover served as an elder statesman of the Republican Party. He died on October 20, 1964.

See also: Reconstruction Finance Corporation; Stock Market Crash

Further Reading

Alef, Daniel. Rappleye, Charles. 2016. *Herbert Hoover in the White House: The Ordeal of the Presidency*, New York: Simon & Schuster; Herbert Hoover Presidential Library and Museum. "Gallery Six: The Great Depression," http://hoover.archives.gov/exhibits/Hooverstory/Gallery06/. Accessed September 1, 2016; Miller Center. "American President: Herbert Hoover," University of Virginia, http://millercenter.org/president/hoover. Accessed September 5, 2016.

Hoover Moratorium

Blaming Germany for the devastation of World War I, the Allied Powers at the Versailles Conference of 1919 decided to punish their former adversary. The Treaty of Versailles saddled Germany with a $56 billion reparations bill for the cost of the war. It was a catastrophically bad decision, for it destabilized the German economy and weakened the rest of Europe as well. By 1924, when it had become obvious that Germany would never be able to pay the bill, the Allied Powers in the Dawes Plan reduced the debt. The Young Plan of 1929 reduced the total reparations debt to $8 billion. Even that, however, was impossibly high once the world's economy entered the Great Depression.

By 1931, with the world's money markets facing collapse, handling the international reparations issue became critical. The French did not want to forgive the German debt until the United States had forgiven the Allied war debt. In May 1931, the central bank of Austria declared bankruptcy, creating a worldwide liquidity crisis. President **Herbert Hoover** then acted. On June 20, 1931, he proposed a twelve-month moratorium on all Allied war debts payments and on German reparations payments. France accepted the plan in July 1931, and the moratorium was imposed. Then, at the Lausanne Conference of 1932, the Allied Powers reduced German reparations to $1 billion. The complete collapse of the U.S. banking system in 1933 and the rise of Adolf Hitler to power in Germany in 1933–1934 all but ended the debt-reparations issue.

Further Reading

Miller Center. "Herbert Hoover: Foreign Affairs," University of Virginia, http://millercenter.org/president/biography/hoover-foreign-affairs. Accessed September 5, 2016; Nash, Lee. 2010. *Herbert Hoover and World Peace*, Lanham, MD: University Press of America.

Hopkins, Harry Lloyd

Harry Lloyd Hopkins was born in Sioux City, Iowa, on August 17, 1890. He graduated from Grinnel College in 1911 and began a career in social work. In New York City, Hopkins worked for Christadora House, a settlement house, and for the Association for Improving the Condition of the Poor. In both positions, he acquired a lifelong sympathy for the problem of urban poverty and a commitment to ameliorating its effects through governmental activism. Hopkins became active in local Democratic Party politics, and in 1931 Governor **Franklin D. Roosevelt** of New York appointed him deputy director of the state's **Temporary Emergency Relief Administration**, a state agency designed to assist the unemployed. Hopkins became a close personal friend and influential adviser to Governor Roosevelt, and in 1933, when FDR became president of the United States, Hopkins went to Washington, D.C., with him to head up a succession of federal government relief agencies—**Federal Emergency Relief Administration** (1933), **Civil Works Administration** (1933–1934), and the **Works Progress Administration** (1935–1938). Hopkins served in Roosevelt's cabinet as secretary of commerce from 1983 to 1940. Although Republicans often criticized Hopkins's administration of federal relief programs, he was a dutiful civil servant who emphasized work relief over the dole.

Much of the criticism Republicans directed at Hopkins came from his conversion to **Keynes**ian economics. Using the power of the federal government, through government spending and taxation policies, to stimulate an ailing economy seemed perfectly logical to Hopkins. It also seemed perfectly logical to use such powers for political reasons—to make sure that the economy was in as good shape as possible during election years. Although such reasoning has become commonplace in recent years, among Republicans as well as Democrats, it was an innovative public policy initiative in the late 1930s and early 1940s and earned Hopkins the wrath of political enemies.

During World War II, Hopkins had an office in the White House, where he worked as a special adviser to the president on foreign and domestic affairs. He often served as FDR's personal emissary to foreign leaders, troubleshooting serious problems and attending all of the major conferences between Allied leaders. Passionately committed to a world at peace and to the right of every individual to a decent standard of living, Harry Hopkins is today considered to be a founding father of the modern federal government and an architect of the **New Deal**. Hopkins died on January 19, 1946.

Further Reading

Cohen, Adam. 2010. *Nothing to Fear: FDR's Inner Circle and the Hundred Days That Created Modern America*, London, UK: Penguin Books; Hopkins, June 2009. *Harry Hopkins: Sudden Hero, Brash Reformer* (The World of the Roosevelts), Basingstoke, Hampshire, UK: Palgrave Macmillan.

Howe, Louis

Louis McHenry Howe was born in Indianapolis, Indiana, on January 14, 1871. He was raised in Saratoga Springs, New York. He attended Yale and then went to work for the *New York Herald* in Albany, New York, where he became an insider in state politics. In 1911 he met state senator **Franklin D. Roosevelt** and came away extremely impressed. Roosevelt had Howe manage his 1912 reelection campaign, and when FDR won a major victory, Howe became his political confidant. In 1913, Howe became secretary to Roosevelt, who had been appointed assistant secretary of the navy. When Roosevelt ran and lost for vice president in 1920, Howe was by his side, and when FDR later came down with polio, Howe encouraged him not to surrender to his paralysis but to come back strong. Howe continued to serve as secretary to FDR when Roosevelt won the governorship of New York and then came to the White House in 1933. Although Howe continued to advise Roosevelt, health problems limited his activities, and he died on April 18, 1936.

Further Reading

Fenster, Julie M. 2009. *FDR's Shadow: Louis Howe, the Force That Shaped Franklin and Eleanor Roosevelt*, New York: St. Martin's Griffin.

I

Investment Company Act of 1940

During the late 1930s, after the revelations of the **Pecora Committee** and such federal regulatory legislation as the **Securities Act of 1933**, the Securities Exchange Act of 1934, and the **Public Utility Holding Company Act of 1935**, the securities industry decided to adopt some self-policing policies. The Investment Bankers Association (IBA) worked to standardize industry-wide practices and eliminate corruption and fraud. The IBA and the **Securities and Exchange Commission** (SEC) jointly drafted the law that became known as the Investment Company Act of 1940. It prohibited "self-dealing" between companies and their affiliates, enforced proportion of independent directorships, and outlawed changes in investment policies without the consent of stockholders. All investment trust companies had to register with the SEC and provide full information to stockholders, and the SEC was empowered to oversee their operations.

See also: Securities and Exchange Commission

Further Reading

Levitt, Aaron. September 3, 2014. "What Is the Investment Company Act of 1940?" Mutual Fund Education, MutualFunds.com, http://mutualfunds.com/education/investment-company-act-of-1940-introduction/. Accessed September 9, 2016.

J

Johnson, Hugh Samuel

Hugh Samuel Johnson, who headed the **National Recovery Administration** (NRA) during the 1930s, was born in Ft. Scott, Kansas, on August 5, 1882. He was raised in Oklahoma's Cherokee Strip, and after earning a degree from Northwestern Teachers' College in Oklahoma in 1901, he went on to the U.S. Military Academy, where he graduated in 1903. Johnson pursued a military career, rising in rank to brigadier general by 1918, and in 1916 he finished a law degree from the University of California. He was a logistical genius, and during World War I, he served on the War Industries Board, where he became a close confidant of Bernard Baruch, a leading figure in the Democratic Party. During the 1920s, Johnson served as vice president and then as chairman of the board of the Moline Plow Company. In 1933, President **Franklin D. Roosevelt** picked Johnson to head up the NRA.

Blessed with the personality of a pit bull, Johnson made friends with difficulty and enemies with ease. He led a heavy-handed crusade to get major industries to sign up to cooperate with the National Recovery Administration's production codes, and he personally designed the "Blue Eagle," which became the NRA's logo. During the spring and summer of 1933, Johnson succeeded in securing the approval and cooperation of the cotton textile, shipbuilding, electrical, wool textile, garment, oil, steel, lumber, and automobile industries. In September 1933, Johnson reached the peak of his popularity because it appeared that the NRA was poised to lead the country out of the Depression.

But the NRA was soon mired in controversy. Southern Democrats criticized the NRA for the huge federal bureaucracy it seemed to be generating, while progressives considered it a government agency that encouraged monopolies. Union leaders criticized Johnson because the NRA did little to enforce the minimum wage and maximum hours standards of the National Industrial Recovery Act of 1933. Some economists also argued that rather than stimulating an economic recovery, the NRA was prolonging the Depression by trying to secure reductions in industrial production. Finally, the National Recovery Review Board, a federal commission headed by famous attorney Clarence Darrow and designed to evaluate the effectiveness of the NRA, concluded that the NRA had become the pawn of big business. Johnson resigned in October 1934. In subsequent years, as a columnist for the Scripps-Howard newspaper chain, Johnson became quite critical of Roosevelt and the **New Deal**. He died on April 15, 1942.

Further Reading

Spartacus Educational. "Hugh S. Johnson," http://spartacus-educational.com/USARjohnson.htm. Accessed September 9, 2016.

Jones, Jesse

Jesse Holman Jones, next to President **Franklin D. Roosevelt** the most powerful man in Washington, D.C., during the 1930s, was born in Robertson County, Tennessee, on April 22, 1874. The family moved to Dallas, Texas, and in 1891 Jones graduated from Hill's Business College. He went to work in his uncle's lumber business and then branched out on his own, moving to Houston and becoming deeply involved in lumber, construction, real estate, oil and gas, and banking. By the early 1920s, he was one of the most successful real estate developers in the country and owned dozens of major Houston properties. He helped found what became the Texas Commerce Bank, the *Houston Chronicle* newspaper, and Exxon. While he made a personal fortune, Jones was also a leading light in Houston politics and in the state Democratic Party. Between 1913 and 1917, he served as chairman of the Houston Harbor Board, which built the Houston ship channel, and during World War I, he played a key role in American Red Cross activities. He also became a close personal friend of President Woodrow Wilson. In 1928, Jones succeeded in bringing the Democratic National Convention to Houston.

When the banking system disintegrated in 1932, President **Herbert Hoover** named Jesse Jones to the board of directors of the **Reconstruction Finance Corporation** (RFC), a federal agency designed to liquefy the money markets by loaning money to troubled banks so they would not have to close. In 1933, President Franklin D. Roosevelt named Jones to head up the RFC, where Jones remained until 1945. The RFC became the most powerful government agency in American history, becoming known as the "Fourth Branch of Government," and as head of the RFC, Jones presided over a government credit empire that, at one time or another, included or funded the **Federal Emergency Relief Administration**, the **Home Owners' Loan Corporation**, the **Farm Credit Administration**, the Federal Home Loan Bank Board, the Regional Agricultural Credit Corporations, the **Federal Housing Administration**, the Rural Electrification Administration, the **Resettlement Administration**, the Federal National Mortgage Association, the Electric Home and Farm Authority, the Disaster Loan Corporation, the **Commodity Credit Corporation**, and the **Export-Import Bank**. In 1939, President Roosevelt added the Federal Loan Agency to Jones's **New Deal** empire. By 1940, the RFC and its subsidiaries had loaned more than $10 billion to tens of thousands of American banks, building and loan associations, industrial banks, municipal savings banks, credit unions, railroads, insurance companies, and private businesses. Jones's responsibilities then grew geometrically during World War II, when the RFC assumed responsibility for funding the expansion of the wartime economy. By 1945 the total volume of RFC loans exceeded $50 billion. Jones returned to private life in 1945 and devoted his energies to his personal business empire and to philanthropy through the Jesse Jones Foundation. He continued to be active in national and state Democratic Party politics. Jesse Jones died on June 1, 1956.

Further Reading

Fenberg, Steven. 2013. *Unprecedented Power: Jesse Jones, Capitalism, and the Common Good*, reprint ed., College Station: Texas A&M University Press.

K

Kerr-Smith Tobacco Control Act of 1934

The Agricultural Adjustment Act of 1933 was designed to address the problem of falling commodity prices by getting American farmers to reduce the number of acres planted each year. The **Agricultural Adjustment Administration** (AAA) paid farmers for the number of acres held out of production. The AAA's goal was to bring the annual production of flue-cured tobacco to 500 million pounds. Individual farmers agreed to reduce acreage and production by 30 percent of their previous three-year average. In return, each farmer received a rental payment of $17.50 per acre and an annual payment of 12 percent of the selling price of his tobacco. Farmers were not compelled to participate.

AAA economists soon became worried, however, that those farmers not participating might increase their own production so much as to defeat the entire purpose of **New Deal** economic policy. The Kerr-Smith Tobacco Control Act of 1934 made participation virtually compulsory. It imposed a tax of 25 to 33 percent on the sale price of all tobacco and then awarded tax-exempt certificates in that amount to participating farmers. In 1935 tobacco production in the United States was 557 million pounds, and the average price of flue-cured tobacco went up to 27.3 cents per pound, making the program a modest success.

See also: Agricultural Adjustment Administration

Further Reading

Biles, Roger. 2006. *The South and the New Deal* (New Perspectives on the South), Lexington: University Press of Kentucky; Yeargin, Billy. 2008. *North Carolina Tobacco: A History*, Charleston, SC: The History Press.

Keynes, John Maynard

John Maynard Keynes, arguably one of the most influential figures of the twentieth century, was born in Cambridge, England, in 1883. A brilliant student at Eton and King's College, Cambridge, he studied economics and after graduation became a civil servant with the India Office. After just two years, he returned to Cambridge and wrote *Indian Currency and Finance* (1913). Considered an intellectual triumph, the book earned Keynes the editorship of the prestigious *Economic Journal*. In 1918, he was involved as a deputy to the chancellor of the exchequer for the Supreme Economic Council in the Versailles negotiations to end World War I. He considered the final treaty, because of its punitive reparations package for Germany, an economic disaster, and in protest he wrote *The Economic Consequences of the Peace* (1918), a book that gave him an international reputation.

During the 1920s Keynes became wealthy, not because of his faculty position at Cambridge but because of successful speculation in international currencies. He hated the world's preoccupation with gold, currency, and money supply and argued so in two books: *Tract on Monetary Reform* (1923) and *Treatise on Money* (1930). But it was his 1936 book *The General Theory of Employment, Interest, and Money* that turned the world of economic theory upside down. He rejected the ideas of classical economic theory that in the long run an economy will balance itself; instead, he argued that in a modern industrial economy declines could go on indefinitely, since declines in employment, production, and purchasing could be mutually reinforcing. Unlike classical economists, who wanted to wait for an economy to rejuvenate itself, Keynes called on government to use its own spending and taxation policies to supplement temporarily private investment, income, and spending. Deficit spending—issuing government bonds to well-to-do investors—and then spending the proceeds on **unemployment** relief and public works construction would stimulate the economy and lift the country out of the Depression.

During the 1930s, Keynes wrote several letters to President **Franklin D. Roosevelt**, and a number of prominent **New Deal** figures, such as **Marriner Eccles** and Leon Keyserling, converted to "Keynesian economics." Roosevelt moved slowly in the direction of Keynes, but it was not until World War II, when massive government spending lifted the country out of the Great Depression, that his theories were demonstrated conclusively. John Maynard Keynes died on April 21, 1946.

Further Reading

Rauchway, Eric. 2015. *The Money Makers: How Roosevelt and Keynes Ended the Depression, Defeated Fascism and Secured a Prosperous Peace*, New York: Basic Books; Scranton, Philip. July 8, 2013. "Why John Maynard Keynes Supported the New Deal," BloombergView, https://www.bloomberg.com/view/articles/2013-07-08/why-john-maynard-keynes-supported-the-new-deal. Accessed September 9, 2016.

L

Lange, Dorothea

Dorothea Lange was born in Hoboken, New Jersey, on May 26, 1895. Although she graduated from the New York Training School for Teachers, she had no intention of going into public education. Instead, she moved to San Francisco and opened her own photography studio. Her business did well, catering to the city's wealthiest families, but the onset of the Great Depression sharpened Lange's social conscience. The gap between the living conditions of her wealthy clients and the city's poorest residents seemed scandalously wide to Lange. She decided to use photography to expose poverty in America. Her exhibitions proved to be political and commercial excesses, and Lange attracted the attention of **Eleanor Roosevelt**. Between 1936 and 1938, as the official photographer of the **Resettlement Administration** and then the **Farm Security Administration**, she traveled widely throughout the country, exposing the poverty of midwestern farm families, southern tenant farmers, and urban ghetto families. Lange's photographs were published widely in books, newspapers, and magazines and appeared in dozens of exhibitions. In 1939 she published a collection

One of Dorothea Lange's famous photos of a migrant worker and her family in Nipomo, California, during the Great Depression in March 1936. Lange wanted to bring to public attention the homeless and migrant workers who were the hardest hit from the economic downturn. She lived with the migrants and used their words to caption her photos. This approach was so successful that California established camps for the workers. (Library of Congress)

of the photographs as *An American Exodus: A Record of Human Erosion*. During World War II, she worked as a photographer for the War Relocation Authority and for the Office of War Information. She retired after the war and died on October 11, 1965.

See also: Farm Security Administration; Resettlement Administration

Further Reading

Burns, Ken. *The Dust Bowl: A Film by Ken Burns*, "Biographies: Dorothea Lange," PBS, http://www.pbs.org/kenburns/dustbowl/bios/dorothea-lange/. Accessed September 9, 2016; Lange, Dorothea. 2015. *Dorothea Lange: 500 FSA Photographs*. Mark Rochkind, compiler. CreateSpace Independent Publishing Platform; Partridge, Elizabeth. 2013. *Dorothea Lange: Grab a Hunk of Lightning*, San Francisco: Chronicle Books.

Lemke, William

William Lemke was born on August 13, 1878, in Albany, Minnesota, but he was raised in the Dakota Territory where the family acquired a large farm. In 1898, Lemke graduated from the University of North Dakota. Three years later, he earned a law degree at Yale. Lemke then practiced law in North Dakota and published a monthly magazine—*The Common Good*. As an attorney for the Non-Partisan League, Lemke developed progressive Republican values and an interest in the plight of farmers. He promoted government regulation of railroads, public utilities, banks, and insurance companies. Lemke won a seat in Congress in the election of 1932, and he was reelected in 1934, 1936, and 1938. Lemke's major accomplishment in Congress was the **Federal Farm Bankruptcy Act of 1934**, also known as the Frazier-Lemke Farm Bankruptcy Act, which brought mortgage relief to troubled farm families.

In 1935, when President **Franklin D. Roosevelt** and the **New Deal** opposed Lemke's inflationary monetary proposals, Lemke became one of the administration's most bitter critics. In the presidential election of 1936, Lemke threw in his lot with **Huey Long**, Francis Townsend, and Father Charles Coughlin and their **Union Party**, but they secured less than a million votes in the election. In 1940, Lemke lost a bid for a seat in the U.S. Senate. He died on May 30, 1950.

See also: Federal Farm Bankruptcy Act of 1934; Long, Huey P.; Union Party

Further Reading

UND Department of Special Collections: Digital Finding Aids. "William Lemke Papers, 1901–2014," Orin G. Libby Manuscript Collection, University of North

Dakota, 2010. https://apps.library.und.edu/archon/index.php?p=collections/controlcard&id=524. Accessed September 9, 2016.

Lewis, John Llewellyn

John L. Lewis, the most prominent labor leader of the 1930s, was born on February 12, 1880, in Lucas, Iowa. Lewis's father was a coal miner, and the younger Lewis pursued the career. As a young man he worked in a variety of coal, lead, and silver mines in the western states, and he became active in union politics. In 1909, Lewis was elected president of the Panama, Illinois, chapter of the United Mine Workers (UMW), and his profile in the national UMW rose steadily. He was smart, tenacious, and tough. Between 1909 and 1920, he served as the UMW's chief statistician, business manager of the *United Mine Workers Journal*, and national vice president of the union. In 1920, Lewis was elected national UMW president.

His initial thirteen years at the helm of the UMW were difficult for the union. Management hostility toward the union during the 1920s caused membership declines, and when the Great Depression hit in 1929, membership slipped even more. Between 1920 and 1933, UMW membership dropped from more than 500,000 workers to less than 75,000. The mining industry was characterized by overproduction, falling prices, massive **unemployment**, and declining wages for those miners who managed to keep their jobs. Although opposition to Lewis's leadership emerged in the union, he was ruthless in crushing rivals and maintaining his control.

When **Franklin D. Roosevelt** and the Democrats came into power in 1933, Lewis suddenly enjoyed access to the seat of power in the United States, and he used that access to promote the labor movement. Lewis promised Roosevelt millions of votes if the **New Deal** would finally underwrite labor's major demands, and Roosevelt agreed. Lewis supported the National Industrial Recovery Act of 1933 and the National Labor Relations Act of 1935, and as a result of the laws, Lewis soon had more than 90 percent of miners in the UMW.

Lewis also had a vision for labor that extended beyond the UMW. The UMW was an affiliate of the American Federation of Labor, which confined its membership to skilled workers in the major craft unions. Lewis was convinced that mass production workers needed to be organized into unions as well, and in 1935 he helped establish the Committee for Industrial Organization (CIO). Lewis was elected president of the CIO in 1936 and changed its name to the Congress of Industrial Organizations. His own party membership was Republican, but in the election of 1936 he endorsed Franklin D. Roosevelt, contributed $500,000 to the president's campaign, and marshaled the CIO's organization behind the reelection bid. Lewis eventually soured on Roosevelt and returned to the Republican Party. John L. Lewis died on June 11, 1969.

See also: Organized Labor

Further Reading

Carnes, Cecil. 2016. *John L. Lewis: Leader of Labor*, South Yarra, Victoria, Australia: Leopold Classic Library; John L. Lewis Memorial Museum of Mining and Labor. "History of John L. Lewis," John L. Lewis Commission, 2009. http://www.coalmininglabormuseum.com/lewis.html. Accessed September 9, 2016.

The Literary Digest

The Literary Digest was a weekly magazine established by Isaac K. Funk and Adam Wagnalls in 1890. By the late 1920s, circulation exceeded 1.5 million copies. It began running informal political polls with the election of 1920, and its first national, presidential poll was published in 1924. Using automobile registration information, magazine subscription lists, and telephone directories, the editors polled prospective voters. The polls proved quite popular, securing newspaper coverage and increased subscriptions. But in the election of 1936, *The Literary Digest* poll predicted a victory for Republican nominee Alf Landon. When President **Franklin D. Roosevelt** was elected by a landslide, the magazine lost credibility. Its polling methodology, of course, was flawed. Most people who voted for Roosevelt did not own automobiles or telephones. In February 1938, *The Literary Digest* suspended publication.

Further Reading

History Matters. "Landon in a Landslide: The Poll That Changed Polling," Roy Rosenzweig Center for History and New Media, George Washington University, http://historymatters.gmu.edu/d/5168/. Accessed September 9, 2016.

Long, Huey P.

Huey Long was born near Winnfield, Winn Parish, Louisiana, on August 30, 1893. Long's family had a streak of populism that ran deep, with equally hostile feelings for the ruling, upper classes, especially big banks, utility companies, and railroads. Long passed the Louisiana bar exam after studying briefly at the University of Oklahoma Law School and the

Louisiana senator Huey Long was a flamboyant orator and referred to himself as the "Kingfish." (Library of Congress)

Tulane University Law School. He then opened a law practice in Winnfield.

But Long had bigger dreams than being a small-town southern attorney. In 1918 he was elected state railroad commissioner, and he was reelected in 1924. He also launched an attack on Standard Oil Company and found that anti–big business rhetoric resonated well with Louisiana's poor, rural farmers. He was elected governor of Louisiana in 1928 and proceeded to create a powerful political machine that dominated the entire state. Long made sure that poor people had public works construction jobs and that rural children attended improved public schools, and in 1930, voters put him in the U.S. Senate. As a U.S. senator, Long began calling for a redistribution of national wealth and then criticized the **Franklin D. Roosevelt** administration for being too conservative.

In 1934, Long established the Share Our Wealth Society, which essentially became a national political vehicle for Long. He called for a living minimum wage for all families to be paid for by high taxes on the rich and the well-to-do. In November 1935, Long announced his intention of seeking the Democratic presidential nomination in 1936. Although his chances of unseating Franklin D. Roosevelt were next to none, FDR took Long's threat seriously, especially when Long agreed to run as the presidential candidate of the new **Union Party**. Roosevelt did not have to worry. On September 8, 1936, Long was assassinated.

See also: Union Party

Further Reading

Brinkley, Alan. 1983. *Voices of Protest: Huey Long, Father Coughlin, and the Great Depression*, New York: Vintage; Burns, Ken. *Huey Long*, Ken Burns America Collection, DVD, 90 min., PBS; White, Richard. 2006. *Kingfish: The Reign of Huey P. Long*, Random House: New York.

Lorentz, Pare

Pare Lorentz, the **New Deal**'s great **film**maker, was born in Clarkburg, West Virginia, in 1905. He began working as a freelance journalist and film critic in West Virginia, but after moving to New York, he acquired a national reputation, writing regularly for *Harper's* and *Fortune*. In 1930, his first book was published—*Censored: The Private Life of Movies*—and in 1934 he wrote a second book—*The Roosevelt Year: 1933*. Lorentz was an unabashed fan of **Franklin D. Roosevelt** and the New Deal, and in 1935, he went to work for the **Resettlement Administration** as a filmmaker. He teamed up with Hollywood director King Vidor and photographer **Dorothea Lange**, and the result was *The Plow That Broke the Plains*, a brilliant description of Great Plains ecology and the impact of dust storms, overgrazing, overplanting, and migrant poverty. The film premiered in May 1936 and was a critical success. Lorentz followed that up with *The River*, an equally compelling portrait of flooding, soil erosion, and poverty in the Mississippi River Valley. Roosevelt was so impressed with *The River* that he established the U.S. Film Service to make more documentaries. Lorentz's third film in his Great Depression trilogy was *The Fight for Life*, a documentary on infant mortality and poverty. During and after World War II, Lorentz made documentaries for the War Department. He died on March 4, 1992.

See also: Lange, Dorothea; Resettlement Administration

Further Reading

Lorentz, Pare, dir. *The Films of Pare Lorentz*, DVD, 125 min.; Pare Lorentz Center. "Biography of Pare Lorentz," Franklin D. Roosevelt Presidential Library, 2015. http://www.parelorentzcenter.org/biography/. Accessed September 9, 2016.

M

Morgan, John Pierpont, Jr.

J. P. Morgan Jr. was heir to one of America's greatest financial fortunes and a key figure in the investment banking community during the early twentieth century. He was born at Irvington-on-Hudson, New York, on September 7, 1867, and in 1889, he graduated from Harvard. Morgan spent two years in Boston with Jacob C. Rogers and Company, a banking firm, and in 1891, he moved to New York and joined his father's firm—Drexel, Morgan & Company. Between 1898 and 1905, he lived in London as a junior partner in J. P. Morgan and Company. When his father died in 1913, Morgan returned to New York as senior partner of J. P. Morgan and Company and within a few years was widely recognized as the world's best international banker.

The company prospered especially during the 1920s, when a huge market for new securities emerged. Morgan also became a specialist in financing government debt and recapitalizing government bonds and national debts. During his tenure, J. P. Morgan floated bond issues for dozens of countries, including Great Britain, France, Belgium, Italy, Austria, Cuba, Canada, and Germany. He played a key role in the negotiations that led to the Dawes Plan of 1924 and the Young Plan of 1929, which reduced German reparations payments.

At first, Morgan praised the efforts of President **Franklin D. Roosevelt** to stabilize the money markets, but he soon soured on the **New Deal**, especially when the Banking Act of 1933 forced him to separate his investment banking operations from his commercial operations. J. P. Morgan and Company functioned thereafter as a commercial bank, and Morgan, Stanley & Company assumed control of the securities underwriting business. Morgan eventually came to see the New Deal as fundamentally an anti-American, antibusiness, pro-bureaucracy operation that stifled incentive and limited private property rights. Higher tax rates on the well-to-do cost Morgan money as well, which did nothing to endear the New Deal to him. During the late 1930s, Morgan went into semiretirement, and he died on March 13, 1943.

Further Reading

Morris, Charles R. 2006. *The Tycoons: How Andrew Carnegie, John D. Rockefeller, Jay Gould, and J. P. Morgan Invented the American Supereconomy*, New York: Owl Books.

Motor Carrier Act of 1935

By the mid-1930s, the nation's transportation industry was in disarray. Most railroads were suffering from heavy debt burdens and increased competition from trucks. At the same time, the trucking industry was suffering from declining freight rates, primarily from cutthroat competition. To settle the problem, Joseph Eastman of the Interstate Commerce Commission (ICC) wanted federal legislation to rationalize the industry. The Eastman bill became the Motor Carrier Act on August 9, 1935.

The Motor Carrier Act gave the ICC new authority over the trucking industry, particularly to control maximum and minimum rates, service, accounting, finances, organization, and management of common carriers. It was also authorized to issue permits to contract carriers. Throughout the decade, however, the Motor Carrier Act had little impact. Because freight rates kept falling, few complaints were received from shippers, and most truckers simply ignored ICC trucking regulations. With relative few employees and a limited budget, the ICC could not really enforce its regulations. Still, the Motor Carrier Act greatly expanded the power of the ICC, and after World War II, that new power was vigorously exercised.

See also: Emergency Railroad Transportation Act of 1933

Further Reading

PBS. "Interstate Commerce Act," American Experience, http://www.pbs.org/wgbh/americanexperience/features/general-article/streamliners-commerce/. Accessed September 9, 2016.

Municipal Bankruptcy Act of 1934

Because of declining tax revenues during the years of the Great Depression, many towns and cities found themselves unable to make payments on their own outstanding bonds. The municipal bond market was in a state of shambles, and many bankers worried that defaults on those bonds would further damage the money markets. Urban mayors and the Investment

Bankers Association demanded federal action, and Congress passed the Municipal Bankruptcy Act, which President **Franklin D. Roosevelt** signed on May 24, 1934. The law allowed cities and towns, with the approval of 51 percent of the holders of outstanding obligations, to seek the assistance of federal courts in scaling down their debts. If the court found the plan equitable and 75 percent of the bondholders approved, the reorganization plan would go into effect. Because of the legislation, the municipal bond market recovered.

Further Reading
Skeel, David A. 2003. *Debt's Dominion: A History of Bankruptcy Law in America*, Princeton, NJ: Princeton University Press.

Muscle Shoals. *See* Tennessee Valley Authority

N

National Association for the Advancement of Colored People

During the 1930s and much of the twentieth century, the National Association for the Advancement of Colored People (NAACP) was the nation's premier civil rights organization. During the 1930s, under the leadership of **Walter White**, the NAACP focused its energies on five distinct goals. First, it provided financial support to the **Southern Tenant Farmers' Union** because so many southern blacks worked as farm tenants, laborers, and sharecroppers. Second, it pursued legal cases, such as that of the so-called **Scottsboro boys**, in order to protect black civil rights. Third, it worked, unsuccessfully as it turned out, to secure a Federal Anti-Lynching Bill to make it easier to prosecute southern whites who had lynched blacks. Fourth, the NAACP worked to make sure that **New Deal** relief agencies provided a fair number of jobs to black workers and a wage equal to that of white workers. Finally, the NAACP worked, with some success, to convince labor unions to organize black workers. The unions of the Congress of Industrial Organizations did so.

See also: White, Walter Francis

Further Reading

Sklaroff, Lauren Rebecca. 2014. *Black Culture and the New Deal: The Quest for Civil Rights in the Roosevelt Era*, Chapel Hill: University of North Carolina Press; Gale: *U.S. History in Context*. http://ic.galegroup.com/ic/uhic/ReferenceDetailsPage/DocumentToolsPortletWindow?displayGroupName=Reference&jsid=7812016b5ea4d6684ea4837e2c6ef921&action=2&catId=&documentId=GALE%7CCX3404500017&u=sand55832&zid=b57acc008e359910d5c24de390bb447b. Accessed September 3, 2016; Trotter, Joe W. 2004. "African Americans, Impact of the Great Depression on." *Encyclopedia of the Great Depression*. Vol 1. Robert S. McElvaine, ed. New York: Macmillan Reference USA.

National Employment System Act of 1933. *See* Wagner-Peyser Act of 1933

National Farmers' Union

During the 1930s, the National Farmers' Union (NFU) was a lobbying organization committed to representing the interests of the small family farm. The American Farm Bureau Federation (AFBF) tended to represent large commercial farmers, so the NFU often found itself at odds with the AFBF. Led by **John A. Simpson**, the NFU at first opposed the drift of **New Deal** farm policy because the Agricultural Adjustment Act of 1933 provided so many benefits to large commercial farmers and so few to small family farmers. But the NFU also praised such New Deal agencies as the **Farm Credit Administration** and the **Commodity Credit Corporation**, which eased the small farmers' burden. Later in the New Deal, when such federal agencies as the **Resettlement Administration**, the Rural Electrification Administration, and the **Farm Security Administration** appeared, the NFU became wholeheartedly pro–New Deal. The NFU also worked to prevent the industrialization of American agriculture, which its leaders knew would favor the capital-rich large commercial farmers. The NFU dream of stopping technological advance and increasing farm size was, of course, a pipe dream. During the last sixty years, the family farm has gradually become an endangered species as large commercial operations have become increasingly common.

See also: Organized Labor

Further Reading

Grubbs, Donald H. 2000. *Cry from the Cotton: The Southern Tenant Farmers' Union and the New Deal*, Fayetteville: University of Arkansas Press; Meyer, Carrie A. 2007. *Days on the Family Farm: From the Golden Age through the Great Depression*, Minneapolis: University of Minnesota Press; Ness, Immanuel. 2000. *Encyclopedia of Interest Groups and Lobbyists in the United States*, Armonk, NY: Sharpe Reference.

National Housing Act of 1934

By 1933, the housing market in the United States was in a state of shambles. Because of the virtual collapse of the money markets, a host of financial institutions—banks, savings banks, building and loan associations, and insurance companies—were trapped in a liquidity crisis, unable and unwilling to extend credit to finance housing construction. At the same time, the unprecedented **unemployment** problem in the economy had badly eroded demand for new housing. To stimulate the housing industry, the **Franklin D. Roosevelt** administration proposed and Congress passed the National Housing Act of 1934. Roosevelt signed the law on June 28, 1934. The legislation created the **Federal Housing Administration** (FHA) to insure banks, mortgage companies, and building and loan associations against losses they sustained as a result of making home improvement and new construction loans. With the FHA willing to assume those losses, so the logic went, financial institutions would be more willing to make the loans. The **Reconstruction Finance Corporation** supplied $200 million in capital to the FHA. An FHA home improvement loan could not exceed $2,000, nor could a new home loan exceed $12,000. No more than 20 percent of any institution's total loan portfolio could consist of FHA-guaranteed loans. Under the law, the FHA could create national mortgage associations to purchase first mortgages from banks and building and loan associations. Finally, the National Housing Act of 1934 increased to $3 billion the borrowing power of the **Home Owners' Loan Corporation**.

The National Housing Act also established the Federal Savings and Loan Insurance Corporation (FSLIC) to do for building and loan associations what the **Federal Deposit Insurance Corporation** had done for banks. By insuring deposits, the FSLIC helped prevent runs on building and loan associations by panic-stricken depositors. The FSLIC insured deposits up to $5,000, and participating building and loan associations had to pay a small annual premium and allow FSLIC examiners to periodically audit their books. By 1940 a total of 2,189 building and loan associations had joined the FSLIC, and bankruptcies among those institutions all but stopped. During the 1930s, the FSLIC had to pay off depositors in only seven failed institutions.

See also: Federal Housing Administration; Home Owners' Loan Corporation; Reconstruction Finance Corporation

Further Reading

Griffith, John. October 11, 2012. "The Federal Housing Administration Saved the Housing Market," Center for American Progress, https://www.americanprogress.org/issues/housing/report/2012/10/11/40824/the-federal-housing-administration-saved-the-housing-market/. Accessed September 9, 2016; Smith, Jason Scott. 2014. *A Concise History of the New Deal* (Cambridge Essential Histories), Cambridge: Cambridge University Press.

National Recovery Administration

Between 1929 and 1933, as the economy sank steadily into a deep depression, explanations of the country's plight abounded. One belief—proposed by such prominent businessmen as Bernard Baruch, Gerard Swope, and Henry I. Harriman—argued that the Depression had been caused by

overproduction and too much competition in the industrial economy, which had brought about price deflation, layoffs, and profit declines. They wanted the federal government to eliminate destructive competition, encourage national economic planning, and improve business confidence. Some business leaders even called for the federal government to suspend the antitrust laws and impose industrial codes regulating production and prices. As their model, they remembered the War Industries Board of World War I, which had worked out cooperative arrangements between the federal government and major industries.

Such prominent labor leaders as **John L. Lewis** of the United Mine Workers and Sidney Hillman of the Amalgamated Clothing Workers supported such proposals. But union leaders also wanted the federal government to establish nationwide labor standards, including a minimum wage and maximum hours regulations for workers. Senator Hugo Black of Alabama was pushing an idea of limiting the workweek to thirty hours so that jobs could be spread around. His legislation—known as the Black-Connery Bill—began moving through Congress late in 1932. Finally, Senator **Robert Wagner** of New York was calling for a massive federal public works construction program to relieve **unemployment**. All of these disparate proposals came together in an omnibus bill passed by Congress and signed by President **Franklin D. Roosevelt** on June 16, 1933.

The National Industrial Recovery Act (NIRA) consisted of several titles. Title I established the National Recovery Administration (NRA) to implement a broad series of government rules to promote cooperative economic action, eliminate unfair trade practices, increase consumer purchasing power, expand production, reduce unemployment, stabilize prices, and conserve national resources. Businesses could enter into cooperative arrangements to achieve the purposes of the law, and the president could establish enforceable codes to implement them. Title I also established basic labor standards, provided for a minimum wage, outlawed yellow-dog contracts, and guaranteed the rights of workers to bargain collectively. Title II of the NIRA established the **Public Works Administration** (PWA) and endowed the PWA with $3.3 billion to finance the construction of highways, dams, federal buildings, naval construction, and other projects.

President Franklin D. Roosevelt established the NRA and named Hugh Johnson as its director. During World War I, Johnson had served on the War Industries Board, and he believed in the NRA's mission. Johnson campaigned for the NRA as if it were a patriotic issue, urging businessmen to cooperate for the good of the country. Each business cooperating with the NRA could display the NRA emblem—a Blue Eagle—in advertising literature or on store and factory windows, and Johnson urged buyers to boycott all non-NRA companies. Johnson eventually wrote codes governing codes, competition, and prices in 541 industries.

But within a matter of months, critics of every stripe were targeting the NRA. Labor leaders accused businessmen of noncompliance with the labor standards provisions of the NIRA, while small businessmen complained that the NRA had been seized by big businessmen who were trying to squeeze small companies out of the market. Many consumer advocates and political leftists complained that the NRA was actually sanctioning monopolies and exploiting the law's suspension of antitrust action. Conservatives accused the NRA specifically and the federal government in general of exercising too much control over economic processes. Finally, many economists held the NRA responsible for the economic downturn of late 1933 and early 1934, arguing that the NRA was actually encouraging cuts in production in order to raise prices and that the cuts in production actually led to more layoffs and a degeneration in the unemployment problem. Under such intense, varied political criticism, public support for the NRA evaporated. Hugh Johnson's personal style did not help matters. The proverbial "bull in a china shop," Johnson managed to offend just about everybody, and in September 1934, Roosevelt eased him out of the NRA.

Actually, the NRA's days were numbered. On May 27, 1935, in the case of **Schechter Poultry Corporation v. United States**, the U.S. Supreme Court declared the NIRA to be unconstitutional. The code system, the justices said, was an illegal delegation of legislative power to the executive branch and an unconstitutional expansion of federal power over interstate commerce. The Roosevelt administration responded with the so-called Little NRA, which attempted to preserve NRA activities in certain limited industries, but it had little effect. The original logic of the NIRA had been so badly flawed that its chances of bringing about a recovery were nil. In fact, many historians argue that the NRA actually made economic matters worse in the United States.

See also: Public Works Administration; *Schechter Poultry Corporation v. United States* (1935)

Further Reading

Himmelberg, Robert. 2000. *The Origins of the National Recovery Administration*, 2nd ed., New York: Fordham University Press; Leuchtenburg, William E. 2009. *Franklin D. Roosevelt and the New Deal: 1932–1940*, New York: Harper Perennial; Simkin, John. August 2014. "National Recovery Administration," Spartacus Educational, http://spartacus-educational.com/USARnra.htm. Accessed September 9, 2016.

National Resources Planning Board

Under Title II of the National Industrial Recovery Act of 1933, President **Franklin D. Roosevelt** established a National Planning Board to consider national economic planning as a way of stimulating the economy and ending the Great Depression. The idea behind the planning board was for experts to supply the White House and Congress with important data to be employed in establishing guidelines and legislation for land-use planning, water-use planning, demographics, mineral policy, energy policy, transportation policy, and technology. But in May 1935, when the Supreme Court declared the National Industrial Recovery Act unconstitutional, the National Planning Board, which had already been renamed the National Resources Board, lost its legislative mandate. It then became known as the National Resources Committee. In 1939 it was renamed again, this time being known as the National Resources Planning Board (NRPB).

But whatever its name, the NRPB became increasingly controversial during the 1930s. Conservative businessmen hated the very thought of national economic planning, seeing in it a loss of their own prerogatives and a subversion of market forces by the federal government. The fact that the NRPB by 1938 was a powerful advocate of **Keynes**ian economics and deficit spending only attracted more criticism. In 1939, Roosevelt failed to get a provision for a permanent national planning board into the **Reorganization Act**. Under fierce attack in Congress because of its liberal tendencies, the NRPB was dissolved in 1943.

Further Reading
Clawson, Marion. 2011. *New Deal Planning: The National Resources Planning Board* (RFF Natural Resource Management Set), Washington, DC: RFF Press;
Reagan, Patrick D. 2000. *Designing a New America: The Origins of New Deal Planning, 1890–1943* (Political Development of the American Nation: Studies in Politics and History), Amherst: University of Massachusetts Press.

National Youth Administration

In June 1935, Congress passed the bill and President **Franklin D. Roosevelt** signed it, creating the National Youth Administration (NYA). The NYA was designed to address an **unemployment** problem among young people that exceeded 5 million. The NYA was authorized to assist college students to continue their education through government work-study programs, and eventually more than 620,000 did so. The NYA also supplied part-time employment to 1,514,000 high school students and to 2,677,000 young people who had either dropped out of school or had just graduated. The NYA was led by **Aubrey Williams**. To make sure that black youths were treated fairly, Williams created a division of Negro affairs in the NYA and named Mary McLeod Bethune to head it. More than any other **New Deal** agency, the NYA worked diligently to deal with the race issue in a fair and equitable manner. Eventually, completed NYA projects included the construction of 2,000 bridges, the paving of 1,500 miles of public roads, the completion of more than 6,000 public buildings, and the construction of 1,429 libraries and public schools.

See also: Williams, Aubrey Willis

Young men working on telephone poles in Maine as vocational training under the National Youth Administration program, ca. 1935–1943 (Library of Congress)

Further Reading

Halstead, Gordon. "Work–Study–Live: The Resident Youth Centers of the NYA," New Deal Network, http://newdeal.feri.org/wsl/index.htm. Accessed September 9, 2016; Schiller Institute. June 2013. "This Week in History: June 23–29, 1935—FDR Launches a Program to Rescue America's Youth," http://www.schillerinstitute.org/educ/hist/eiw_this_week/v5n25_jun23_1935.html. Accessed September 9, 2016.

New Deal

The term "New Deal" has become politically synonymous among historians and public officials with the first two presidential administrations of **Franklin D. Roosevelt** (1933–1941). Among political conservatives, the term "New Deal" has also become synonymous with big government and a bloated federal bureaucracy. The term was first heard in June 1932 when Governor Franklin D. Roosevelt of New York, working from a speech drafted by Samuel Rosenman, accepted the Democratic presidential nomination in Chicago and said, "I pledge you, I pledge myself, to a new deal for the American people. Let us all here assembled constitute ourselves prophets of a new order of competence and courage." Stuart Chase, a writer for *The New Republic*, picked up on the phrase and published a series of articles entitled "A New Deal for America." By mid-1933, the term was firmly ensconced in American political culture as a synonym for the political and economic policies of Franklin D. Roosevelt.

See also: First 100 Days

Further Reading

Kennedy, David M. 2003. *The American People in the Great Depression: Freedom from Fear, Part I* (Oxford History of the United States). New York: Oxford University Press; Leuchtenburg, William E. 2009. *Franklin D. Roosevelt and the New Deal: 1932–1940*, New York: Harper Perennial; Smith, Jason Scott. 2014. *A Concise History of the New Deal* (Cambridge Essential Histories), Cambridge: Cambridge University Press.

O

Organized Labor

Labor unions seemed to be on the decline in the early years of the Great Depression. Union membership had decreased by almost one-third from the previous decade. Despite attempts to grow membership in the up-and-coming sectors of automobiles, textiles, mining, and steel, most union members were still skilled craft workers, enrolled under the American Federation of Labor (AFL), the most successful national labor union in U.S. history. Founded in 1886, the union had secured real leverage over employers by focusing its attention only on the organization of skilled workers. Previous labor unions, such as the National Labor Union and the Knights of Labor, had failed in part because they tried to organize unskilled workers as well. It was relatively easy for management to bring in strikebreakers to fill in for striking unskilled workers. The AFL also focused only on what founding union president Samuel Gompers called the "bread and butter" issues—better wages, shorter workweeks, and safer working conditions—and eschewed all forms of radicalism.

Unions made dramatic gains, however, under pro-labor **New Deal** legislation. The National Industrial Recovery Act of 1933 protected labor's right to engage in collective bargaining. The National Labor Relations Act of 1935 (Wagner-Connery Act), also known as the "Magna Carta of Labor in the United States," guaranteed the right of labor unions to engage in collective bargaining; required management to bargain in good faith with union representatives; and prohibited management from engaging in strikebreaking and other antiunion activities (the Norris-La Guardia Act of 1932 had already outlawed "yellow-dog contracts"—the management tactic of securing from employees, as a condition of employment, a promise not to join a labor union). The 1935 act also prohibited management from interfering in the operations of company unions; required that the union elected by a majority of workers in free elections would be recognized as the sole bargaining agent for those workers; and established a new National Labor Relations Board (NLRB) to serve as a "Supreme Court" in adjudicating labor disputes with management. Unlike the earlier National Labor Board and the first National Labor Relations Board, the new NLRB enjoyed administrative and statutory authority to enforce its decisions. Not surprisingly, business groups argued that the measure was unconstitutional, but in *National Labor Relations Board v. Jones & Laughlin Steel Corporation* (1937), the Supreme Court upheld the constitutionality of the law. Because of the National Labor Relations Act of 1935, union membership in the United States boomed, reaching more than 9 million people in 1940.

In 1935, **John L. Lewis**, head of the United Mine Workers (UMW), an AFL member union, founded, along with David Dubinsky, the Committee for Industrial Organization to organize unskilled and semiskilled mass production workers in the automobile, steel, mining, and rubber industries. Such a plan undermined the AFL's commitment to skilled workers. Lewis was undeterred, however, and in 1936 the committee became the Congress of Industrial Organizations (CIO), with Lewis as president. The AFL promptly expelled the CIO constituent unions and their 561,000 members.

The CIO also actively campaigned to organize industrial workers. In June 1936 Philip Murray, who served as Lewis's assistant in the UMW, established the Steel Workers Organizing Committee (SWOC), and Sidney Hillman formed the Textile Workers Organizing Committee. Late in 1936, the United Automobile Workers staged sit-down strikes against the major automobile companies, and in February 1937 General Motors agreed to bargain with the union. UAW membership jumped from 30,000 workers to 400,000 workers. In March 1937, United States Steel Corporation recognized the SWOC, and within a few months, SWOC membership exceeded 350,000 workers. Other industrial unions that enjoyed similar success in 1937 included the United Rubber Workers, United Electrical and **Radio Workers**, and the Textile Workers Organizing Committee. By 1940, the CIO unions had a total membership of 2,654,000 workers.

Even the AFL recovered thanks to the National Industrial Recovery Act, and by 1940 AFL membership exceeded 4 million. World War II, with its huge demand for labor, further strengthened the union. By the end of World War II, over 12 million workers belonged to unions.

See also: American Farm Bureau Federation; Lewis, John Llewellyn; National Farmers' Union

Further Reading

Rees, Jonathan, and Jonathan Z. S. Pollack. 2004. *The Voice of the People: Primary Sources on the History of American Labor, Industrial Relations, and Working-Class Culture*, Hoboken, NJ: Wiley-Blackwell; White, Ahmed. 2016. *The Last Great Strike: Little Steel, the CIO, and the Struggle for Labor Rights in New Deal America*, Oakland: University of California Press.

P

Panama Refining Company v. Ryan (1935)

During the years of the Great Depression, price deflation afflicted the economy, wreaking havoc with corporate strategic planning and profit margins. Economists discussed at length what might be done to stem the deflation tide, and in the spring of 1933, during the famous **first 100 days** of the early **New Deal**, Congress passed the National Industrial Recovery Act (NIRA), which created the **National Recovery Administration** (NRA), a large federal bureaucracy, to help businesses cut production and, so the logic went, raise prices and profit margins. Republican conservatives, enraged at such an expansion of federal power, condemned the legislation in no uncertain terms.

The oil industry found itself in deep economic troubles. Oil-producing states, which could not muster up the strength to create a cartel and limit production, turned to the NRA for help. In an administrative order, the NRA prohibited the transport across state lines of so-called hot oil—oil produced in excess of state-mandated production quotas. One case contesting the constitutionality of the "hot oil" provisions of the NIRA was *Panama Refining Company v. Ryan*, which claimed the law defied the Constitution by violating the principle of separation of powers. The NIRA delegated essential legislative powers to the executive branch.

The case was argued before the U.S. Supreme Court on December 10–11, 1934, and decided on January 7, 1935. The conservative, tradition-bound Court voted 8 to 1 to overturn the hot oil provision of the NIRA, agreeing that it was an unconstitutional delegation of legislative powers to the president. The decision in *Panama Refining Company* boded ill for the rest of the New Deal's attempts to lift the country out of the Great Depression, and the Supreme Count soon confirmed those fears, declaring the entire NIRA unconstitutional in the ***Schechter Poultry Corporation v. United States*** in 1935.

Further Reading

Hall, Kermit L., and James W. Ely Jr. 2009. *The Oxford Guide to United States Supreme Court Decisions*, 2nd ed., New York: Oxford University Press; Leuchtenburg, William E. 2009. *Franklin D. Roosevelt and the New Deal: 1932–1940*, New York: Harper Perennial.

Parity

"Parity" is an economic concept that has been central to farm activism since the early twentieth century and to federal agricultural policy since the 1930s. The real issue surrounding parity was whether or not a farmer was getting a fair price for his commodities, that is, a price fairly connected to the labor invested in production. Government economists created a series of indexes designed to establish a ratio between the price, or gross income, from a commodity and an index of the prices of nonfarm commodities, which allowed for a measurement of farmer costs. Government policy during the **New Deal** worked to restore farmer purchasing power by restoring the ratio between income and costs that had existed during the early 1900s.

See also: Agricultural Adjustment Administration

Further Reading

Ganzel, Bill. "Farming in the 1930s—Parity," Wessels Living History Farm, http://www.livinghistoryfarm.org/farminginthe30s/money_24.html. Accessed September 9, 2016; Gilbert, Jess. 2015. *Planning Democracy: Agrarian Intellectuals and the Intended New Deal*, New Haven, CT: Yale University Press; White, Ann Folino. 2014. *Plowed Under: Food Policy Protests and Performance in New Deal America*, Bloomington: Indiana University Press.

Pecora Committee

The **stock market crash** of 1929 and subsequent collapse of the nation's money markets precipitated concern in the United States about endemic fraud in the banking system. In 1933, Republican senator Peter Norbeck of North Dakota, chair of the Senate Banking and Currency Committee, engaged progressive Republican Ferdinand Pecora to head up an investigation of the nation's securities markets. The investigation, which came to be known as the Pecora Committee hearings, continued through 1933 and 1934. Pecora subpoenaed Wall Street's major figures, including **J. P. Morgan**, Richard Whitney, Winthrop Aldrich, Albert H. Wiggin, and Thomas W. Lamont.

Congressman Pecora's investigators discovered numerous instances of fraud. Albert H. Wiggin had created dummy affiliated companies to help Chase National Bank avoid federal stock market regulations, had sold short on his own stock during the 1929 crash, and had dipped into Chase money to finance his own personal stock speculations. Charles Mitchell's reputation suffered when the committee exposed a series of shady loan deals and bank fraud at National City Bank, and revealed that he had speculated in the bank's stock as well. Mitchell, in what was certainly a public relations disaster, defended the bank's practices as an example of the rights of private property and liberty and urged laissez-faire on the federal government. J. P. Morgan, one of the world's wealthiest international bankers and a founder of U.S. Steel, owed two years' worth of back taxes. Richard Whitney, head of the New York Stock Exchange, resolutely maintained the industry's innocence.

Pecora exposed the existence of widespread fraud in the securities markets, including rigged stock market pools, tax evasion, byzantine holding company networks, and outright criminal activity. The Pecora Committee's findings led directly to the Securities Exchange Act of 1934. President **Franklin D. Roosevelt** then appointed Pecora as an original member of the **Securities and Exchange Commission** board.

Further Reading

King, Gilbert. November 29, 2011. "The Man Who Busted the Bankers," Smithsonian, http://www.smithsonianmag.com/history/the-man-who-busted-the-banksters-932416/?no-ist. Accessed September 9, 2016; Perino, Michael. 2011. *The Hellhound of Wall Street: How Ferdinand Pecora's Investigation of the Great Crash Forever Changed American Finance*, reprint edition, New York: Penguin Press.

Peek, George Nelson

George N. Peek, a leading figure in American agriculture during the 1930s, was born on November 19, 1873, in Polo, Illinois. He was raised in Oregon, Illinois, attended Northwestern University, and then became a farm equipment salesman in Minneapolis, Minnesota, for Deere and Company. He rose steadily through the company, becoming general manager of John Deere Plow Company in Omaha, Nebraska, in 1901. Peek was a fine businessman, and in 1911, he was named vice president of sales for Deere and Company. The first two decades of the twentieth century were generally quite good for farmers, and when World War I broke out, Peek was named to the War Industries Board, a powerful government agency charged with organizing the economy to maximize industrial and agricultural production. In 1918 and 1919 Peek headed up the federal government's Industrial Board, which was to ease the economy back into peacetime production; he then returned to Moline, Illinois, to serve as president of the Moline Plow Company.

When the American farm economy cratered during the 1920s, Peek emerged as an influential spokesman for farm interests. He developed a comprehensive program to rescue farmers that involved an activist federal government. He wanted the federal government to implement protective tariffs, marketing cooperatives, farm loans, and a domestic price support system. More specifically, he wanted the federal government to purchase farm surpluses at market prices and export them abroad, and if the domestic price was higher than the export price, the government would collect an equalization fee. In Congress, the proposal became the McNary-Haugen Bill. Peek left Moline Plow to lobby full-time for the legislation, and the bill passed once in 1927 and again in 1928, but on both occasions, President Calvin Coolidge vetoed it.

Disgusted with the Republican Party, Peek endorsed for president Democrats Al Smith in 1928 and **Franklin D. Roosevelt** in 1932. In 1933, newly elected president Franklin D. Roosevelt placed Peek in charge of the **Agricultural Adjustment Administration** (AAA), a government agency committed to dealing with the farm crisis by cutting production. Peek soon loathed the AAA, finding it to be a cumbersome bureaucratic arrangement that completely defied market realities. He remained committed to his own idea of solving the farm crisis—export marketing. Peek resigned from the AAA late in 1933 for a brief tenure as head of the **Export-Import Bank**. In 1935 he retired to private relief and returned to the Republican Party. George Peek died on December 17, 1943.

Further Reading

Gilbert, Jess. 2015. *Planning Democracy: Agrarian Intellectuals and the Intended New Deal*, New Haven, CT: Yale University Press; White, Ann Folino. 2014. *Plowed Under: Food Policy Protests and Performance in New Deal America*, Bloomington: Indiana University Press.

President's Organization on Unemployment Relief

As **unemployment** steadily grew worse in 1930, Democrats and liberal Republicans clamored for federal action to provide unemployment relief. President **Herbert Hoover**, however, worried about the long-term implications of a large federal relief bureaucracy, and he opted for private initiatives. In 1930 he established the President's Emergency Committee for Employment (PECE) to coordinate the relief efforts of the federal government, business, labor unions, state and local governments, women's groups, and social welfare agencies. He appointed Arthur Woods to head the group. Woods quickly grew frustrated by PECE's inadequacies, and early in 1931, he urged the president to support a $375 million congressional appropriation to fund relief efforts. Hoover rejected the proposal out of hand. Woods then resigned from the organization. It had become clear to him that the unemployment problem was severe and getting worse and that the private sector did not have the resources or the will to address the problem in a serious way.

On August 13, 1931, PECE was absorbed by the new President's Organization on Unemployment Relief (POUR). Hoover put AT&T president Walter S. Gifford in charge of the government's unemployment relief effort. POUR deemphasized direct federal relief action in favor of private efforts, but time quickly proved that Arthur Woods's fears were being realized. The unemployment crisis dwarfed private resources. The nation's unemployment rate reached 15 percent in 1931 and 20 percent early in 1932. It was obvious that POUR's campaign was hopelessly inadequate, and President Hoover, with the presidential election of 1932 looming on the horizon, had to do something to provide real unemployment relief to retain any chance of reelection. In July 1932, POUR was eclipsed when Congress passed the **Emergency Relief and Construction Act**.

See also: Emergency Relief and Construction Act of 1932; Hoover, Herbert Clark; Unemployment

Further Reading

Herbert Hoover Presidential Library and Museum. "Gallery Six: The Great Depression," http://hoover.archives.gov/exhibits/Hooverstory/gallery06/. Accessed September 1, 2016; Miller Center. "American President: Herbert Hoover," University of Virginia, http://millercenter.org/president/hoover. Accessed September 5, 2016; Rappleye, Charles. 2016. *Herbert Hoover in the White House: The Ordeal of the Presidency*, New York: Simon & Schuster.

Public Utility Holding Company Act of 1935

During the 1920s, the public utility industry had behaved quite irresponsibly in making money by creating and issuing new securities for multiple holding companies stacked on top of a single operating company. The public utility holding company empire of Samuel Insull had been especially

egregious, and when the stock market fell in 1929, the multiple holding companies collapsed in value. Many **New Deal**ers, especially those with a Brandesian faith in the obligation of the federal government to maintain a competitive economic environment through antitrust action, called for government regulation. President **Franklin D. Roosevelt** had **Benjamin Cohen** and **Thomas Corcoran** draft the bill. Congressman Sam Rayburn of Texas and Senator Burton K. Wheeler sponsored the legislation in Congress. The bill contained the so-called death sentence clause that allowed the **Securities and Exchange Commission** (SEC) to dissolve any public utility holding company that could not justify its own existence. In other words, a public utility holding company could not exist simply as a device for issuing new securities.

Not surprisingly, the public utility industry marshaled all of its resources in fighting the Public Utility Holding Company Act, also known as the Wheeler-Rayburn Bill. In the end, industry lobbyists managed to eliminate the "death sentence" clause. Roosevelt signed it into law on August 28, 1935. The law awarded the Federal Power Commission the authority to regulate interstate shipments of electrical power and extended similar authority over natural gas to the Federal Trade Commission. The law also eliminated all holding companies twice removed from their public utility operating companies. The law required all public utility holding companies to register with the SEC, which also enjoyed the power to supervise the financial activities of holding companies. The SEC also enjoyed the power to dissolve any holding company that could not justify its own existence after a five-year period. That power, however, was severely limited by the fact that the burden of proof rested on the SEC. By 1952, under the authority of the Public Utility Holding Company Act, the SEC had forced public utilities to divest themselves or to dissolve 753 affiliated holding companies with a total value of more than $10 billion.

See also: Cohen, Benjamin; Corcoran, Thomas; Securities and Exchange Commission

Further Reading

Hyman, Leonard S., Andrew S. Hyman, and Robert C. Hyman. 2005. *America's Electric Utilities: Past, Present, and Future*, 8th ed., Public Utilities Reports; PBS. "Regulation: Public vs. Private Power: From FDR to Today," *Frontline*, http://www.pbs.org/wgbh/pages/frontline/shows/blackout/regulation/time line.html. Accessed September 9, 2016; Smithsonian. "Emergence of Electric Utilities in America," American History, http://americanhistory.si.edu/power ing/past/h1main.htm. Accessed September 9, 2016.

Public Works Administration

As far back as the depression of 1893, when Jacob Coxey led a march of unemployed men to Washington, D.C., to demand a federal public works program for unemployed workers, social welfare advocates have seen in government jobs programs a way to alleviate the suffering caused by downturns in the economy. During the 1920s, such progressive politicians as senators Robert La Follette of Wisconsin, **Robert Wagner** of New York, and Edward P. Costigan of Colorado endorsed the idea, as did a well-received 1930 book by William T. Foster and Waddill Catchings—*The Long Range Planning of Public Works*. Foster and Catchings called for creation of a federal reserve fund for the construction of new highways, public buildings, and other projects. They argued that such a program would relieve the suffering of the unemployed and augment consumer purchasing power.

In July 1932, Congress passed the **Emergency Relief and Construction Act** to provide **unemployment** relief, and among its provisions was authority for the **Reconstruction Finance Corporation** (RFC) to establish a public works division to construct "self-liquidating" projects, such as water

A PWA construction site in Washington, D.C., 1933. (Franklin D. Roosevelt Presidential Library)

and sewage systems and toll roads and bridges, that would pay for themselves in a few years. When **Franklin D. Roosevelt** was inaugurated, Congress passed the National Industrial Recovery Act of 1933, and Title II of the law created a Public Works Administration (PWA) to take over the RFC's work. The PWA had an appropriation of $3.3 billion. By 1940, the PWA had constructed more than 34,000 projects, including Grand Coulee Dam, Queens Midtown Tunnel, and the All American Canal.

See also: Emergency Relief and Construction Act of 1932; Reconstruction Finance Corporation; Unemployment

Further Reading

Cohen Adam. November 13, 2007. "Public Works: When 'Big Government' Plays a Role," *New York Times*, http://www.nytimes.com/2007/11/13/opinion/13tues4.html?_r=0. Accessed September 9, 2016; Smith, Jason Scott. 2009. *Building New Deal Liberalism: The Political Economy of Public Works, 1933–1956*, New York: Cambridge University Press.

R

Radio

The first commercially licensed radio station in the United States began broadcasting in 1920. By 1930, over 40 percent of households in America owned at least one radio. The medium, with its mix of comedies, dramas, variety shows, and news programming, became a steady source of entertainment and escape for people who increasingly could not afford other leisure activities. As Irving Settel wrote in *A Pictorial History of Radio* (1967), "Movie houses closed, night clubs languished, and theatrical stock companies disappeared, [but] radio boomed. . . . Thousands of families who had purchased much of their household equipment on credit gave up their vacuum cleaners, their cars, and their furniture, but kept up payments on their radios."

Radio was one of the earliest and most effective forms of mass media, creating a more cohesive national identity. People would go to one another's homes to listen to their favorite programs; often a single radio in a town could draw people from miles away. Not only did radio provide a distraction, but it helped Americans feel connected to one another during the desolate and trying years of the Great Depression.

Radio programs offered heroes, feel-good stories, action, adventure, news, politics, and, in the form of President **Roosevelt**'s informal radio addresses known as **fireside chat**s, guidance and clarity during the early years of the crisis. In the first fireside chat, delivered just eight days into his presidency, Roosevelt discussed the banking crisis and his decision to declare a bank holiday, explaining the steps that would be taken to ensure financial security once the banks opened. Over 60 million people heard that address, which is credited with restoring confidence in capitalism and the banking system, and giving birth to the age of media politics.

As the **Rural Electrification Administration** helped bring electricity to remote areas of the United States, more and more Americans were exposed to radio programming. The most popular radio program of the period was *Amos 'n' Andy*, a show with vaudeville roots about two owners of a Harlem taxicab company that operated with just a single vehicle, an all-but-broken-down jalopy. Amos was a hardworking, conservative family man,

Atwater Kent stands by a radio while others listen in the Hamilton Hotel, Washington, D.C. Kent operated one of the largest radio manufacturers of the time. (Library of Congress)

while Andy was a playful, irresponsible ne'er-do-well. Both of the show's key sponsors, Pepsodent toothpaste and Campbell Soup, enjoyed growing market shares because of the program. *Amos 'n' Andy* was so popular that movie theaters would stop their projectors when the show began and broadcast it to the theater audiences. Otherwise, people would have stayed home in order to hear the program. Historians today recognize *Amos 'n' Andy* as the first radio program to achieve a truly national audience, and as such, it occupies a unique place in the rise of a mass culture in the United States.

Radio also gave rise to soap operas—emotional serial dramas initially sponsored by soap manufacturers. Soap operas were marketed to women and tended to occupy late-afternoon weekday time slots, when women would listen while doing household chores. The melodramatic *Betty and Bob* was one such program, centered around lower-class secretary Betty and her boss, tycoon Bob Drake. *Betty and Bob* plotlines revolved around love, hate, hubris, jealousy, greed, betrayal, divorce, and madness. Other dramatic adventure programs included *Rin Tin Tin*, featuring a German shepherd dog who battled desperadoes and helped rescue women and children from natural disasters; and *The Lone Ranger*, about a Texas ranger who, along with his Native American sidekick, Tonto, and his horse, Silver, fought for truth and justice. The Lone Ranger himself was known for being the ultimate do-gooder, and parents tuned in not only to enjoy Western drama but also to have values taught to their children.

Other popular radio genres included science fiction, like *Buck Rogers in the Twenty-Fifth Century*, whose title character fights and foils galactic villains 500 years in the future, and crime/mystery, like *The Shadow*, *Calling All Cars*, *Gang Busters*, and *Sherlock Holmes*. *The Shadow* revolved around the exploits of Lamont Cranston, a crime-fighting social scientist with the power to cloud people's minds. *Calling All Cars* tracked the investigation of a different fictional crime each week. *Gang Busters* exploited an almost obsessive public interest in criminal celebrities like John Dillinger and Pretty Boy Floyd, and the FBI agents who pursued them. *Sherlock Holmes* was based on the popular detective novels by Sir Arthur Conan Doyle about a detective with unparalleled deductive reasoning skills, and his faithful sidekick, Dr. John Watson.

One of the best-loved and enduring radio programs in American history was the vaudeville-based *Fibber McGee and Molly*. The main characters were Fibber McGee, an unrealistic-but-gentle blowhard who dreamed implausible dreams and told tall tales, and his long-suffering wife, Molly. The episodes revolved around life in the McGee household. Such signature comments as Molly's "heavenly days" became common pop-culture phrases. Another incredibly popular series *Lux Radio Theater* began by airing anthologies of Broadway plays and then shifted to movie themes, basing its weekly broadcasts on popular films. In 1936, famed Hollywood director Cecil B. DeMille took over directorship, and the show's ratings skyrocketed. DeMille attracted Hollywood's most prominent names to the program, including Clark Gable, Marlene Dietrich, Gary Cooper, and John Wayne. The *Major Bowes' Original Amateur Hour* (later renamed *The Original Amateur Hour*) was also a broadcasting phenomenon in the 1930s. Desperate to hit it big during the Depression, literally hundreds of thousands of amateur acts applied for the chance to perform on the show, win a prize, and perhaps get noticed by big-time producers. *Death Valley Days* was another highly rated show, set in late-nineteenth- and early-twentieth-century California, where traders and settlers were trying to settle in the west. Depression-era Americans saw their struggles mirrored in the hardscrabble life of the desert frontier, and the courage and perseverance of the *Death Valley* pioneers inspired them with hope.

During World War II, radio became even more popular, keeping Americans informed about the war effort and introducing more patriotic dramas. By the 1950s, however, radio gave way to TV as the more popular medium; in fact, several popular radio shows of the 1930s and 1940s went on to become successful television shows as well.

See also: Coughlin, Charles Edward; Fireside Chats

Further Reading

Dickstein, Morris. 2010. *Dancing in the Dark: A Cultural History of the Great Depression*, New York: W. W. Norton & Company; Douglas, Susan J. 2004. *Listening In: Radio and the American Imagination*, Minneapolis: University of Minnesota Press; Hilmes, Michelle. 2010. *Only Connect: A Cultural History of Broadcasting in the United States*, 3rd ed., Boston: Wadsworth Publishing; Settel, Irving. 1967. *A Pictorial History of Radio*, New York: Grosset & Dunlap; Smith, Stephen. November 10, 2014. "Radio: The Internet of the 1930s," American RadioWorks, http://www.americanradioworks.org/segments/radio-the-internet-of-the-1930s/. Accessed September 9, 2016.

Railroad Retirement Board et al. v. Alton Railroad Company et al. (1935)

In 1934, Congress passed the Railroad Retirement Act, which established a federal government retirement program for railroad workers. The law established a Railroad Retirement Board to administer the retirement program, whose pensions were financed by a 2 percent payroll tax on all railroad workers and a 4 percent tax on all railroad carriers. The law required 150,000 railroad workers to retire at age sixty-five. Many **New Deal**ers hoped such a measure would make that many new jobs available to ease the country's **unemployment** problem.

But railway executives hated the measure, and the Association of Railway Executives filed a lawsuit in federal court. They labeled the law unconstitutional on the grounds that it violated their Fifth Amendment rights to private property. The case of *Railroad Retirement Board et al. v. Alton Railroad Company et al.* reached the Supreme Court in 1935. The Court declared the Railroad Retirement Act of 1934 unconstitutional, siding with the Association of Railway Executives. The justices claimed that mandatory pensions did not come under the commerce clause of the U.S. Constitution and therefore Congress did not have the power to enact such a law.

Congress almost immediately responded with the Railroad Retirement Act of 1935, also known as the Wagner-Crosser Railroad Retirement Act of 1935. The replacement legislation exempted railroad employees from provisions of the **Social Security Act of 1935** and financed railroad pensions by an excise tax of 3.5 percent on employee payrolls and an income tax of an equal amount on the carriers. But in June 1936, a federal district court declared the Railroad Retirement Act of 1935 unconstitutional.

Congress again reacted, though not so quickly. In 1937, a new Railroad Retirement Act became law. Before the law was passed, President **Franklin D. Roosevelt** had asked the railway unions and railway executives to work out a compromise pension plan. The Railroad Retirement Act of 1937 represented that compromise. A companion bill—the Carriers' Taxing Act—financed the pension plan by income taxes levied on carriers and employees. The Association of Railway Executives did not contest the law.

See also: Social Security Act of 1935

Further Reading

Huibregtse, Jon R. 2010. *American Railroad Labor and the Genesis of the New Deal, 1919–1935* (Working in the Americas), Gainesville: University Press of Florida; Wolmar, Christian. 2014. *The Great Railroad Revolution: The History of Trains in America*, New York: Public Affairs.

Recession of 1937–1938

By mid-1937, the **unemployment** rate had fallen dramatically from its highs in 1932, and the stock market had risen. Many **New Deal** economists concluded that the end of the Great Depression was in sight, that the New Deal's recovery measures were finally yielding results. But what they did not realize was that a series of fiscal decisions by the **Roosevelt** administration and monetary decisions by the **Federal Reserve Board** had undermined the prosperity. Out of a misguided fear of the possibility of inflation, the Federal Reserve Board in 1936 pursued tight money policies, doubling reserve requirements and putting a damper on the money markets. At the same time, Social Security taxes began to be collected without benefits yet being paid, which removed purchasing power from the economy. Declining federal spending on relief and work relief also cut purchasing power.

These policies combined to drive the economy into recession. Beginning in September 1937 and lasting until June 1938, the economy headed back into the Depression. Industrial production and payrolls declined by a third, manufacturing employment by a quarter, and industrial stocks by more than half. The economic downturn precipitated a huge debate inside the Roosevelt administration, with conservatives like **Jesse Jones**, Daniel

Roper, and Henry Morgenthau Jr. calling for balanced budgets and pro-business policies, and such liberals as **Leon Henderson**, Robert Jackson, **Thomas Corcoran**, **Benjamin Cohen**, Harold Ickes, and **Marriner Eccles** advocating deficit spending and antitrust action to stimulate the economy. In April 1938, President Franklin D. Roosevelt announced that he was siding with the liberals. It was not until the spring of 1940, however, with war raging in Europe, that federal government spending finally pulled the economy out of the Depression.

See also: Eccles, Marriner; Federal Reserve Board; Keynes, John Maynard

Further Reading

Ganzel, Bill. 2003. "New Financial Laws," Ganzel Group, http://www.livinghistoryfarm.org/farminginthe30s/money_15.html. Accessed September 9, 2016; Meltzer, Allan H. 2004. *A History of the Federal Reserve, Volume 1: 1913–1951*, Chicago: University of Chicago Press.

Reciprocal Trade Agreements Act of 1934

During the 1920s, tariff policies in the United States and abroad restricted trade and stimulated declines in industrial production. In the United States, the Republican administrations of Warren G. Harding, Calvin Coolidge, and **Herbert Hoover** pursued high tariff policies, symbolized by the Fordney-McCumber Tariff of 1921 and the **Hawley-Smoot Tariff of 1930**. The Republican logic was simple: by keeping European industrial products out of U.S. markets, American manufacturing jobs would be protected. But the opposite happened. Europeans retaliated with high tariffs of their own, and the combined effect was to discourage economic activity.

By the early 1930s, it was obvious to many economists and Democrats that U.S. tariff policy had to be drastically revised downward if there was going to be any hope of stimulating the economy. Between 1929 and 1932 American exports had fallen by a third. Secretary of State Cordell Hull led the fight for tariff reductions, which he believed would improve U.S. foreign relations and stimulate the economy. He proposed a bill that would authorize the State Department to negotiate bilateral tariff reductions with other countries. Congress passed the measure in June 1934, and President **Franklin D. Roosevelt** signed it.

The Reciprocal Trade Agreements Act of 1934 authorized the president to negotiate bilateral tariff agreements with other nations without seeking congressional approval, as long as those tariffs did not raise or lower rates by more than 50 percent from the levels of the **Hawley-Smoot Tariff**. Congress renewed the legislation in 1937, 1940, 1943, and 1945, by which time a total of thirty-seven bilateral tariff reductions had been negotiated.

See also: Hawley-Smoot Tariff of 1930

Further Reading

Economist. December 18, 2008. "The Battle of Smoot-Hawley," http://www.econ omist.com/node/12798595. Accessed September 5, 2016; Irwin, Douglas A. 2011. *Peddling Protectionism: Smoot-Hawley and the Great Depression*, Princeton, NJ: Princeton University Press.

Reconstruction Finance Corporation

The Reconstruction Finance Corporation (RFC) was perhaps the most important federal agency of the Great Depression, although historians have tended to ignore it. The RFC had its beginnings in the collapse of the banking system early in the 1930s. Because of long-term problems with the banking system during the 1920s—more than 5,000 banks had failed during the decade—depositors had completely lost confidence, and their demands for deposits created a liquidity crisis in the economy. In October 1931, to keep banks from closing their doors or selling off their assets at panic-level prices, President **Herbert Hoover** established the National Credit Corporation (NCC), a private organization of major banks designed to loan money to troubled financial institutions. If depositors realized that banks could come up with the cash to redeem deposits, they would be less likely to launch runs on the banks.

The NCC, however, proved inadequate to the task. The weaknesses in the banking system in particular and the money markets in general proved to be deep and endemic, and to prevent bankruptcy throughout the entire system, President Hoover proposed and Congress created the RFC in January 1932. The RFC received an appropriation of $500 million and the right to issue its own bonds to raise another $2 billion. It could then loan that money to troubled banks, savings banks, industrial banks, insurance companies, credit unions, and building and loan associations. With the money, the president hoped, the banks would enjoy greater liquidity, depositors would be reassured, and bankers could increase their volume of commercial loans. With credit again flowing in the economy, Hoover presumed, industrial production and employment would increase too. The RFC could also make loans to railroads. During the previous two decades, banks had invested heavily in railroad bonds, but when automobiles and trucks cut into railroad freight revenues, many railroads found themselves in serious financial difficulties and defaulted on their bond payments, which seriously compromised the investment portfolios of thousands of financial institutions.

Hoover named prominent banker and Republican politician Charles Dawes to head the RFC, and RFC loans did restore some stability, temporarily, to the money markets. Many liberal Democrats, however, pilloried the RFC because a substantial volume of its loans went to large commercial banks, big insurance companies, and high-profile railroads. They accused the RFC of bailing out the rich and powerful while the poor and the unemployed suffered without any federal assistance. The president insisted that the economy would not recover until the money markets recovered, and he was probably right, but it was a tough position to sell politically. When Charles Dawes quit the RFC in June 1932 and the RFC turned around and loaned $90 million to Dawes's troubled Central Republic Bank of Chicago, the Democrats howled in protest and talked scandal, and Hoover lost even more ground politically.

In response to the political criticism, Congress passed the **Emergency Relief and Construction Act** in July 1932, which authorized the RFC to loan $300 million to state and local governments for **unemployment** relief and up to $1.5 billion to the states for public works construction. The legislation was politically imperative since the unemployment rate had hit 25 percent.

Within a few months, however, virtually all of the RFC's programs were bankrupt. Late in December 1932 and in January and February 1933, the money markets collapsed, and it appeared that the entire banking system was about to go bankrupt, in spite of billions of dollars in RFC loans. Unemployment continued to rise, and the RFC relief funds proved pitifully inadequate. The $1.5 billion in public works construction money had little impact because the projects, many of them very complex, had not even gotten under way yet. The RFC had failed. Frightened depositors were hoarding currency in even greater volumes; bankers were accumulating large volumes of excess reserves at Federal Reserve Banks; and businessmen were laying off workers in record numbers. The RFC had failed because all of its loans had to be repaid, and borrowers were cautious about undertaking such obligations during hard times.

By February 1933, a series of banking panics were spreading throughout the country, and to deal with the crisis, the RFC would have literally needed billions more dollars to loan out. When President Hoover left office in March 1933, nearly all of the banks in the country had shut down, and the RFC, one of the largest federal agencies in U.S. history, had failed.

But the RFC was resurrected during the years of the **New Deal**. For President **Franklin D. Roosevelt**, the RFC became an all but ubiquitous agency, used for a variety of purposes. He named Houston banker **Jesse Jones** to head the RFC. Under the authority of the Emergency Banking Act of 1933, the RFC was authorized to purchase the preferred stock and capital notes of troubled banks. In the previous year, RFC loans had not helped that much because bankers had to pay them off on a short-term basis. But by buying preferred stock and only receiving annual dividends on the stock, the RFC essentially supplied banks with long-term capital, which allowed them to hold on to assets until values had recovered. By the mid-1930s, the RFC owned stock in more than 6,000 American banks. The RFC also created and supervised the work of such other New Deal agencies as the **Commodity Credit Corporation**, the Federal National Mortgage Association, the Disaster Loan Corporation, the **Export-Import Bank**, and the RFC Mortgage Company. Another subsidiary, the Electric Home and Farm Authority, purchased installment contracts from retailers and finance companies to help make electric appliances affordable to poorer consumers. With an expanded secondary market available for the contracts, retailers were more willing to finance appliance purchases, increasing production and sales of appliances and electricity consumption.

Finally, the RFC was a funding agency for such New Deal agencies as the **Works Progress Administration**, the **Civil Works Administration**, and the **Federal Emergency Relief Administration**. By 1940, the RFC had loaned more than $10 billion, making it by far the most powerful of the New Deal agencies.

See also: Commodity Credit Corporation; Emergency Relief and Construction Act of 1932; Export-Import Bank; New Deal; Unemployment

Further Reading

Folsom, Burton W. November 30, 2011. "The First Government Bailouts: The Story of the RFC," Foundation for Economic Education (FEE), https://fee.org/articles/the-first-government-bailouts-the-story-of-the-rfc/. Accessed September 1, 2016; Rothbard, Murray N. 2002. *A History of Money and Banking in the United States: The Colonial Era to World War II*, Auburn, AL: Mises Institute.

Reno, Milo

Milo Reno was born near Agency, Iowa, on January 5, 1866. He attended William Penn College in Oskaloosa, Iowa, in order to study for the ministry, but he left school after losing interest in a ministerial career. Reno

tried his hand at selling insurance and farm equipment, but the plight of midwestern farmers steadily consumed more of his attention, and in 1918, he joined the National Farmers' Union (NFU). A popular, engaging individual, Reno became quite influential in the NFU, and he began speaking to larger and larger audiences, always insisting that farmers "deserved the cost of production plus a reasonable profit."

In 1932, Reno was elected president of the National Farmers' Holiday Association (NFHA), a group dedicated to holding crops off the market until farmers received fair prices for them. In August 1932, the NFHA took militant action by preventing milk and livestock trucks from delivering crops to market. The strike spread from Iowa to four other states, and in the process, Reno became a national figure. Reno called off the strike in March 1933 when President **Franklin D. Roosevelt** was president, hoping that the new administration would address the farm problem. But the **New Deal** soon disappointed Reno, who believed that the acreage reduction plans of the **Agricultural Adjustment Administration** would benefit only large commercial farmers, not troubled family farmers. In September 1933, he tried to resurrect the strikes again, but few farmers were willing to listen to him anymore. The movement collapsed, and Reno retreated into obscurity. He died on May 5, 1936.

See also: Agricultural Adjustment Administration; Organized Labor

Further Reading

Meyer, Carrie A. 2007. *Days on the Family Farm: From the Golden Age through the Great Depression*, Minneapolis: University of Minnesota Press; Ness, Immanuel. 2000. *Encyclopedia of Interest Groups and Lobbyists in the United States*, Armonk, NY: Sharpe.

Reorganization Act of 1939

As governor of New York, **Franklin D. Roosevelt** had earned a reputation as an advocate of government efficiency, but when he became president, the impact of the Great Depression put a premium on federal government activism and federal spending, both of which militated against Roosevelt's reputation as a conservative. In fact, two months into the **New Deal**, both liberals and conservatives would have found it laughable to describe the president as a supporter of government reorganization, retrenchment, and efficiency. In the **Economy Act of 1933**, the president had gained the authority to implement government reorganization schemes, but he could not act upon that authority because of the compelling need for government relief and recovery programs.

In 1936, however, President Roosevelt began paying more attention to issues of efficiency and administrative management. He established the President's Committee on Administrative Management, under the leadership of Louis Brownlow, head of the public administration committee of the Social Science Research Council. In 1937 the committee produced its report—*Report of the President's Committee on Administrative Management*—which was delivered to Congress. After more than two years of congressional debate and maneuvering, Congress passed the Reorganization Act of 1939. Roosevelt signed it on April 3, 1939.

Roosevelt began to implement the legislation three weeks later. The president submitted Reorganization Plan No. 1 to Congress, which created the Federal Security Agency, the **Federal Works Agency**, the Federal Loan Agency, and an executive office of the president. The Federal Security Agency consolidated into one agency more than a dozen federal agencies, including the Social Security Board, the Public Health Service, the **National Youth Administration**, the U.S. Office of Education, the Civilian Conservation Corps, the Food and Drug Administration, and the U.S. Employment Service. The Federal Works Agency consolidated into one agency the **Works Progress Administration**, the **Public Works Administration**, the Bureau of Public Roads, and the U.S. Housing Agency. The Federal Loan Agency consolidated the **Reconstruction Finance Corporation**, the **Export-Import Bank**, the **Federal Housing Administration**, the **Home Owners' Loan Corporation**, the RFC Mortgage Company, the Disaster Loan Corporation, the Federal National Mortgage Association, and the Electric Home and Farm Authority.

Further Reading

Calabresi, Stephen G., and Christopher S. Yoo. 2008. *The Unitary Executive: Presidential Power from Washington to Bush*, New Haven, CT: Yale University Press; Leuchtenburg, William E. 2009. *Franklin D. Roosevelt and the New Deal: 1932–1940*, New York: Harper Perennial.

Resettlement Administration

The great problem facing American agriculture during the 1920s and 1930s was overproduction. Commodity production exceeded demand in the United States, and mechanisms for marketing surpluses abroad with profitable margins were not available. Commodity prices and the purchasing power of farm families steadily declined between World War I and the early 1930s. As farm income declined, millions of farmers found themselves unable to meet mortgage payments and ended up losing their land in foreclosure proceedings. **New Deal** farm policy addressed these two problems by trying to reduce production and to liquefy the credit markets.

The programs implemented under the Agricultural Adjustment Act of 1933, the **Soil Conservation and Domestic Allotment Act of 1936**, the **Bankhead Cotton Control Act**, the **Warren Potato Control Act**, and the Agricultural Adjustment Act of 1938 all worked to reduce the number of acres in production, and farmers were compensated for the acreage removed. In some areas, especially the labor-intensive cotton fields of the South, the acreage reductions wreaked havoc with poor farm laborers and tenant farmers. While the large commercial landowners received government checks for their acreage reductions, farm laborers ended up with crops to pick and tenant farmers and sharecroppers found themselves without land to work. Displaced from the land and unable to find work in other sectors of the economy, they suffered a numbing poverty.

The rise of the **Southern Tenant Farmers' Union** and its activities brought their plight to the attention of the public, and in 1935, President **Franklin D. Roosevelt** established the Special Committee on Farm Tenancy to investigate their situation and to make recommendations. The Resettlement Administration grew out of the committee's recommendation that the federal government assume some responsibility for what New Deal farm policy had done to poor farm families, especially in the South. Of course, the larger commercial farmers resisted any such efforts because they feared losing access to a supply of cheap, easily exploitable labor. But Congress nevertheless responded and in 1935 created the Resettlement Administration and placed **Rexford G. Tugwell** at its head.

The Resettlement Administration was the most class-conscious of New Deal agencies. Its mission was to upgrade the lives of the poorest of Americans, at the expense of wealthy commercial landowners, and of many black Americans, at the expense of wealthy whites. Tugwell initially wanted to resettle more than 500,000 poor families on their own land or in suburban developments; provide decent camps and sanitary living conditions for migratory farmworkers; and initiate farm rehabilitation and land utilization projects to assist poor farmers who owned small amounts of land to maximize their assets. The Resettlement Administration even organized large collective farms in Casa Grande, Arizona; Lake Dick, Arkansas; Walker Country, Alabama; and New Madrid, Louisiana. The collective farms were complete with project managers, family cottages, medical cooperatives, and heavy farm machinery. Finally, the Resettlement Administration, through its Suburban Resettlement Division, worked to depopulate urban slums and tenant farm slums and build twenty-five new towns in suburban areas.

The Resettlement Administration never even came close to achieving its goals because it upset so many entrenched interest groups. Conservatives labeled these collective farms **socialist**ic or communistic, and large commercial farmers resented the assistance given to poor tenant farmers, primarily because they feared it would raise their labor costs. The American Medical Association protested the medical cooperatives, real estate developers protested the new suburban towns, and labor unions complained that the federal government was assuming some of their functions.

Because of all the opposition, the Resettlement Administration's actual achievements were quite meager. Instead of relocating 500,000 families, the Resettlement Administration actually relocated only 4,441 families. Instead of twenty-five new towns, the Resettlement Administration built only three: Greenbelt, Maryland, near Washington, D.C.; Greendale, Wisconsin, near Milwaukee; and Green Hills, Ohio, near Cincinnati. In the end, the **Farm Security Administration** absorbed the Resettlement Administration and its programs.

See also: Dust Bowl and California Migration; Farm Security Administration; Southern Tenant Farmers' Union; Tugwell, Rexford Guy

Further Reading

Grubbs, Donald H. 2000. *Cry from the Cotton: The Southern Tenant Farmers' Union and the New Deal*, Fayetteville: University of Arkansas Press; Maloney, C. J. 2011. *Back to the Land: Arthurdale, FDR's New Deal, and the Costs of Economic Planning*, Hoboken, NJ: Wiley; Roberts, Charles Kenneth. 2015. *The Farm Security Administration and Rural Rehabilitation in the South*, Knoxville: University of Tennessee Press.

Revenue Act of 1932

Because of declining industrial production and increasing **unemployment** during the early 1930s, federal government revenues dropped precipitously, leaving the **Hoover** administration with a deficit. For President Herbert Hoover, the deficit only increased public skepticism about the health of the economy and made a recovery less likely. The only answer, the president was convinced, was a tax increase, which would balance the federal budget and restore confidence to the economy. Congress passed the Revenue Act of 1932, which raised the corporate income tax to 13.75 percent, the maximum surtax from 25 to 55 percent, and general tax rate schedules from 4 to 8 percent. President Hoover signed the bill on June 6, 1932.

In one way, the Revenue Act of 1932 marked a watershed in the history of public policy in the United States. The idea of raising taxes during an economic downturn, exactly what the Revenue Act of 1932 accomplished, would soon be discredited by the advent of **Keynes**ian economics and the use of deficit spending to stimulate the economy. Never again would policymakers raise taxes during a recession.

See also: Keynes, John Maynard

Further Reading

Miller Center. "American President: Herbert Hoover," University of Virginia, http://millercenter.org/president/hoover. Accessed September 5, 2016; Rappleye, Charles. 2016. *Herbert Hoover in the White House: The Ordeal of the Presidency*, New York: Simon & Schuster; Herbert Hoover Presidential Library and Museum. "Gallery Six: The Great Depression," http://hoover.archives.gov/exhibits/Hooverstory/gallery06/. Accessed September 1, 2016.

Roosevelt, Anna Eleanor

Anna Eleanor Roosevelt, arguably the most influential woman of twentieth-century America, was born in New York City on October 11, 1884, to one of the country's most distinguished families. To put it mildly, she suffered in a dysfunctional family. Although the family put on a facade of strict Victorian morality and respectability, her father was a drunk and her mother a woman who withheld love and affection from her daughter. Eleanor was orphaned by the time she was ten years old. She attended the Allenswood School outside of London, where she managed to recover, or least begin to develop, her identity. In 1905, Eleanor married **Franklin D. Roosevelt**, a distant cousin. They had five children and eventually forged one of the greatest political partnerships in U.S. history.

In 1913 the Roosevelts moved to Washington, D.C., when Franklin was appointed assistant secretary of the navy in the Woodrow Wilson administration. The normal routine of their marriage was shattered when Eleanor learned that her husband had had an affair with her social secretary. The affair was an emotional catastrophe for Eleanor, but it forced her to develop an independent identity, one quite distinct from that of her husband. Their marriage never again enjoyed any physical intimacy but survived because it suited the political objectives of both partners.

Franklin D. Roosevelt ran unsuccessfully for the vice presidency in the election of 1920, but after his defeat, they returned to New York City, where Eleanor became active in the Women's Trade Union League and in

Democratic politics, especially in the party's women's division. She actively campaigned for federal minimum wage and maximum hours legislation, outspokenly opposed child labor, and crusaded for the Sheppard-Towner Act, which provided modest government protections for working women. Eleanor also took a firm stand against the Equal Rights Amendment, which she believed would actually hurt working-class women by removing gender-based protective legislation. When her husband was elected governor of New York in 1928, Eleanor's political profile increased even more.

On March 4, 1933, Eleanor became First Lady when her husband was inaugurated president of the United States. Over the years, she became the liberal conscience of the **New Deal**, serving as the country's most powerful lobbyist for civil rights, Social Security, **unemployment** relief, and labor standards legislation. She was outspoken in her opposition to lynching and in her support for a federal anti-lynching law. Her role was a critical one in the history of the New Deal, since her husband so often found himself trying to balance the demands of liberal Democrats in the Northeast and conservative Democrats in the South. Because of Eleanor, legislation that might never have garnered the support of the president managed to do so.

Eleanor Roosevelt photographed on July 20, 1933. Roosevelt was the first wife of a president to use her unique position to fight for the rights of minorities, women, and the destitute. After her husband died, Roosevelt expanded her responsibilities, playing an important role in the fledgling United Nations. (Library of Congress)

After Franklin D. Roosevelt's death in 1945, Eleanor Roosevelt emerged as the most famous and influential woman in the world. She became the matron of the Democratic Party and an icon for liberals interested in civil rights and social welfare legislation. She also was an avowed internationalist who realized that the United States possessed a moral responsibility to use its economic and military power to promote education, civil rights, and social welfare around the world. Eleanor Roosevelt died on November 7, 1962.

Further Reading

Beasley, Maurine. 2010. *Eleanor Roosevelt: Transformative First Lady*, Wichita: University Press of Kansas; Beasley, Maurinea H., Holly C. Shulman, and Henry R. Beasley. 2001. *The Eleanor Roosevelt Encyclopedia*, Westport, CT: Greenwood; Burns, Ken. 2014. *The Roosevelts: An Intimate History*, Blu-ray, 7 discs, 840 min., PBS; Columbian College of Arts and Sciences. Eleanor Roosevelt Papers Project, https://erpapers.columbian.gwu.edu/. Accessed September 12, 2016; Golay, Michael. 2013. *America 1933: The Great Depression, Lorena Hickok, Eleanor Roosevelt, and the Shaping of the New Deal*, New York: Free Press.

Roosevelt, Franklin Delano

In most surveys of professional historians, Franklin D. Roosevelt joins the ranks of George Washington and Abraham Lincoln as one of America's three greatest presidents. Blessed with enormous political talent, he led the country through two crises—the Great Depression and World War II—and in the process earned the esteem of most Americans. To be sure, his **New Deal** was anathema to most conservatives and big businessmen, but he provided middle-of-the-road leadership at a time when, because of the suffering caused by the Great Depression, he could have taken the country down the path to socialism. In that sense, Franklin D. Roosevelt can be credited with saving capitalism in the United States.

Franklin D. Roosevelt was born in New York City on January 30, 1882, to a prominent, prosperous family. He was an only child and as such enjoyed and endured the close attention of an elderly, indulgent father and a doting mother who made his life her life. The wealth of the Roosevelt family reached back to the mercantile and shipping industries of the colonial period, and as such it was "old money," which gave Franklin a patrician outlook on life. He remembered growing up on the family estate at Hyde Park. He grew up competitive but not really acquisitive, as if money had always been available and therefore not something to scramble after. In 1905 he married **Eleanor Roosevelt**, a distant cousin, and they had five children.

Roosevelt had a gilt-edged education—at Groton, Harvard, and Columbia, where he earned a law degree. He practiced law privately but had no real passion for it. The money had no real interest to him, but he did have a sense of noblesse oblige that pushed him toward politics. Roosevelt had no ideology or any fixed political philosophy. He was generally conservative but certainly not dogmatic, and a real pragmatic streak governed his thinking about the world. Such values, or lack thereof, prepared him for a political world where compromise and the art of the possible governed reality.

In 1911, Roosevelt was elected to the state legislature on a platform that opposed the political corruption so endemic to Tammany Hall, the Democratic political machine in New York City. But he soon realized that opposing Tammany Hall might win him votes in upstate New York, but it would surely keep him from winning statewide office, since Tammany Hall controlled so much of the New York City vote. So Roosevelt made peace with Tammany Hall. In 1913, President Woodrow Wilson picked Roosevelt as assistant secretary of the navy, a post that brought Roosevelt and his family to Washington, D.C., where they resided for the next seven years. Roosevelt's stature in the Democratic Party grew steadily, and in 1920 he was nominated as James Cox's vice presidential running mate. They lost in a landslide to Republican nominee Warren G. Harding.

The Roosevelts then returned to New York City, but in the summer of 1921, their lives changed dramatically. While vacationing at the family compound at Campobello, Roosevelt came down with a case of infantile paralysis, or polio, that attacked his legs and left him a paraplegic. Confined to a wheelchair, he retreated into a depression and farther into a private life. The depression proved to be short-lived. With the assistance of his wife Eleanor, he reevaluated his life and decided to return to politics. He became active in New York Democratic politics, and at the conventions of 1924 and 1928, he delivered the formal speeches nominating New York governor Al Smith for president. In 1928, Al Smith lost to **Herbert Hoover**, and Roosevelt won the New York governorship, becoming overnight the most prominent Democrat in the country.

Roosevelt's first term as governor of New York was a distinguished one. He emphasized conservation, state regulation of major public utilities, prison reform, and old-age pensions. When the economy fell into the Great Depression, New York became a model for **unemployment** relief, public works construction, and social welfare legislation. New York's **Temporary Emergency Relief Administration** paved the way for much of the New Deal's subsequent unemployment relief program. Roosevelt's administration in New York stood in stark contrast to President Herbert Hoover's administration in Washington, D.C., where procrastination, delay, and doubt characterized the approach to unemployment.

By 1932, Republicans were in desperate political circumstances. The national unemployment rate had reached an unprecedented 25 percent, corporate profits had collapsed, industrial production had cratered, and the money markets were in a state of meltdown, with banks, savings banks, building and loan associations, and credit unions failing by the thousands. Public confidence in the economy and in the Hoover administration had all but evaporated. Roosevelt won the Democratic nomination for president in 1932, and he immediately became the frontrunner. In the election, Roosevelt shattered all records when he won 22,809,638 popular votes to Hoover's 15,758,901, and Democrats came to control Congress by huge margins. The victory was the most stunning and complete in American history.

Roosevelt immediately set about rewarding the political constituencies that had put him in office. He knew that President Hoover had been too slow to move on federal unemployment relief projects, leaving Americans with the distinct impression that he did not care about the suffering of the poor, and Roosevelt was committed to portraying exactly the opposite. He also knew that Americans expected him to do something to stimulate the economy and lift the economy out of the Depression. Finally, Roosevelt realized that the federal government would have to undertake important initiatives to prevent future economic collapses. The early New Deal, therefore, soon became known for its commitment to "Relief, Recovery, and Reform."

Between March 9 and June 16, 1933, in the **first 100 days** of Roosevelt's presidency, Congress engaged in a flurry of legislative activity, much of it at the instigation of President Roosevelt. During those three months, Congress passed more major legislation than at any other time in U.S. history, including the Emergency Banking Act, the Economy Act, the Civilian Conservation Corps Reforestation Relief Act, the Federal Emergency Relief Act, the Agricultural Adjustment Act, the **Tennessee Valley Authority**, the **Securities Act**, the National Employment System Act, the Home Owners' Refinancing Act, the Banking Act, the Farm Credit Act, the **Emergency Railroad Transportation Act**, and the National Industrial Recovery Act. Compared to the Hoover administration, the early New Deal seemed, and was, bold and confident, and most Americans soon endowed Franklin D. Roosevelt with heroic status.

The so-called Second Hundred Days in 1935–1936 only cemented the president's reputation. The Supreme Court's decision in 1935 and 1936 to outlaw the **Agricultural Adjustment Administration** and the **National Recovery Administration** had gutted the New Deal's recovery programs, which enraged Roosevelt and only committed him to more activism and a change in focus. At the heart of the early New Deal had been the idea of national economic planning and business–government cooperation, but the later New Deal had a different focus, which included antitrust activity, social reform, and **Keynes**ian deficit spending. The later New Deal involved a shift to the left, indicated in such social reform legislation as the **Social Security Act of 1935**, the National Labor Relations Act of 1935, and the Wealth Tax Act of 1935, and a new emphasis on Brandesian antitrust activity through such items as the **Public Utility Holding Company Act of 1935**. In the presidential election of 1936, FDR was reelected over Republican nominee Alf Landon in a landslide.

Roosevelt's second term in office witnessed a shift in emphasis from the first. He all but abandoned the balanced budget rhetoric of the early New Deal in favor of the deficit spending philosophy of British economist John Maynard Keynes. Roosevelt also gave a new boost to antitrusters in his **Temporary National Economic Committee** hearings and new antitrust activity in the Department of Justice. But he also learned that there were limits to his popularity. In 1937, when he embarked on his **court-packing scheme** to liberalize the Supreme Court, he ran into a political roadblock of opposition, even from supporters who resented many of the Court's anti–New Deal decisions. What FDR learned was that Americans did not want him tampering with the Court, even if they disagreed with it. In the election of 1938, when he intervened in many primary elections to try and help defeat conservative Democrats, Americans again let him know that he had overstepped his bounds.

Some Republicans had high hopes of defeating Roosevelt when he decided to run for a third term in 1940, but events in Europe guaranteed FDR's reelection. Most Americans viewed Roosevelt as a father figure who had led the country through the pain of the Great Depression and had eased their suffering, and they trusted him to do the same in case of war. He was reelected in 1940 and again in 1944, dying in office on April 12, 1945. A grief-stricken nation mourned his passing.

Further Reading

Burns, Ken. 2014. *The Roosevelts: An Intimate History*, Blu-ray, 7 discs, 840 min., PBS; Leuchtenburg, William E. 2009. *Franklin D. Roosevelt and the New Deal: 1932–1940*, New York: Harper Perennial; Miller Center. "American President: Presidential Speech Archive," http://millercenter.org/president/speeches#fdroosevelt. Accessed September 12, 2016; Smith, Jean Edward. 2007. *FDR*. New York: Random House; *Time*. "The Legacy of FDR," http://content.time.com/time/specials/packages/0,28757,1906802,00.html. Accessed September 12, 2016.

Rural Electrification Administration

By the 1930s, there were two Americas, at least in terms of access to electricity. In cities and towns throughout the country, most Americans enjoyed electrical power systems in their homes, with the convenience of electric lights, home appliances, **radios**, and affordable heat. The major public utilities generated the power and constructed the delivery systems—poles and utility lines—to serve customers. Naturally, they preferred constructing such delivery systems in heavily populated areas, where the return on investment in terms of kilowatt hours of energy consumed would be high. Rural areas lagged behind in such service because the expense of constructing utility lines into sparsely populated areas was not cost-effective. A lone farm family living in a house several miles from their nearest neighbor would never be able to consume enough electricity to cover the up-front capital required to get the electricity into their home.

President **Franklin D. Roosevelt** decided to do something about the problem. Using funds from the Emergency Relief Appropriation Act of 1935, Roosevelt issued Executive Order No. 7037 on May 11, 1935, establishing the Rural Electrification Administration (REA). The president named Morris Cooke, a longtime advocate of public power, to head the REA. In May 1936, Congress passed the Rural Electrification Act, which gave the REA statutory authority to function for ten years.

Since private power companies would not expand service into rural areas, the REA formed rural electric cooperatives. The REA extended low-interest, long-term loans to cooperatives that then built the delivery systems. The cooperatives then purchased electricity from private utilities. By 1939, the REA had helped form 417 rural electric cooperatives and had delivered electric power service to 268,000 homes. The REA continued to function, and by the 1950s, few homes in the United States were without electricity.

See also: Tennessee Valley Authority

Further Reading

Manganiello, Christopher J. 2015. *Southern Water, Southern Power: How the Politics of Cheap Energy and Water Scarcity Shaped a Region*, Chapel Hill: University of North Carolina Press; Popeson, Pamela. March 22, 2012. "Lester Beall and the Rural Electrification Administration," Inside Out: A MoMA/MoMa PS1 Blog, http://www.moma.org/explore/inside_out/2012/03/22/lester-beall-and-the-rural-electrification-administration/. Accessed September 9, 2016.

S

Schechter Poultry Corporation v. United States (1935)

The National Industrial Recovery Act of 1933 was the linchpin of early **New Deal** economic policy. The law established a new government agency—the **National Recovery Administration** (NRA)—to address the problem of price deflation in the economy, which made corporate planning difficult, reduced business investment, and sliced into profit margins. The logic behind the NRA was that prices were falling because of industrial overproduction. The solution, therefore, was to cut industrial production, which supposedly would increase prices, raise profits, and stimulate the hiring of workers. The economic logic, of course, was badly flawed, since cutting industrial production would only lead to more **unemployment**.

Serious legal and political opposition also materialized against the NRA. Conservatives considered the NRA an unacceptable increase in the power of the federal government, and they opposed the legislation on constitutional grounds. A host of lawsuits against the NRA found their way into the federal judicial system, and *Schechter Poultry Corporation v. United States* became the premier example. The NRA accused Schechter of violating several provisions of the agency's codes in its Brooklyn chicken processing business and levied a fine against them. In return, Schechter sued.

The case reached the U.S. Supreme Court and was decided, by a unanimous vote, on May 27, 1935. Writing for the Court, Chief Justice Charles Evans Hughes declared the National Industrial Recovery Act unconstitutional. Hughes based his opinion on three principles. First, the existence of extraordinary economic conditions did not justify an attempt to enlarge the constitutional powers of the federal government. Second, the legislation delegated essential legislative powers to the executive branch, which violated the principle of separation of powers and amounted to "delegation run riot." Finally, the Schechter poultry operations were essentially a local matter, not a question of interstate commerce, and therefore Congress did not possess jurisdiction.

The *Schechter* decision gutted the early New Deal and enraged President **Franklin D. Roosevelt**, who soon launched his **court-packing scheme** to reorganize and reform the federal judiciary. Although Roosevelt did not succeed in his crusade to restructure the federal court system, the controversy and political battle did allow him to replace the U.S. Supreme Court's conservative majority with more liberal justices who upheld the right of the federal government to regulate the economy.

See also: National Recovery Administration

Further Reading

Hall, Kermit L., and James W. Ely Jr. 2009. *The Oxford Guide to United States Supreme Court Decisions*, 2nd ed., New York: Oxford University Press; Himmelberg, Robert. 2000. *The Origins of the National Recovery Administration*, 2nd ed., New York: Fordham University Press.

Scottsboro Boys

It was not uncommon during the years of the Great Depression for unemployed men to hitch rides in railroad boxcars as they scoured the countryside looking for work. But in March 1931, riding the rails led to one of the century's most notorious criminal cases. Nine young black men

Nine African American youths, known as the Scottsboro Boys, confer with civil rights activist Juanita Jackson Mitchell (fourth from left) and her female colleague. The Scottsboro Boys were imprisoned in Scottsboro, Alabama after being falsely accused of raping two white women in a freight car. The boys' convictions were overturned in *Powell v. Alabama* (1932), when the U.S. Supreme Court declared that the defendants, who had not been given adequate time to prepare a defense, were denied due process. (Library of Congress)

between the ages of thirteen and twenty hitched a ride on a train in Alabama, but during the trip, they got into a fight with a group of white youths. The white young men, after being ejected from the train, complained to the local sheriff, and at the next stop, deputy sheriffs arrested the nine blacks and two white women traveling with them. The women, perhaps worried about being prosecuted for prostitution, claimed to have been gang-raped by the blacks, and the deputies then hustled the accused rapists to the county seat in Scottsboro. Thus began the saga of the so-called Scottsboro boys.

The nine young black men went on trial in April. Although the Sixth Amendment guarantees legal representation to indigent criminal defendants, the Scotttsboro boys received what can best be described as scandalously inadequate counsel. Also, the judge systematically excluded blacks from the jury, denying the defendants another dimension of their Sixth Amendment rights. Although the two women's stories were riddled with inconsistencies and physicians could find no physical evidence of rape, the first two defendants were convicted in a one-day trial after being given only a twenty-minute discussion with attorneys before the trial. Outside the courtroom, when the verdict was announced, 10,000 spectators cheered wildly and a brass band began playing marching music. In the next three weeks the other defendants, except the thirteen-year-old, were convicted. The judge declared a mistrial in his case. All the others were sentenced to death.

The case soon became a cause célèbre for civil rights advocates. Lawyers for the **National Association for the Advancement of Colored People** (NAACP) joined the battle for the Scottsboro defendants, as did attorneys for the Communist Party. Attorneys for the NAACP and the communist-backed International Labor Defense worked up an appeal, and the case of *Powell v. Alabama* went to a higher court. The Alabama Supreme Court upheld seven of the convictions while reversing the conviction of the youngest defendant. The case then entered the federal courts. The case of *Powell v. Alabama* was argued before the Supreme Court on October 10, 1932. And on November 7, 1932, by a vote of 7 to 2, the U.S. Supreme Court reversed all of the convictions on the grounds that the defendants, by not having access to legal counsel, had been denied their Fourteenth Amendment right to due process.

The national controversy over the Scottsboro case ricocheted through the federal court system. On April 1, 1935, the Supreme Court decided the fate of Clarence Norris, one of the Scottsboro defendants who had been retried in the wake of the *Powell v. Alabama*, convicted again, and then sentenced to death. Norris's NAACP attorneys argued that because Alabama had systematically excluded African Americans from the trial jury and from the grand jury that had returned the indictment, they had not received a fair trial as dictated by the Fifth, Sixth, and Fourteenth Amendments to the Constitution. By a unanimous vote, the Court overturned the conviction, agreeing that Norris had been denied his rights to due process.

During the next several years, the Scottsboro defendants were tried again and again. By 1937, under intense political pressure and international scrutiny, the state of Alabama dropped charges against five of the young men. Several others were paroled from prison between 1937 and 1940. The last Scottsboro defendant was paroled in 1946. By that time the Scottsboro case had become one of the most notorious violations of civil rights in American history.

See also: National Association for the Advancement of Colored People

Further Reading
Carter, Dan T. 2007. *Scottsboro: A Tragedy of the American South*, Baton Rouge: Louisiana State University Press; PBS. 2001. *Scottsboro: An American Tragedy. American Experience*, DVD, 90 min.; Sklaroff, Lauren Rebecca. 2009. *Black Culture and the New Deal: The Quest for Civil Rights in the Roosevelt Era*, Chapel Hill: University of North Carolina Press.

Second New Deal

Journalists and historians have used the term "Second New Deal" to describe the burst of legislative activity that characterized the **Franklin D. Roosevelt** administration from 1935 to 1939. The so-called **First New Deal** focused on relief and recovery measures when the president and Congress tried to relieve the suffering of **unemployment** by creating such agencies as the **Federal Emergency Relief Administration**, the **Civil Works Administration**, the **Public Works Administration**, and the Civilian Conservation Corps, to end the Depression through such agencies as the **National Recovery Administration**, the **Agricultural Adjustment Administration**, and the **Tennessee Valley Authority**; to reconstruct the financial system through the **Reconstruction Finance Corporation**, the Banking Act of 1933, and the Emergency Banking Act of 1933; and to strengthen labor standards through the National Industrial Recovery Act. Historians decided that the First New Deal ended in May 1935 when the Supreme Court handed down its decision in the **Schechter Poultry Corporation v. United States**, invalidating the National Industrial Recovery Act and declaring the National Recovery Administration unconstitutional.

The Second New Deal then began, but its focus shifted. The change of focus resulted from the Supreme Court's conservative decisions, criticism of the New Deal from the business community, and the persistence of the Depression. At the core of the early New Deal was the idea of national economic planning and business–government cooperation, but the Second New Deal had a different focus, which included antitrust activity, social reform, and **Keynes**ian deficit spending. The Second New Deal involved a shift to the left, indicated in such social reform legislation as the **Social Security Act of 1935**, the National Labor Relations Act of 1935, and the Wealth Tax Act of 1935, and a new emphasis on Brandesian antitrust activity through such items as the **Public Utility Holding Company Act of 1935** and the **Temporary National Economic Committee** of 1937–1938. The Second New Deal also abandoned the balanced budget rhetoric of the First New Deal in favor of the deficit spending philosophy of British economist John Maynard Keynes.

See also: Keynes, John Maynard; Public Utility Holding Company Act of 1935; *Schechter Poultry Corporation v. United States* (1935); Social Security Act of 1935

Further Reading

Badger, Anthony J. "The Hundred Days and Beyond: What Did the New Deal Accomplish?" *History Now: The Journal of the Gilder Lehrman Institute*, https://www.gilderlehrman.org/history-by-era/new-deal/essays/hundred-days-and-beyond-what-did-new-deal-accomplish. Accessed September 9, 2016; Phillips-Fein, Kim. 2010. *Invisible Hands: The Businessmen's Crusade against the New Deal*, New York: W. W. Norton & Company; Rauchway, Eric. 2015. The *Money Makers: How Roosevelt and Keynes Ended the Depression, Defeated Fascism and Secured a Prosperous Peace*, New York: Basic Books.

Securities Act of 1933

The huge losses sustained by investors in the **stock market crash** of 1929 convinced many politicians that the securities markets needed government regulation in order to prevent corporate abuses. The stock market in the 1920s had been characterized by fraudulent investment companies, high-pressure salesmanship, corruption, greed, dishonest securities disclosures, misrepresentation, margin buying, and highly inflated promises of guaranteed investment returns. In 1932, the **Pecora Committee**—led by Ferdinand Pecora for Senator Peter Norbeck of North Dakota—delved into the secrets of the securities industry. The hearings lasted for more than two years and exposed to public scrutiny just how corrupt the securities industry had become. Newspapers published headline after headline exposing the fraud, and by the time President **Franklin D. Roosevelt** was inaugurated in March 1933, the public was more than ready for reform.

Late in March 1933, just three weeks after his inauguration, President Roosevelt called for reform legislation requiring full disclosure on all new securities issues, with the burden of responsibility resting on the seller, not the buyer. The eventual legislation that was drafted gave the Federal Trade Commission the power to investigate new securities issues and to postpone their sale if full disclosure had not taken place. The law—known as the Securities Act—was sponsored by Congressman Sam Rayburn of Texas and senators Joseph Robinson of Arkansas and Duncan Fletcher of Florida. Congress passed the measure, and Roosevelt signed it on May 27, 1933.

The press referred to the legislation as the Fletcher-Rayburn Bill. Corporations issuing new stock as initial public offerings first had to file with the Federal Trade Commission all possible information about the prospective securities. Among the law's requirements were information about all commissions or discounts paid by the issuer to the underwriter, the names of people who held more than 10 percent of any other securities issued by that company, the names of the company's directors and officers, and detailed financial statements about the health and stability of the company. Hiding information or issuing bogus information carried criminal penalties. The Federal Trade Commission enjoyed quasi-judicial powers to investigate and to punish violators of the law. For the first time, the federal government had acquired real power over the securities industry.

See also: Pecora Committee; Securities and Exchange Commission

Further Reading

Securities and Exchange Commission Historical Society. "431 Days Joseph P. Kennedy and the Creation of the SEC (1934–35)," http://www.sechistorical.org/museum/galleries/kennedy/politicians_c.php. Accessed September 10, 2016.

Securities and Exchange Commission

When Congress passed the **Securities Act of 1933**, investment bankers and Wall Street traders howled in protest. The law, they argued, was too punitive because of its criminal and civil penalties, which even included innocent mistakes and omissions. They also argued that the burdensome disclosure requirements would take too much time and money to implement. They insisted that the language of the bill was so vague that it subjected securities industries professionals to dangerous legal vulnerability. Finally, they had real concerns about the fact that the law essentially awarded legislative authority to an agency of the executive branch. They warned that the Securities Act would destabilize the securities markets and discourage the issuance of new securities, which would make it difficult for industrial concerns to acquire capital for investment. They also decried the great expansion of federal power that the legislation represented. Of course, there were some investment bankers who welcomed the Securities Act because they thought it would clean up the industry by driving unscrupulous competitors out of the market.

In 1934, **New Deal** lawyers fine-tuned the language, and Congress passed new legislation—the Securities Exchange Act. It established a Securities and Exchange Commission (SEC) to replace the Federal Trade Commission as the governing federal agency in the securities markets. To reassure investment bankers and traders about their criminal liability, the language of the law was tightened and the disclosure and liability provisions of the Securities Act of 1933 were modified. President **Franklin D. Roosevelt** appointed Boston banker Joseph P. Kennedy to head the SEC. Kennedy's leadership of the SEC was quite enlightened and helped revive private capital investment. He relied mostly on industry self-regulation and established consistent, industry-wide accounting rules, but at the same time he was not hesitant to investigate and prosecute fraud. James M. Landis, who had helped draft the bill that created the SEC, succeeded Kennedy as head of the agency in 1937. Some critics on the left claimed that the SEC was too pro-industry, while many Wall Street conservatives found it way too liberal. Like so much of the New Deal, the Securities and Exchange Commission followed a middle-of-the-road set of public policies.

See also: Securities Act of 1933

Further Reading

Securities and Exchange Commission Historical Society. http://www.sechistorical.org/. Accessed September 9, 2016; Seligman, Joel. 2003. *The Transformation of Wall Street: A History of the Securities and Exchange Commission and Modern Corporate Finance*, 3rd ed., New York: Aspen Publishers.

Shahn, Benjamin

Ben Shahn was born to a Jewish family in Kaunas, Lithuania, on September 12, 1898. The Shahns immigrated to the United States in 1906 and settled in Brooklyn, New York. When he was fifteen, Shahn apprenticed out to a commercial lithographer, attending art classes at night. Shahn rejected what he called the "passionless amorality" of abstract art and picked social themes for his work—paintings of Sacco and Vanzetti, striking workers, Middle America farmworkers, poor immigrants, and industrial workers in foundries and plants. Some critics accused him of being "didactic" or "preachy" in his art, but Shahn considered himself the artist of the masses and for the masses.

Mexican muralist Diego Rivera became enchanted with Shahn's work, and they came together to work on the *Man at the Crossroads* fresco for the RCA Building at Rockefeller Center in New York City. During the later 1930s, Shahn became the most prominent painter of the **Federal Art Project** in the **Works Progress Administration**. His most memorable work for the Federal Art Project was the mural on immigration at the Jersey Homesteads housing project in New Jersey. Other memorable Shahn murals were completed at the Bronx Central Post Office in New York City and the Social Security Building in Washington, D.C. During World War II, Shahn designed posters for the Office of War Information. He died on March 14, 1969.

See also: Federal Art Project

Further Reading

Egan, Timothy. 2008. *The Photographs of Ben Shahn* (Library of Congress: Fields of Vision), London: Giles; Hapke, Laura. 2008. *Labor's Canvas: American Working-Class History and the WPA Art of the 1930s*, Newcastle, UK: Cambridge Scholars Publishing; Linden, Diana L. 2015. *Ben Shahn's New Deal Murals: Jewish Identity in the American Scene*, Detroit: Wayne State University Press.

Shelterbelt Project

The so-called Shelterbelt Project was a personal favorite of President **Franklin D. Roosevelt**, who had long maintained an interest in conservation and tree planting on the family estate at Hyde Park, New York. Ever since 1913, as part of the Department of Agriculture's "shelterbelt program," North Dakota farmers had planted belts of trees around their exposed fields to soil wind erosion. In 1934, Roosevelt tried to secure support for what he called the "Great Plains Shelterbelt," a vision of 3 billion trees planted on a 100-mile-wide strip of land extending from the Canadian border to central Texas. Within that swath of land, the U.S. Forest Service would plant tree belts 1-mile long and eight rods wide at half-mile intervals. In 1935, the Forest Service planted 125 miles of shelterbelts on land the **Agricultural Adjustment Administration** had withdrawn from farm production.

The program did attract serious criticism from nursery owners and from eastern foresters, who felt the government program would compete with their interests. Eventually, the president acquired only a few million dollars for the program, but the money was used well, and by World War II, a total of 217 million trees had been planted on 232,212 acres.

See also: Agricultural Adjustment Administration; Civilian Conservation Corps

Further Reading
Brinkley, Douglas. 2016. *Rightful Heritage: Franklin D. Roosevelt and the Land of America*, New York: HarperCollins; Rothbard, Murray N. 2002. *A History of Money and Banking in the United States: The Colonial Era to World War II*, Auburn, AL: Ludwig von Mises Institute; Rutkow, Eric. 2013. *American Canopy: Trees, Forests, and the Making of a Nation*, New York: Scribner.

Silver Purchase Act of 1934

Ever since the 1880s and 1890s, midwestern and southern farmers and western miners had pitched currency expansion as the answer to deflation, and when the Great Depression of the 1930s pushed prices down, they resurrected the idea of expanding currency volumes through purchases of silver. During the 1920s, western mining and farming interests had suffered when agricultural commodity and metal prices declined while costs held steady. In the U.S. Senate, western senators—particularly Key Pittman of Nevada, Burton K. Wheeler of Montana, William Borah of Idaho, and William King of Utah—argued that expanding the stock of monetary silver would ease the gold shortage, increase the money supply, raise silver prices, and increase farm purchasing power. U.S. government purchases of silver would also boost employment in western silver mines. Some of the proposals bordered on the ludicrous. Congressman Martin Dies of Texas demanded the export of all agricultural surpluses in exchange for silver. Senator Wheeler resurrected the old Populist proposal for free coinage of silver at the rate of sixteen to one. Congressman William Fiesinger of Ohio went even further, calling for the federal government to buy 50 million ounces of silver monthly until 1 billion ounces had been purchased.

President **Franklin D. Roosevelt** found all of these proposals too radical, but he also understood political reality. Large numbers of Americans in the western states wanted some federal action on the silver question, and FDR needed to appease them. He approved Senator **Elmer Thomas**'s amendment to the Agricultural Adjustment Act of 1933, which empowered the Department of the Treasury to exchange silver certificates for silver bullion. And to ratify the Silver Agreement the United States had signed at the London Economic Conference of 1933, the president ordered the Treasury to purchase all newly mined domestic silver. Roosevelt also decided to sign the Silver Purchase Act of 1934, which ordered that the ratio of silver to gold in the money supply be increased until it reached one-third or until the price of silver hit $1.29 an ounce. Under the law, the Department of the Treasury would then issue silver certificates equal to the amount of silver purchased. The president would also nationalize silver stocks at a price not to exceed $0.50 per ounce.

Farm interests hailed the legislation, as did western mining interests, but the only real beneficiaries of the Silver Purchase Act of 1934 were miners and mining companies. The president had pursued the silver plan for political, not economic, reasons. After his experiences in 1933–1934 with the commodity dollar schemes of **Irving Fischer** and **George Warren**, he had no faith in monetary tinkering to stimulate the economy.

The Silver Purchase Act had little impact on the domestic economy, but it wreaked havoc overseas in countries whose monetary systems were based on the silver standard. Because silver prices in the United States were artificially high, silver moved from overseas markets to the United States. As those countries lost bullion to the United States, their own money markets destabilized.

See also: Fischer, Irving; Gold Standard; Thomas, Elmer; Warren, George Frederick

Further Reading

Rothbard, Murray N. 2002. *A History of Money and Banking in the United States: The Colonial Era to World War II*, Auburn, AL: Mises Institute.

Simpson, John A.

John Simpson, the champion of poor farmers during the 1920s and 1930s, was born on July 4, 1871, in Salem, Nebraska. In 1896 he graduated from the University of Kansas with a teaching degree and then spent four years in the public schools. Simpson then became an accountant for the state. In 1907, he got a job as a banker, and it introduced him to farm economics and farm politics. In 1917, he was elected president of the Oklahoma Farmers' Union.

Simpson spent the next fourteen years with the Oklahoma Farmers' Union, and in 1931, he was elected president of the National Farmers' Union.

During the 1920s, Simpson had become increasingly politicized as he watched small farmers suffer the consequences of heavy debt burdens, overproduction, and falling commodity prices. Large commercial farmers, though pressured, seemed to survive the economic storm, but small farmers went bankrupt by the millions. Simpson especially resented the policies of the American Farm Bureau Federation, which represented the interests of large commercial farmers. He made the National Farmers' Union the political organ of small family farmers.

With the advent of the **New Deal**, Simpson backed the **Agricultural Adjustment Administration**, even though he felt that it was primarily beneficial to large commercial farmers. He also urged upon President **Franklin D. Roosevelt** a series of measures designed to relieve the mortgage and credit problems of small farmers. John Simpson died on March 15, 1934.

See also: Agricultural Adjustment Administration; Organized Labor

Further Reading

Ness, Immanuel. 2000. *Encyclopedia of Interest Groups and Lobbyists in the United States*, Armonk, NY: Sharpe Reference; Truelsen, Stewart R. 2009. *Forward Farm Bureau: Ninety Year History of the American Farm Bureau Federation*, Washington, DC: American Farm Bureau Federation.

Socialist Party

The Socialist Party of America was founded in 1901, with Eugene V. Debs at its head. Debs remained at the helm until 1928, when Norman Thomas succeeded him. In the presidential election campaigns of 1928, 1932, and 1936, Thomas called for nationalization of major American industries; increased federal public works construction and relief programs; minimum wage and maximum hours legislation for workers; government refinancing of farm and home mortgages; U.S. membership in the League of Nations; and federal systems of **unemployment**, old-age, and medical insurance.

Although Thomas was convinced that the Great Depression would usher in an era of socialism in the United States, most Americans had no interest in any political scheme that purported to take away people's private property. Thomas managed 267,835 votes in the presidential election of 1928 and then lost ground. He won only 881,951 votes in 1932 and 187,720 in 1936. In 1940, when he added isolationism to his socialism, he secured only 99,557 votes, proving the bankruptcy of socialism as a political philosophy in the United States. He simply could not overcome the boundless faith Americans had in the future, their respect for private property, and the popularity of **New Deal** reforms.

Further Reading

Ross, Jack. 2015. *The Socialist Party of America: A Complete History*, Lincoln: Potomac Books.

Social Security Act of 1935

Ever since the early 1900s, social welfare advocates had called for the creation of a federal system of old-age insurance. By the 1920s, compulsory social insurance programs had become common in Europe, but bills submitted to Congress in the 1920s by Congressman William Connery of Massachusetts and Senator Clarence Dill of Washington failed. Too many Americans believed that family and local charities should take care of the elderly, not the federal government. The onset of the Great Depression after 1929 had intensified the demands, and in 1929 Abraham Epstein established the American Association for Old-Age Security to promote a comprehensive federal insurance program. Pressure for a federal pension system became more politically compelling when **Francis Townsend** established his Old-Age Revolving Pensions, Ltd., which campaigned for pensions and attracted substantial political support. In 1932 the American Federation of Labor had endorsed the idea.

In June 1934, President **Franklin D. Roosevelt** established the **Committee on Economic Security**, headed by Secretary of Labor Frances Perkins, to study the issue. The committee came up with a national system of federal old-age insurance financed by contributions from farm employers and workers. They also called for a federal-state system of **unemployment** insurance. Senator **Robert Wagner** of New York and Congressman David Lewis of Maryland introduced the legislation to Congress. The bill inspired intense opposition. Conservative businessmen argued that the taxes would break them and lead the country down the road to socialism. Many southerners rejected the bill because it offered benefits to African Americans. Followers of Francis Townsend said the benefits were inadequate, far below the $200 per person per month Townsend had proposed. Such social welfare advocates as Abraham Epstein and Isaac Rubinow did not like the financing scheme. They preferred funding the program out of general revenues, not from taxes on workers and employers.

But the idea of old-age pensions enjoyed growing public support. Congress passed the law and President Roosevelt signed it on August 14, 1935. It established a Social Security Board to provide for unemployment compensation; old-age insurance; assistance to the destitute blind; and assistance for homeless, crippled, dependent, and delinquent children. The legislation established a federal-state system of unemployment compensation, financed by a federal tax on employer payrolls equal to 1 percent in 1936, 2 percent in 1937, and 3 percent thereafter. Each state administered its own program. The program for old-age and survivor's insurance was financed by equal taxes on employers and employees of 1 percent in 1937 and increasing to 3 percent by 1949. The money would accumulate in a national fund until January 1, 1942, when pensions would begin to be paid to people sixty-five years of age and older.

See also: Committee on Economic Security; Townsend, Francis Everett

Further Reading

Altman, Nancy J. 2005. *The Battle for Social Security: From FDR's Vision to Bush's Gamble*, Hoboken, NJ: Wiley; Beland, Daniel. 2005. *Social Security: History and Politics from the New Deal to the Privatization Debate* (Studies in Government and Public Policy), Lawrence: University Press of Kansas; Ray, Ruth, and Toni Calasanti. 2011. *Nobody's Burden: Lessons from the Great Depression on the Struggle for Old-Age Security*, Lanham, MD: Lexington Books; Stern, Mark, and June Axinn. 2011. *Social Welfare: A History of the American Response to Need*, 8th ed., Upper Saddle River, NJ: Pearson.

Soil Conservation Act of 1935

In 1934 and 1935, devastating droughts hit the Great Plains; and then rain, when it came, resulted in severe flooding and soil erosion. Midwestern farming interests began demanding federal action to deal with the problem, and Congress responded with the Soil Conservation Act of 1935. The law established soil conservation districts throughout the country, and using workers from the Civilian Conservation Corps and later the **Works Progress Administration**, a Soil Conservation Service in the Department of Agriculture conducted research on wind and water erosion and land-use planning; loaned funds to farmers to plant grasses and trees to hold down soil; and taught farmers how to employ strip cropping, terracing, and crop rotation techniques, all of which helped reduce soil erosion.

See also: Agricultural Adjustment Administration; Civilian Conservation Corps

A Dust Bowl farm north of Dalhart, Texas. The U.S. government hoped to combat soil erosion–related dust storms through the Soil Conservation Act, which supported environmental research and taught farmers soil conservation techniques. (Library of Congress)

Further Reading

Brinkley, Douglas. 2016. *Rightful Heritage: Franklin D. Roosevelt and the Land of America*, New York: HarperCollins; Maher, Neil M. 2009. *Nature's New Deal: The Civilian Conservation Corps and the Roots of the American Environmental Movement*, New York: Oxford University Press.

Soil Conservation and Domestic Allotment Act of 1936

On January 6, 1936, in its **United States v. Butler** decision, the Supreme Court declared the Agricultural Adjustment Act of 1933 unconstitutional, which all but destroyed the **New Deal**'s farm recovery program. The Court ruled that the law's provisions placing federal controls on crop production and its tax on processors were unconstitutional. President **Franklin D. Roosevelt** and the New Deal responded immediately, and Congress passed the Soil Conservation and Domestic Allotment Act. Roosevelt signed it into law on February 29, 1936. Instead of using a tax on processors to force reductions in production, the new measure used general revenues to take land out of production for "conservation" reasons. Everybody knew what Roosevelt was trying to do, and most farmers did not miss a check in the transition from one program to the other. The legislation authorized payments to farmers not to grow such "soil-depleting" crops as cotton, corn, tobacco, and wheat and to plant "soil-preserving" crops like alfalfa, clover, or hay. Another payment to farmers was authorized if they would purchase lime, potash, and phosphate fertilizers to restore soil fertility and to terrace their fields. In the end, the legislation did not succeed in really cutting the number of acres planted or the yields per acre. Large production increases in 1937 led to the Agricultural Adjustment Act of 1938.

See also: Agricultural Adjustment Administration; *United States v. Butler* (1936)

Further Reading
Gilbert, Jess. 2015. *Planning Democracy: Agrarian Intellectuals and the Intended New Deal*, New Haven, CT: Yale University Press; Maher, Neil M. 2009. *Nature's New Deal: The Civilian Conservation Corps and the Roots of the American Environmental Movement*, New York: Oxford University Press.

Southern Tenant Farmers' Union

During the 1930s, rural poverty became a terrible problem, and some **New Deal** programs actually made matters worse for the poorest farm families. The **Agricultural Adjustment Administration** (AAA) paid farmers not to grow in order to reduce crop surpluses, and although the Agricultural Adjustment Act of 1933 contained provisions to make sure that farm tenants saw some of that money, large landowners found ways to keep the bulk of the money for themselves. Also, by taking land out of production, the AAA increased **unemployment** among farm tenants, who no longer had land to work.

In 1934, the plight of poor tenant farmers in the South inspired Henry Clay East and Harry Leland Mitchell of Tyronza, Arkansas, to establish the Southern Tenant Farmers' Union (STFU). Both men were **socialist**s who had taken a suggestion from Socialist leader Norman Thomas to found the group. The STFU had a racial open-door policy, welcoming black and white tenant farmers into the union. In doing so, the STFU inspired the wrath of white racists and large commercial farmers who feared losing their economic prerogatives.

At first, the STFU concentrated on investigating and complaining about abuse of AAA policies by large commercial farmers, and planters reacted with hostility. STFU organizers were harassed, beaten up, and arrested on charges of anarchy. Some were murdered. Hostility increased in 1935 when the STFU urged its members to strike for higher wages for picking cotton. The STFU implemented the strike during picking season when the planters were most vulnerable economically. The strike succeeded, and planters agreed to nearly double the pay of pickers.

The existence of the STFU brought media attention to the problem of rural poverty, and in November 1936, President **Franklin D. Roosevelt** established the Special Committee on Farm Tenancy to investigate the problem of rural poverty. As a result of the committee's report, Roosevelt proposed and Congress created the **Farm Security Administration** in 1937. Later in the decade, the STFU fell victim to jurisdictional disputes within its own membership. STFU communists wanted to affiliate with the United Cannery, Agricultural, Packing, and Allied Workers of America, while socialists in the STFU simply wanted to become an independent affiliate of the Congress of Industrial Organizations. During World War II, the STFU disintegrated.

See also: Agricultural Adjustment Administration; Farm Security Administration; Organized Labor

Further Reading

Grubbs, Donald H. 2000. *Cry from the Cotton: The Southern Tenant Farmers' Union and the New Deal*, Fayetteville: University of Arkansas Press; Roberts, Charles Kenneth. 2015. *The Farm Security Administration and Rural Rehabilitation in the South*, Knoxville: University of Tennessee Press.

 ## Steinbeck, John Ernst

John Steinbeck, perhaps America's most prominent literary figure during the 1930s, was born in Salinas, California, on February 27, 1902. He attended Stanford University sporadically between 1919 and 1925 and then lived for several years in New York City, where he tried his hand at writing fiction. After moving back to California, Steinbeck in 1929 published his first novel—*Cup of Gold*. A romantic piece of historical fiction based loosely on the life of Sir Henry Morgan, it was not exactly high-quality literature. His first real literary success came in 1935 with the publication of *Tortilla Flat*, a bittersweet comedy about farmworkers in Monterey, California. At that time, Steinbeck became active in the Cannery and Agricultural Workers Industrial Union, which was dominated by communists and gave Steinbeck his sense of class consciousness and sympathy for working-class people. His 1936 book *In Dubious Battle* was about a labor strike and attracted considerable literary and political attention. But Steinbeck was no ideologue. In *In Dubious Battle*, he pilloried Communist Party organizers who simply used workers to advance their own political objectives.

In 1937, Steinbeck's book *Of Mice and Men* portrayed two poor migrant California farmworkers, one a retarded young man and the other his friend. Poverty-stricken and yet optimistic, they dreamed of getting some land of their own. It was, of course, a pipe dream and disintegrated when the retarded young man killed a woman who happened to be the daughter-in-law of the ranch boss. To protect his retarded friend from prosecution, the other young man shoots him.

After the release of *Of Mice and Men*, Steinbeck traveled widely through the valleys of central California, observing the plight of poor workers. Confined to shanty towns and living in homes made of cardboard or even in lean-tos, they suffered a numbing poverty, and Steinbeck wrote a series of newspaper articles about them. He decided to convert the stories into a novel—*The Grapes of Wrath*—which was published in 1939. It became a runaway bestseller and made Steinbeck's name a household word. The novel described one family—the Joads—of tens of thousands who abandoned Texas, Arkansas, and Oklahoma in the 1930s for California. Of course, Steinbeck became persona non grata to chambers of commerce in Arkansas, Oklahoma, and Texas and to the large commercial farmers in California. *The Grapes of Wrath* became an icon of the Great Depression.

Steinbeck continued to write and played out the role of cause célèbre in the United States. In 1962 he received the Nobel Prize for his work, even though most critics felt his work after the depression was mediocre. John Steinbeck died on December 20, 1968.

See also: Dust Bowl and California Migration

Further Reading

A&E Home Video. 2004. *John Steinbeck: An American Writer* (Biography series), DVD, 50 min.; Bragg, Melvin. November 21, 2011. "John Steinbeck's Bitter Fruit," *Guardian*, https://www.theguardian.com/books/2011/nov/21/melvyn-bragg-on-john-steinbeck. Accessed September 9, 2016; Meltzer, Milton. 2008. *Up Close: John Steinbeck*, New York: Viking.

Stock Market Crash

During the 1920s, the stock market in the United States underwent unprecedented, sustained growth, creating a speculative bubble that burst

Stock Market Crash

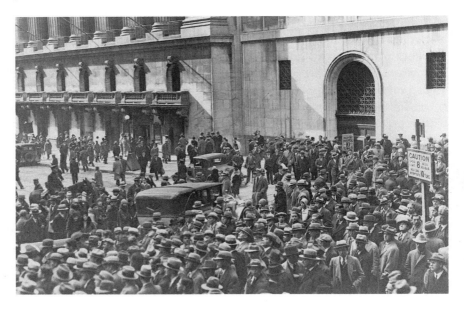

Distressed investors and speculators mobbed the New York Stock Exchange in 1929 in the wake of the great stock market crash. (Library of Congress)

in October 1929. An unusual infusion of cash drove stock market prices ever higher during the early 1920s. Billions of dollars of corporate profits from World War I found their way into the market, and when the Warren Harding administration (1921–1923) cut taxes on the rich, even more money flowed into Wall Street. The decision of the Harding administration to pay off the national debt removed U.S. Treasury securities from the money markets, and the cash traditionally flowing there was rerouted to Wall Street. Finally, as the market gained steadily in the early 1920s, many corporations foolishly invested working capital there, as did many middle-class Americans, who removed money from bank accounts and bought stocks. Finally, Americans borrowed billions of dollars, often in margin purchases, in the form of broker loans to buy even more stocks. The collective impact of such huge cash flows was enormous. *The New York Times* stock index stood at 65 in 1921 and jumped to 134 by the end of 1924, 180 at the end of 1926, 245 at the end of 1927, and 331 at the end of 1928. On August 31, 1929, the index peaked at 449.

The basic problem, however, was that market fundamentals did not justify such gains. Corporate profits rose steadily, but modestly, during the 1920s, as did dividends, but such modest dividend growth did not drive the huge capital gains stockowners experienced. Also, investors had become accustomed to double-digit annual gains and had become used to no bad stock market news. The securities markets were extremely vulnerable. On October 23, 1929, the stock market underwent a severe correction, with *The New York Times* index falling from 415 to 384. The next day, in which historians remember as "Black Thursday," the rout became a panic, with a record 12,894,650 shares changing hands and the index plummeting to 372. On "Black Monday," October 28, the date economic historians point to as the day the Great Crash went into full speed, the index dropped 49 points more, and on "Black Tuesday" another 43 points. By mid-November 1929, the index hit 224. The crash had wiped out 50 percent of all asset values in just a few months. The slide continued intermittently for the next four years, with the index bottoming out at 58 in June 1932. The stock market crash, when combined with weaknesses in the banking system and chronic problems on farms, sent the entire economy into a tailspin that morphed into the Great Depression of the 1930s.

Further Reading

Galbraith, John Kenneth. 2009. *The Great Crash 1929*, reprint ed., New York: Mariner Books; Parker, Selwyn. 2008. *The Great Crash: How the Stock Market Crash of 1929 Plunged the World into Depression*, London: Piatkus; Payne, Phillip G. 2015. *Crash! How the Economic Boom and Bust of the 1920s Worked* (How Things Worked), Baltimore: Johns Hopkins; Piatkus; PBS, 2009. *American Experience: The Crash of 1929*, DVD, 60 min.

Taylor Grazing Act of 1934

Throughout U.S. history, homesteading and relatively free use of the public domain had characterized federal government public policy. Over the years, the federal government had gradually allowed title to public domain land to shift from public to private hands, while permitting grazing on land still owned by the federal government. But the uncontrolled grazing on public lands had a price—deterioration of the range because of overstocking and cutthroat competition among livestock interests to get access to the grass. All attempts at federal planning, however, fell victim to interest group lobbying and appeals to states' rights.

But reform interests gained ground in the 1930s. The severe drought in the west exacerbated range environmental problems, and Congressman Edward Taylor of Colorado finally converted to the idea of planning. In 1934, he submitted what became known as the Taylor Grazing Act to Congress, and the bill enjoyed the backing of President **Franklin D. Roosevelt**, Secretary of the Interior Harold Ickes, and Secretary of Agriculture **Henry Wallace**. The bill passed. It authorized the secretary of the interior to divide the west up into grazing districts and to then issue grazing permits to livestock owners, who would then pay fees for grazing rights. At first, a total of 80 million acres was parceled out into grazing districts, and each permit gave a stockman rights to the grass for ten years. A board composed of local stockmen advised the Department of the Interior on management of the program, and fees collected were to be used for range improvements. The Taylor Grazing Act was a landmark piece of legislation in the history of the federal government. No longer would the public domain be considered a "free" resource available to any businessman wishing to exploit it.

See also: Shelterbelt Project; Wallace, Henry Agard

Further Reading

Bureau of Land Management. "The Taylor Grazing Act," U.S. Department of the Interior, http://www.blm.gov/wy/st/en/field_offices/Casper/range/taylor.1.html. Accessed September 12, 2016; Freyfogle, Eric T. 2003. *The Land We Share: Private Property and the Common Good*, Washington, DC: Island Press; Robbins,

William G., and James C. Foster. 2000. *Land in the American West: Private Claims and the Common Good*, Seattle: University of Washington Press.

Technocracy

The so-called Technocracy movement emerged in mid-1932 as a unique, if ineffectual, response to the Great Depression. Howard Scott was the leader of the movement. He argued that capitalism was dying because its increasingly efficient production led to decreasing manpower requirements in the economy, which had precipitated the Great Depression. With some backing from Columbia University, Scott conducted a study of the role of technology in the American economy. He eventually predicted the coming of an era of extraordinary prosperity after the collapse of capitalism because the country's natural resources and technological assets would be widely shared through what Scott called the distribution of "energy certificates." His ideas had no logic in economic reality, but his ideas generated considerable attention in a country desperate for answers to the Depression. Scott's movement, however, collapsed in 1933 when he accused newly elected President **Franklin D. Roosevelt** of leading the country down the road to fascism. At the time, FDR was the most popular man in the country, and Scott's accusations irritated most Americans. When journalists discovered that Scott had forged his academic credentials, he lost what little support he had left. Scott's organization—Technocracy, Inc.—survived until 1941, by which time it had become a protofascist group.

Further Reading

Whisenhunt, Donald W. 2013. *Utopian Ideas and Movements of the Great Depression: Dreamers, Believers, and Madmen*, Lanham, MD: Rowman and Littlefield.

Temporary Emergency Relief Administration

The Temporary Emergency Relief Administration (TERA) was established in September 1931 in New York by Governor **Franklin D. Roosevelt**. With **unemployment** surpassing all predictions and hundreds of thousands of New Yorkers suffering, Roosevelt knew that the state government needed to provide relief programs, particularly since no such relief programs were forthcoming at the federal level from the **Hoover** administration. **Harry L.**

Hopkins headed the TERA. The TERA provided matching grants to local government agencies to provide relief to the unemployed. TERA issued bonds to generate its own revenues and encouraged cities to do the same to raise relief and public works construction revenues.

The TERA helped Governor Roosevelt project a political image as a caring reformer and contrasted sharply with Herbert Hoover's image as a tight-fisted, insensitive conservative. Once Roosevelt was elected president in 1932, he used the TERA as a prototype for such **New Deal** federal relief agencies as the **Federal Emergency Relief Administration**, the **Civil Works Administration**, and the **Works Progress Administration**.

See also: Civil Works Administration; Federal Emergency Relief Administration; Works Progress Administration

Further Reading
Stern, Mark, and June Axinn. 2011. *Social Welfare: A History of the American Response to Need*, 8th ed., Upper Saddle River, NJ: Pearson.

Temporary National Economic Committee

Although the early **New Deal** focused on national economic planning and cooperative relationships between the federal government and the business community as the best way to stimulate the economy and end the Depression, the later New Deal became less visionary, more conservative, and increasingly interested in antitrust activity. Concern about monopoly and declining competition in the modern economy became a preoccupation of President **Franklin D. Roosevelt** and the New Deal later in the 1930s. Some of FDR's closest advisers, including **Thomas Corcoran** and **Benjamin Cohen**, urged antitrust activities upon him, and the president agreed. In an April 29, 1938, message to Congress, he suggested the need for an investigation of antitrust activity and enforcement practices by the Department of Justice. In response, Congress established the Temporary National Economic Committee (TNEC).

Members of the TNEC included congressmen and representatives from the **Securities and Exchange Commission**, the Federal Trade Commission, and the Departments of Justice, Commerce, Labor, and the Treasury. The committee members were all enthusiastic in their belief that economic concentration had gone too far in the United States and that the federal government needed to be more aggressive in its antitrust activities.

Between December 1938 and March 1941, the TNEC convened a series of fifteen hearings, investigating potential monopolies in the liquor, petroleum, construction, iron and steel, milk, poultry, and investment banking industries. But in the end, the TNEC achieved very little. Those industries were not controlled by visible, powerful monopolies, and antitrust activity did not enjoy universal support in Congress. The TNEC produced very few policy recommendations and served mostly to relieve President Roosevelt of political criticism from antitrusters. The TNEC ended up producing dozens of technical volumes of statistics but nothing of lasting public policy value.

After 1940, President Roosevelt's interest in antitrust activity flagged as well. The outbreak of World War II in Europe had stimulated the economy, and foreign policy issues crowded domestic concerns from the president's mind. The TNEC became an abstraction to him as World War II stimulated new levels of cooperation between private business and a big-spending federal government.

See also: Cohen, Benjamin; Corcoran, Thomas; Securities and Exchange Commission

Further Reading
Lind, Michael. 2013. *Land of Promise: An Economic History of the United States*, New York: HarperCollins; Rothbard, Murray N. 2002. *A History of Money and Banking in the United States: The Colonial Era to World War II*, Auburn, AL: Mises Institute.

Tennessee Valley Authority

The Tennessee Valley Authority (TVA) remains today the most comprehensive economic development project of the federal government in U.S. history. The federal government had long owned a huge swath of land that included Muscle Shoals in northern Alabama, where the Tennessee River drops approximately 140 feet over a distance of 30 miles, creating enormous potential for hydroelectric power development. Early in the 1900s, the federal government constructed two dams and two nitrate plants at Muscle Shoals, but World War I erupted before those projects became operational and stalled more comprehensive projects, and during the 1920s the Muscle Shoals property became embroiled in political controversy.

Senator George Norris, a progressive Republican from Nebraska, made development of Muscle Shoals his pet project. Private power companies afraid of the federal government generating cheap hydroelectric power in competition with them fought development of Muscle Shoals and called for the federal government to sell the land. Senator Norris kept submitting bills to Congress allowing the federal government to continue to develop the region, but when his bills survived committee and passed, they received quick vetoes from President Calvin Coolidge, who did not think it was the business of government to generate hydroelectric power in competition with private business. The debate over the project and whether it should be publicly or privately owned continued during the **Herbert Hoover** administration.

But the onset of the Great Depression after 1929 boosted Norris's chances of success. The Tennessee River Valley was one of the poorest regions of the United States, and **unemployment** and economic plight there were worse than anywhere else in the country. When **Franklin D. Roosevelt** took office as president in 1933, the chances of completing the Muscle Shoals project improved even more because he backed the idea and enjoyed widespread political support throughout the country. In April 1933, Roosevelt formally asked Congress for legislation establishing a federal agency to construct a comprehensive project at Muscle Shoals and along the entire Tennessee River Valley that would produce hydroelectric power and promote industrial and agricultural development through reforestation, flood control, and irrigation projects. Congress responded, and on May 18, 1933, the president signed a bill creating the TVA.

The TVA encountered bitter, ongoing opposition from the private power industry, which resented the cheap electricity TVA planned to generate. **Wendell Willkie** of Commonwealth and Southern Company led the opposition of the utility companies. They accused the federal government of unfair competition and of trying to put them out of business, and they filed dozens of lawsuits. Although the TVA survived the lawsuits in the federal courts, the litigation forced a change of direction, and TVA began to place more emphasis on flood control and navigation than on power generation as its central mission. A different type of opposition came from property owners bitter about having their land condemned for flooding when the TVA built dams and created reservoirs. They also filed lawsuits. So did private fertilizer manufacturers who accused TVA of unfair competition. TVA also attracted criticism from other regions that claimed that the vast outpouring of federal funds attracted business from other areas into the Tennessee Valley.

In addition to external criticism, the TVA board was characterized during the 1930s by bitter internecine, ideological warfare, and the political infighting reflected changes in the direction of the **New Deal**. At first, the head of the TVA was Arthur Morgan, a former president of Antioch College. Morgan was a believer in the business commonwealth in which the federal government and the private business community engaged in cooperative economic planning. His views fit right in with the philosophy of the National Industrial Recovery Act of 1933 and the activities of the **National Recovery Administration**. But the TVA's two other board members had decidedly different views. Harcourt Morgan championed the needs of large commercial farmers and was suspicious of big government. He wanted to place limits on the TVA, to curtail its activities. David Lilienthal, on the other hand, wanted the TVA to aggressively produce electricity and to compete directly with private companies. Only then would poor people enjoy low electricity prices. Both Harcourt Morgan and David Lilienthal opposed Arthur Morgan's belief in planning. By 1936 the battles on the TVA board had become public, with Lilienthal and Harcourt Morgan teaming up against Arthur Morgan, whose influence rapidly declined. At the same time, of course, the New Deal was abandoning the planning schemes it had emphasized in 1933–1935. In 1938, Harcourt Morgan became head of the TVA.

The bickering and external criticism, however, did not keep the TVA from transforming the Tennessee River Valley. A series of nine large dams were constructed on the Tennessee River, with dozens of smaller dams along its tributaries, and the Tennessee River actually became a series of large lakes with a 300-foot-wide channel that could be navigated by ships of 9-feet draft or less. The channel reached a total of 640 miles from Knoxville, Tennessee, to the Ohio River at Paducah, Kentucky. TVA became the most important economic and environmental force in the region. It was the largest producer of electrical power in the United States, and it manufactured chemicals for fertilizer; engaged in reforestation programs and projects to limit soil erosion; funded experimental farms to test fertilizers, crops, and new methods of production; constructed roads, bridges, and model cities; and developed enormous projects for irrigation and flood control.

See also: *Ashwander v. Tennessee Valley Authority* (1936); Willkie, Wendell Lewis

Further Reading

Glaser, Leah S. 2009. *Electrifying the Rural American West: Stories of Power, People, and Place*, Lincoln: University of Nebraska Press; Manganiello, Christopher J. 2015. *Southern Water, Southern Power: How the Politics of Cheap Energy and Water Scarcity Shaped a Region*, Chapel Hill: University of North Carolina Press.

Thomas, Elmer

Elmer Thomas was born on September 8, 1876, in Green-castle, Indiana. In 1897 he graduated from Central Normal College, and three years later he earned a degree from DePauw University. Between 1900 and 1911, he practiced law in Lawton, Oklahoma, and between 1907 and 1920 he served in the state senate. In 1922 Thomas won a seat in Congress as a Democrat, and he was elected to the U.S. Senate in 1926. During the 1930s, Thomas served as a leader of the inflationary bloc of Congress—men who believed that the answer to the Great Depression was to inflate the currency, which they thought would bring about an increase in prices and stimulate an economic boom. Along with other farming interests and silver producers out West, he wanted to devalue the dollar. To appease those interests and to experiment with the commodity dollar ideas of economists like **George Warren** and **Irving Fischer**, **Franklin D. Roosevelt** had Thomas draft the legislation in 1933 that permitted the president to devalue the dollar, monetize silver, and print more money. It was passed as an amendment to the Agricultural Adjustment Act. Because of his support of Thomas's ideas, President Roosevelt enjoyed the support of the Oklahoma senator on other **New Deal** issues. Thomas remained a member of the U.S. Senate until 1951. He died on September 19, 1965.

See also: Gold Standard

Further Reading

David D. Webb. 2009. "Thomas, John William Elmer," Encyclopedia of Oklahoma History and Culture, www.okhistory.org. Accessed September 9, 2016.

Townsend, Francis Everett

Francis Townsend, who many historians consider to be a key player in the origins of Social Security, was born in 1866 outside Fairbury, Illinois. His family was poor and deeply religious and raised Townsend with a concern for the welfare of people less fortunate than he was. He tried his hand at farming in California but then moved to Omaha where he studied at the University of Nebraska Medical School. He graduated there in 1903 and then practiced medicine in Bear Lodge, South Dakota, for the next twenty years, except for a tour of duty as an army physician during World War I.

Dr. Francis Townsend was a respected physician and demagogue that worked on creating a pension to aid the elderly. (Library of Congress)

In 1923 Townsend opened a medical practice in Long Beach, California, but he had a difficult time making ends meet. Nearly seventy years old and destitute, he began speaking and writing articles for local newspapers urging the federal government to establish a program where senior citizens—over the age of sixty—received a monthly pension of $200. The message resonated with large numbers of people, and Townsend received more and more invitations to write and speak. He argued that the pension plan, to be financed by a tax on businesses, would pump purchasing power into the economy and end the Depression.

In January 1934, Townsend joined hands with realtor Robert Earl Clements and turned his idea into a political movement. They founded Old-Age Revolving Pensions, Ltd., to promote the idea. With money coming in from supporters and subscribers to their newspaper—*The Townsend National Weekly*—the movement for a federal pension plan gained real momentum. They formed "Townsend Clubs" around the country, and by early 1935, the more than 3,000 clubs boasted of a membership of more than 500,000 people. The clubs lobbied for federal pensions.

At the time, only twenty-eight states had pension plans of any kind, ranging from $7.28 a month in Montana to $30 a month in Maryland. People listened. At the same time, Clements turned Old-Age Revolving Pensions, Ltd., into a profitable business. He marketed Townsend buttons, badges, banners, license plates, tire covers, radiator emblems, pictures, pamphlets, and songs. The newspaper had 300,000 subscribers by 1936 and turned an annual profit of $250,000.

In January 1935, Congressman John Steven McGroarty introduced the Townsend Plan to Congress, and supporters collected more than 20 million petition signatures backing the idea. President **Franklin D. Roosevelt** considered Townsend a political threat, so he vigorously pushed the **Social Security Act of 1935** as a means of silencing Townsend. It worked, even though Townsend participated in the ill-fated, anti-Roosevelt third-party **Union Party** ticket in the presidential election of 1936. In the end, Townsend lost much of his political base when he endorsed Republican candidate Alf Landon for president.

Eventually, Congress decided to investigate Old-Age Revolving Pensions, Ltd., since Clements's tactics proved to be shady and ridden with fraud. Townsend refused to testify and was held in contempt of Congress, but President Roosevelt commuted the sentence. Townsend still had millions of Americans who admired him. He then slowly drifted into obscurity and died on September 1, 1960.

See also: Social Security Act of 1935; Union Party

Further Reading

Amenta, Edwin. 2006. *When Movements Matter: The Townsend Plan and the Rise of Social Security*, Princeton: Princeton University Press; DeWitt, Larry. December 2001. "Research Note #17: The Townsend Plan's Pension Scheme," Agency History: Research Notes & Special Studies by the Historian's Office. Social Security Administration, https://www.ssa.gov/history/townsendproblems.html. Accessed September 10, 2016; Ray, Ruth, and Toni Calasanti. 2011. *Nobody's Burden: Lessons from the Great Depression on the Struggle for Old-Age Security*, Lanham, MD: Lexington Books.

Transportation Act of 1940

The Great Depression was a financial disaster for the country's railroad companies, who found themselves caught in a terrible economic squeeze because of increased competition from trucks, depressed freight rates and declining freight volume, and huge fixed costs because of enormous debt burdens. The Motor Carrier Act of 1935 had tried to address the problem of competition from the trucking industry by setting minimum freight rates, but it really did little to address the problem, other than enrage motor carriers. In March 1938 a conference was held among representatives of the Interstate Commerce Commission (ICC), the **Reconstruction Finance Corporation** (RFC), and the Departments of Treasury, Agriculture, and Commerce to look at the problems facing railroads, and a Committee of Three was established under the leadership of ICC chairman Joseph Eastman.

The committee recommended that the RFC continue to make cheap equipment and credit loans to the railroads and that the ICC carry out a consolidation of the railroad industry to make it more efficient. The proposal immediately encountered the wrath of the railroad brotherhoods, which believed that the consolidation would eliminate too many jobs, and the railroad companies themselves, since many corporate entities would actually disappear. Eventually, the proposal was severely modified and passed as the Transportation Act of 1940. It gave the ICC control over coastal, inland waterways, and Great Lakes common and contract watercarriers, but it did little to address the railroad problem. The outbreak of World War II would eventually create huge demands for railroad freight and passenger service and temporarily solve many railroad problems, although those problems would reassert themselves after 1945.

See also: Emergency Railroad Transportation Act of 1933

Further Reading

Huibregtse, Jon R. 2010. *American Railroad Labor and the Genesis of the New Deal, 1919–1935* (Working in the Americas), Gainesville: University Press of Florida; Wolmar, Christian. 2012. *The Great Railroad Revolution: The History of Trains in America*, London: Atlantic Books.

Tugwell, Rexford Guy

Rexford Tugwell, one of the **New Deal**'s most influential economists, was born in Sinclairville, New York, on July 10, 1891. A brilliant student, he received bachelor's, master's, and Ph.D. degrees in economics from the Wharton School of the University of Pennsylvania. Between 1920 and 1931, he taught economics at Columbia University and published prolifically. Among his major contributions were *The Economic Basis for Public Interest* (1922), *The Trend of Economics* (1924), *American Economic Life* (1925), *Industry's Coming of Age* (1927), and *Soviet Russia* (1928). He became one of the country's premier experts in agricultural economics and a strong proponent of national economic planning. Because of his friendship with Professor Raymond Moley, a political science professor at Columbia and adviser to Governor **Franklin D. Roosevelt** of New York, Tugwell eventually became a member of the "**Brains Trust**" of academics who advised the governor during his presidential campaign of 1932 and the transition to the White House in 1932–1933.

In March 1933, Tugwell was appointed as assistant secretary of agriculture under Secretary of Agriculture **Henry Wallace**, but his real function was to advise the president on economic matters. Tugwell had no faith in laissez-faire and the balancing effects of the market, and he believed that the federal government needed to go beyond progressivism's antitrust and regulating agenda to become the principal institution in the modern industrial economy, establishing production goals, allocating resources, and determining prices and wages. Only then, Tugwell was convinced, would prices stabilize, full employment be achieved, and the poor receive a decent lifestyle. His economic and political philosophies were far too liberal for most Americans and for most people in the Franklin D. Roosevelt administration, but Tugwell was nevertheless a powerful voice for change and reform. He helped draft the Agricultural Adjustment Act of 1933, which tried to address the problem of agricultural overproduction and falling commodity prices by paying farmers not to grow.

In 1934, the president named Tugwell undersecretary of agriculture, and one year later, Tugwell became head of the **Resettlement Administration**, a newly created federal government agency designed to help the rural poor relocate to other areas; to fund programs to reforest certain areas, build flood control systems, and prevent stream pollution and soil erosion; to provide loans so that poor farmers could buy land and farm equipment; and to construct "Greenbelt towns" of subsistence homestead communities that would provide low-income housing. Real estate interests bitterly protested the Resettlement Administration, fearing it would undermine rent prices, and large commercial farmers feared that it would limit their access to cheap labor. Tugwell's unapologetic administration of the Resettlement Administration did not endear him to critics. In 1937, the new **Farm Security Administration** assumed control of the Resettlement Administration.

Tugwell then left Washington, D.C., to become head of the New York City Planning Commission. In 1941 he became chancellor of the University of Puerto Rico but served for only a brief period of time because President Roosevelt named him governor of Puerto Rico. Tugwell spent World War II in Puerto Rico, and his 1946 book *The Stricken Land* analyzed the political and economic challenges facing the island. He then returned to academe as a professor of economics at the University of Chicago. During his tenure at Chicago, Tugwell wrote *The Place of Planning in Society* (1954),

A Chronicle of Jeopardy (1955), and *The Democratic Roosevelt* (1957). He retired from Chicago in 1957 but continued to write and consult. Among his later books were *The Art of Politics* (1958), *The Brains Trust* (1968), and *Tugwell's Thoughts on Planning* (1975). Tugwell died on July 21, 1979.

See also: Brains Trust; Resettlement Administration

Further Reading

Eleanor Roosevelt Papers Project. "FDR's Brains Trust," Teaching Eleanor Roosevelt Glossary, https://www.gwu.edu/~erpapers/teachinger/glossary/brains-trust.cfm. Accessed September 1, 2016; Smith, J. Y. July 2, 1979. "Rexford Tugwell, Adviser in FDR's 'Brains Trust,' Dies," *New York Times*, https://www.washingtonpost.com/archive/local/1979/07/25/rexford-tugwell-adviser-in-fdrs-brains-trust-dies/68a9b1c6-d8c3-44f7-b7d0-2599bada50c4/. Accessed September 1, 2016.

Unemployed Leagues

The plight of the unemployed had become a national trauma, and scandal, by 1931, and in the face of inaction on the part of the **Herbert Hoover** administration, local governments and private groups tried to take matters into their own hands. In 1931 Carl Branin of the Seattle Labor College established the Unemployed Citizens' League (UCL) of Seattle. The group organized a drive—through barter, labor exchange, and private donations—that raised 120,000 pounds of fish, 10,000 cords of firewood, and eight carloads of fruit and potatoes. The fish, produce, and firewood were then distributed to the unemployed.

But as successful as the effort was, it had little long-term impact. Branin himself realized that for all the effort it had taken to raise the products, they supplied the needs of unemployed families for only a week or so. The **unemployment** problem was too vast for private action to ameliorate, and Branin decided that only direct political action would be required to address the nation's economic challenge.

Abraham Muste of the Conference on Progressive Labor Action (CPLA) had taken note of the UCL's energy. A **socialist** and pacifist, Muste wanted to develop a powerful working-class movement in the United States, one capable of taking over the federal government and implementing a socialist economy. Muste sent CPLA organizers throughout the country trying to replicate the UCL of Seattle. The plan was to organize local self-help programs and then move on to left-wing political organizations. Muste's organizers experienced some success among Pittsburgh steelworkers, Pennsylvania and West Virginia coal miners, and North Carolina textile workers. They staged demonstrations, sit-ins, petition drives, and picket lines to protest the suffering of the poor and the insensitivity of the rich in America.

In July 1933, 800 delegates from local unemployed councils met in Columbus, Ohio, and established the National Unemployed League (NUL). They claimed a membership of 150,000 people in thirteen states, but the NUL could never really sustain itself at the national level. **New Deal** relief programs took some steam out of the movement, and Muste's own political meanderings hurt as well. His followers organized the American Workers

Party and then the Trotskyite Workers Party, arguing incessantly about socialist theory and rendering themselves increasingly irrelevant. Unemployed League membership eroded steadily throughout the 1930s, and in 1936, the NUL joined with the Workers' Alliance, a socialist organization, and the Unemployed Councils, a communist-led organization, and formed the Workers' Alliance of America. The NUL then ceased to function at the national and local levels.

See also: Socialist Party; Unemployment

Further Reading

Ness, Immanuel. 2015. *Encyclopedia of American Social Movements*, 4 vols., New York: Routledge; University of Washington. "The Great Depression in Washington State: Unemployed Citizens League and Poverty Activism," Pacific Northwest Labor & Civil Rights Projects, http://depts.washington.edu/depress/Unemployed_Citizens_League.shtml. Accessed September 16, 2016.

Unemployment

Hungry people line up in New York City to receive government-provided bread in 1932. (Franklin D. Roosevelt Library)

Economists still argue about the causes of unemployment during the 1930s, but most agree that the economy had become mired in a liquidity trap where underconsumption led to production declines, deflation, and layoffs. Around the industrial world, by 1930, more than 21 million people were out of work. The numbers of the homeless skyrocketed, and urban centers from New York City to London to Tokyo to Sydney became scenes of makeshift, cardboard homes, bread lines, begging, malnutrition, and suffering. Divorce rates fell because people could not afford to start up a new household, and so did birthrates. Suicide and desertion, on the other hand, jumped dramatically.

When President **Franklin D. Roosevelt** came into office in March 1933, the unemployment rate in the United States exceeded 25 percent. And this was in an age when the vast majority of women did not work outside the home, meaning that nearly one in four American households was without an income. Also, there was no national program of unemployment compensation, social security, or welfare. In order to solidify his political support among the working classes, Roosevelt embarked on an ambitious program of unemployment relief through such government agencies as the **Federal Emergency Relief Administration**, the **Civil Works Administration**, the Civilian Conservation Corps, and the **Works Progress Administration**. The great contribution of the **New Deal** to modern public policy is that the federal government assumed responsibility for guaranteeing full employment in the economy, and when the goal of full employment could not be met, the federal government was obligated to provide public sector jobs for those Americans out of work.

Further Reading

Donkin, R. 2010. *The History of Work*, New York: Palgrave Macmillan; Leuchtenburg, William E. 2009. *Franklin D. Roosevelt and the New Deal: 1932–1940*, New York: Harper Perennial; Ravallion, Martin. 2016. *The Economics of Poverty: History, Measurement, and Policy*, New York: Oxford University Press.

Union Party

By 1934, **Franklin D. Roosevelt**'s political honeymoon was over and the **New Deal** began to attract criticism from the right and the left. Critics on the left—like Norman Thomas of the **Socialist Party** and **Huey Long** and his Share Our Wealth crusade—accused Roosevelt of doing too little to relieve the suffering of the poor and the unemployed, while critics on the right, such as the National Association of Manufacturers, charged him with creating a huge federal bureaucracy and leading the country down the road to socialism.

When Roosevelt looked at his critics, four of them in particular worried him politically: Huey Long and the Share Our Wealth plan; Francis E. Townsend and Old-Age Revolving Pensions, Ltd.; Father **Charles Coughlin** and the National Union for Social Justice; and **William Lemke** and the Non-Partisan League. Gerald L. K. Smith succeeded to the helm of Share Our Wealth in 1935 after Huey Long's assassination. Collectively, the critics proposed dramatic changes in the American political economy. Coughlin proposed the taking of monetary control from the hands of private bankers and the printing of vast amounts of paper currency through a new central bank. Smith called for government confiscation of large fortunes and the redistribution of those assets to poor people. Townsend wanted to establish a system of federal old-age pensions. Lemke proposed the printing of more paper currency and government programs to refinance home and farm mortgages.

What united the critics was a hatred of Franklin D. Roosevelt and the New Deal. In 1936, to oppose his reelection, they formed the Union Party and nominated William Lemke of North Dakota for president and Thomas C. O'Brien of Massachusetts for vice president. They endorsed high protective tariffs, foreign policy isolationism, inflation of the currency, the refinancing of all home and farm mortgages, a federal system of old-age pensions, higher federal appropriations for work relief, high taxes on the rich and well-to-do, and vigorous federal antitrust action.

The Union Party was a complete fiasco. Smith's anti-Catholic, pro–Ku Klux Klan rhetoric offended Charles Coughlin, who was a Roman Catholic priest, and in October 1936, when Smith called for the organization of a paramilitary group to overthrow the U.S. government, he was expelled from the Union Party. Francis Townsend then endorsed the candidacy of Republican Alf Landon. The Vatican condemned the activities of Charles Coughlin. When the votes were counted, Lemke secured only 882,479 votes, compared to Landon's 16,674,665 and Roosevelt's 27,752,869. The Union Party then rapidly declined and officially dissolved in 1939.

See also: Coughlin, Charles Edward; Lemke, William; Long, Huey P.

Further Reading

Brinkley, Alan. 1983. *Voices of Protest: Huey Long, Father Coughlin, and the Great Depression*, New York: Vintage Books.

United States v. Butler (1936)

During the **first 100 days** of the **New Deal**, the **Franklin D. Roosevelt** administration launched a concerted, if helter-skelter, crusade to ameliorate the effects of the Great Depression and to turn the economy around. Roosevelt was especially worried about hard times in rural America, where commodity prices had fallen below cost of production for many farmers. Most agricultural economists recognized overproduction as the key to the problem. The supply of farm products reaching the market was so huge that price levels were overwhelmed. To deal with the problem, Congress passed in 1933 the Agricultural Adjustment Act, which established the **Agricultural Adjustment Administration** (AAA). The AAA, by imposing processing taxes on middlemen, generated cash to pay farmers to reduce production or not to raise crops at all.

Conservatives, of course, were aghast at such an increase in the power and scope of the federal government. Many believed the legislation was unconstitutional. Food processors—canneries, packinghouses, and wholesalers—especially resented the tax they had to pay, and many of them sued. One case—*United States v. Butler*—reached the Supreme Court, which decided the case on January 6, 1936. In a 6 to 3 vote, the Court declared the law unconstitutional, arguing that regulating and controlling agricultural production was a state, not a federal, concern. As a result, the Agricultural Adjustment Administration violated the Tenth Amendment to the Constitution. The decision triggered a storm of controversy and quickly led to President Franklin D. Roosevelt's misguided attempt to "pack" the Supreme Court.

See also: Agricultural Adjustment Administration

Further Reading
Hall, Kermit L., and James W. Ely Jr. 2009. *The Oxford Guide to United States Supreme Court Decisions*, 2nd ed., New York: Oxford University Press.

V

Vann, Robert Lee

Robert L. Vann, one of the most influential African Americans of his time, was born in Ahoskie, North Carolina, on August 27, 1879. He attended the Western University of Pennsylvania in Pittsburgh, where he edited the school newspaper. Vann graduated there in 1906 and then earned a law degree in 1909. He then served for a time as the legal counsel to *The Pittsburgh Courier*, a black newspaper. In 1918, he was named editor of the paper. Vann remained at the helm of *The Pittsburgh Courier* until his death in 1940.

Under Vann's direction, *The Pittsburgh Courier* became the most influential black newspaper in the country. In the process, Vann became the most prominent black journalist in the United States. In the presidential election of 1932, Vann, although a Republican, endorsed **Franklin D. Roosevelt** and began the process that soon saw most African Americans becoming Democrats. **Herbert Hoover** and the Republicans, Vann wrote frequently, had responded tepidly to the Depression and did little while millions of people suffered. FDR then named Vann a special assistant in the Justice Department. In 1936, when he endorsed FDR again, Vann urged black people to "turn Lincoln's picture to the wall. That debt has been paid in full."

But Vann eventually grew disenchanted. He felt that he was being used as a token by the Roosevelt administration to attract the African American vote and that the **New Deal** had done little to really help black people. In 1940, Vann returned to the Republican fold and endorsed **Wendell Willkie** for president. Robert Vann died on October 24, 1940.

Further Reading

Greenberg, Cheryl Lynn. 2009. *To Ask for an Equal Chance: African Americans in the Great Depression*, Lanham, MD: Rowman & Littlefield; Gale. *U.S. History in Context*. http://ic.galegroup.com/ic/uhic/ReferenceDetailsPage/DocumentToolsPortletWindow?displayGroupName=Reference&jsid=7812016b5ea4d6684ea4837e2c6ef921&action=2&catId=&documentId=GALE%7CCX3404500017&u=sand55832&zid=b57acc008e359910d5c24de390bb447b. Accessed September 3, 2016; Trotter, Joe W. 2004. "African Americans, Impact of the Great Depression on." *Encyclopedia of the Great Depression*. Vol. 1. Robert S. McElvaine, ed. New York: Macmillan Reference USA.

W

Wagner, Robert Ferdinand

Robert F. Wagner, a political icon for liberal Democrats in the first half of the twentieth century, was born on June 8, 1877, in Hesse-Nassau, Germany. He was eight years old when the family emigrated from Germany, and they settled in New York City. Wagner became active as a young man in local ward politics and rose in the ranks of Tammany Hall's Democratic machine. In 1904 he won a seat in the state legislature, and by 1911 he was president pro tem of the state senate. In the state legislature, Wagner soon became known as an urban, progressive reformer interested in improving the lot of the poor and the working class. He believed in the rights of **organized labor** and of the role of state and federal government in stabilizing the economy.

In 1926, Wagner won a seat in the U.S. Senate, and his reputation as a pragmatic liberal only grew there. When the country slipped into the Great Depression, Wagner became an early advocate of federal legislation to provide relief to the unemployed. During the **Herbert Hoover** administration, he submitted three bills to Congress on the issue. In 1930, Hoover signed a Wagner bill allowing the federal government to collect **unemployment** statistics, and in 1931 the president signed another bill establishing the Federal Employment Stabilization Board. Hoover vetoed another Wagner bill that would have reorganized the U.S. Employment Service. Several of Wagner's proposals for unemployment relief were implemented, however, in the **Emergency Relief and Construction Act of 1932**.

When **Franklin D. Roosevelt** was elected president in 1932, Wagner became a leading architect of the **New Deal**. His commitment to unemployment relief was implemented in the Federal Emergency Relief Act of 1933, and the National Industrial Recovery Act of 1933 included Wagner's proposal for $3.3 billion in public works construction to assist the unemployed. Wagner also played the key role crafting the National Industrial Recovery Act's labor standards provisions and the National Labor Relations Act of 1935, which guaranteed labor's right to collective bargaining. He was also very influential in securing passage of the **Social Security Act of 1935**. Wagner served in the U.S. Senate until 1949. He died on May 4, 1953.

Robert F. Wagner guided so many key New Deal bills through the U.S. Senate that he was dubbed the "legislative pilot of the New Deal." (Library of Congress)

See also: Wagner-Peyser Act of 1933

Further Reading

Rees, Jonathan, and Jonathan Z. S. Pollack. 2004. *The Voice of the People: Primary Sources on the History of American Labor, Industrial Relations, and Working-Class Culture*, Hoboken, NJ: Wiley-Blackwell; Stern, Mark, and June Axinn. 2011. *Social Welfare: A History of the American Response to Need*, 8th ed., Upper Saddle River, NJ: Pearson.

Wagner-Peyser Act of 1933

The Wagner-Peyser Act, or National Employment System Act, of 1933 established the U.S. Employment Service and authorized federal matching grants to states for establishing and maintaining employment offices. It was part of New York senator **Robert Wagner**'s vision of a nationwide federal government employment service. It would match workers with available jobs on a national basis and, Wagner hoped, serve as a prerequisite to a national system of **unemployment** compensation. Throughout his administration, President **Herbert Hoover** had blocked Wagner's attempts to implement such a program, but President **Franklin D. Roosevelt** enthusiastically supported it. When the **Social Security Act of 1935** was passed, it contained provisions for using the public employment offices as distribution points for unemployment compensation.

See also: Social Security Act of 1935; Wagner, Robert Ferdinand

Further Reading

U.S. Department of Labor. "Wagner-Peyser Act of June 6, 1933," November 10, 2010. https://www.doleta.gov/regs/statutes/wag-peys.cfm. Accessed September 12, 2016.

Wagner-Steagall Housing Act of 1937

With passage of the Wagner-Steagall Housing Act of 1937, the federal government first recognized housing as a social need and assumed some responsibility for providing it. Urban reformers, labor leaders, and social welfare advocates had long promoted public housing as a necessity in a modern industrial state, but their demands fell on deaf ears until the advent of the **New Deal**. Once the country slipped into the Great Depression, the movement for public housing gained momentum because it would stimulate real estate and construction and provide jobs. Opposition came from rural areas, where politicians assumed they would receive none of the benefits. The Wagner-Steagall Housing Act became law on September 1, 1937.

The legislation established the U.S. Housing Authority within the Department of the Interior and appropriated $500 million for loans to promote low-cost housing construction. The U.S. Housing Authority could loan up to 90 percent of the cost of a housing project. Nathan Straus was appointed to head the U.S. Housing Authority, and to drum up rural support, he made sure that at least one-quarter of the agency's loans went to towns with less than 25,000 people. By 1940, the U.S. Housing Authority had made a total of $691 million in loans and had completed 344 projects with 188,045 units.

See also: Federal Housing Administration; National Housing Act of 1934

Further Reading

Vale, Lawrence J. 2007. *From the Puritans to the Projects: Public Housing and Public Neighbors*, Cambridge, MA: Harvard University Press.

Wallace, Henry Agard

Henry A. Wallace was born on October 7, 1888, near the town of Orient in Adair County, Iowa. Intellectually precocious as a child, he began as a teenager a systematic study of plants, and at the age of sixteen, he began experimenting with seed corn, a step that would eventually make him one of the world's premier plant geneticists. In 1910, he graduated from Iowa State College in Ames, Iowa.

Wallace's father—Henry Cantwell Wallace—was a leading figure in American agriculture and publisher of *Wallace's Farmer*. The younger Wallace became editor of the journal in 1910 and remained in the post until 1933. In 1923, the younger Wallace's genetic experiments with corn produced the world's first commercially successful hybrid seed corn. To promote the invention, in 1926 he founded the Hi-Bred Seed Company and served as the company's president until 1933. Wallace's father served as secretary of agriculture in the Warren Harding administration. During the 1920s, Henry Agard Wallace became a strong exponent of federal action to address the farm problem. He supported the McNary-Haugen Bill, called on presidents Calvin Coolidge and **Herbert Hoover** to develop federal grain storage and marketing systems for farmers, and planned cuts in commodity production, which would help stem the problem of falling prices. When Wallace's father died in 1924, Henry Agard emerged as the most influential figure in American farm policy. In 1928, although he had been a lifelong Republican, Wallace endorsed Al Smith for president.

In 1933, President **Franklin D. Roosevelt** appointed Wallace to his cabinet as secretary of agriculture. In that position, Wallace presided over the **New Deal**'s cornucopia of farm programs, none of them more important than the acreage reduction agenda of the **Agricultural Adjustment Administration**. Wallace remained at agriculture until 1940, when President Roosevelt selected him as his vice presidential running mate. In 1944, Roosevelt replaced Wallace with Harry Truman as his running mate, and Wallace was appointed secretary of commerce. It was a short-term assignment because Wallace's politics were increasingly moving to the left, distancing himself from President Truman. Wallace left commerce in 1946.

In 1948, Wallace was becoming increasingly outspoken about the issue of civil rights and urged the federal government to pass legislation to end discrimination against black people. At the height of the Red Scare, he also became more vocal about his feelings that the United States should end the Cold War and reach a rapprochement with the Soviet Union. In the election of 1948, Wallace bolted the Democratic Party and formed his own Progressive Party. He proposed a vigorous, expanded program of social welfare legislation, but his views were far too liberal for the vast majority of Americans. In the election, Wallace won only 2.4 percent of the popular vote, and President Truman was reelected. Wallace then returned to private life and his scientific experiments in plant genetics. He died on November 18, 1965.

See also: Agricultural Adjustment Administration

Further Reading

Culver, John C., and John Hyde. 2001. *American Dreamer: A Life of Henry A. Wallace*, New York: W. W. Norton & Company.

Walsh-Healey Public Contracts Act of 1936

In May 1935, the Supreme Court rendered its decision in the *Schechter* case and declared the National Industrial Recovery Act unconstitutional. That automatically killed the labor standards, or wages and hours, provisions of the law as well. Labor leaders denounced the Court's decision, and Secretary of Labor Frances Perkins decided that the least the federal government could do was enforce minimum wage and maximum hours regulations in companies receiving federal contracts. Senator David Walsh of Massachusetts and Congressman Arthur Healey, also of Massachusetts, sponsored the necessary legislation in Congress, and President **Franklin D. Roosevelt** signed the Walsh-Healey Public Contracts Act on June 30, 1936.

The law required that all federal contractors pay their workers a minimum wage as established by the Department of Labor. Any contract for more than $10,000 required employers to pay overtime for more than eight hours of work a day or forty hours a week. Until Congress passed the **Fair Labor Standards Act of 1938**, the Walsh-Healey Public Contracts Act was the federal government's key piece of labor standards legislation.

See also: Fair Labor Standards Act of 1938

Further Reading

U.S. Department of Labor. "Compliance Assistance: Walsh-Healey Public Contracts Act (PCA)," https://www.dol.gov/whd/govcontracts/pca.htm. Accessed September 12, 2016.

Warburg, James

James Warburg, one of the few wealthy financiers in the United States to support **Franklin D. Roosevelt** and the **New Deal**, was born in Hamburg, Germany, on August 18, 1896, to a wealthy, prominent family. In 1917 he graduated from Harvard University and joined the National Metropolitan Bank in New York City. Warburg soon found himself at the First National Bank of Boston and a prominent young man in Wall Street circles. In 1929, he was named president of the International Manhattan Company. But he did not fit the mold on Wall Street because of his political beliefs. A faithful Democrat, he eschewed laissez-faire and supported the notion that the federal government had an important role to play in stabilizing the money markets. In 1933, suspicious of newly elected President Franklin D. Roosevelt's monetary views, Warburg turned down FDR's offer to become secretary of the Treasury.

But the president kept in close contact with Warburg and used him frequently as an economic adviser, particularly during the difficult months of 1933 when the banking system was being reconstructed. Warburg played a key role in drafting the National Industrial Recovery Act of 1933, the Emergency Banking Act of 1933, and the Banking Act of 1933. That same year the president appointed Warburg as a delegate to the World Monetary Conference in London.

But Warburg's suspicions of FDR's monetary views were confirmed late in 1933 when the president launched the ill-fated gold-buying scheme, an attempt to stimulate prices and the economy by manipulating the world price of gold. He was convinced that the so-called commodity dollar plan would undermine business confidence and restrict the flow of credit. Warburg and the president engaged in a vigorous debate over the issue, but FDR soon tired of it, deciding that Warburg was simply too bound to tradition. Warburg then left the administration. In the end, of course, Warburg had been right about the gold-buying, commodity dollar idea, and Roosevelt abandoned it in 1934.

By that time Warburg had become a vocal critic of the New Deal. His pamphlets *Hell Bent for Election* (1935) and *Still Hell Bent* (1936) accused FDR of being power hungry and likely to take the United States down the road to socialism and dictatorship. In the presidential primaries of 1936 Warburg served as an adviser to Frank Knox, a former Bull Moose Progressive, but when the Republican Party nominated Alf Landon, Warburg returned to the New Deal camp. He apologized to the president, and FDR accepted, but Warburg had lost his influence over public policy. Warburg continued his successful business career, serving as president of the Bydale Company and later for years as director of the Polaroid Corporation. He died on June 3, 1969.

See also: Gold Standard

Further Reading

Simkin, John. "James P. Warburg," Spartacus Educational, http://spartacus-educational.com/SPYwarburg.htm. Accessed September 9, 2016.

Warren, George Frederick

George Frederick Warren was born in Harvard, Nebraska, on February 16, 1874. He was raised on the family's farm and then worked his way through the University of Nebraska, where he graduated in 1897 with a degree in farm management. He went on to earn a master's degree and a Ph.D. at New York State College of Agriculture at Cornell. After a year as a horticulturalist at the New Jersey Experiment Station, Warren returned to Cornell as an assistant professor of agronomy. In 1920, he became professor of agricultural economics at Cornell.

During the 1920s, Warren and his colleague at Cornell, Frank A. Pearson, had met Governor **Franklin D. Roosevelt** of New York. Warren and Pearson coauthored the book *Prices* in 1933, in which they argued that the prices of wheat, cotton, tobacco, and other agricultural commodities rose and fell automatically because they were connected to the price of gold in relation to paper currency. It was possible, therefore, for public officials to set commodity prices by manipulating the price of gold. If the government bought gold in large amounts and then raised the price of gold gradually, the value of the dollar would fall and the prices of farm commodities would rise. Warren and Pearson called their theory the "commodity dollar."

President Roosevelt became enamored of the theory and in 1933 decided to try and implement it. He brought Warren to Washington as an economic adviser and gave him a job in the Department of Commerce. The critics of Warren proved to be correct. The 1933–1934 experiment with the commodity dollar through government gold-buying schemes failed, and Warren returned to Cornell. He died on May 24, 1938.

See also: Gold Standard

Further Reading

Eichengreen, Barry. 1996. *Golden Fetters: The Gold Standard and the Great Depression, 1919–1939*, New York: Oxford University Press; Stanton, B. F. 2007. *George F. Warren, Farm Economist*, Ithaca, NY: Cornell University Press; Warren, George F., and Frank A. Pearson. 1938. *Prices*. New York: Wiley.

Warren Potato Control Act of 1935

One of the great challenges facing the **Agricultural Adjustment Administration** (AAA) in 1933–1934 was the number of farmers planting noncontract crops. For the AAA to have any hope of reducing production and boosting commodity prices, most farmers had to be participating in it. Only compulsory controls could stem the production tide. Congress had already passed the **Bankhead Cotton Control Act** and the **Kerr-Smith Tobacco Control Act**, and potato farmers in Idaho, Maine, Virginia, and North Carolina expected similar protections for themselves. Congressman Lindsay Warren of North Carolina, with the cosponsorship of Senator William Borah of Idaho, submitted legislation to Congress, and the Warren Potato Control Act was passed on August 24, 1935. It imposed a burdensome tax on all noncontract potatoes, which made them noncompetitive in terms of price and therefore forced farmer participation.

See also: Agricultural Adjustment Administration; Bankhead Cotton Control Act of 1934; Kerr-Smith Tobacco Control Act of 1934

Further Reading

Gilbert, Jess. 2015. *Planning Democracy: Agrarian Intellectuals and the Intended New Deal*, New Haven, CT: Yale University Press; White, Ann Folino. 2014. *Plowed Under: Food Policy Protests and Performance in New Deal America*, Bloomington: Indiana University Press.

Wealth Tax Act of 1935

The Wealth Act of 1935, also known as the Revenue Act of 1935, marked a different direction in **New Deal** political and economic policy. In June 1935, President **Franklin D. Roosevelt** proposed a major revision of the federal tax code. He was convinced that it was far too complex and actually contributed to the concentration of wealth in the United States. Roosevelt sought a modest redistribution of wealth through tax policies. Such tax policies, he thought, might stimulate the economy by putting money in the hands of working-class people and provide the necessary dollars to fund relief programs, which would also be spent by poor people. The proposal indicated that the president was drifting toward the left, a move stimulated by Supreme Court decisions that had dismantled several New Deal programs, rabid business opposition to New Deal policies, and political pressure from the likes of Father **Charles Coughlin**, **Francis Townsend**, and **Huey Long**. Political support for the Wealth Tax also came from such old-line progressives as senators William E. Borah, Robert M. La Follette Jr., Gerald P. Nye, and Hiram M. Johnson. The American Federation of Labor also backed the idea.

As first proposed, the measure was comprehensive and capable of curbing the transmission of great wealth from one generation to another. It called for inheritance and gift taxes, enhanced surcharges on large personal incomes, and the imposition of a major graduated tax schedule on corporations. FDR also proposed a constitutional amendment permitting the federal government to levy taxes on the interest earned from issues of state and local securities.

The Wealth Tax Act emerged from Congress much altered. It imposed a 12.5 percent rate on small corporations and a 15 percent rate on companies earning more than $50,000 annually. The law also imposed a 6 percent excess profits tax on earnings of more than 10 percent annually and 12 percent on earnings exceeding 15 percent. It did not include FDR's request for a constitutional amendment or an inheritance tax. In the end, the Wealth Tax Act achieved few, if any, of its objectives. It certainly did not redistribute wealth, and it raised little extra revenue for the federal government. Nevertheless, it was of great political significance. In an act of great hyperbole, conservatives proclaimed it unconstitutional and a form of class warfare, and liberals hailed it as a watershed in the history of public policy in that it at least declared the legitimacy of using the power of the federal government to decentralize wealth. Still, even after the legislation, the poor continued to be responsible for a disproportionate share of the tax burden.

See also: Coughlin, Charles Edward; Long, Huey P.; Townsend, Francis Everett

Further Reading

Olson, James S., and Abraham O. Mendoza. 2015. *American Economic History: A Dictionary and Chronology*, Santa Barbara, CA: ABC-CLIO; Simkin, John. "1935 Wealth Tax Act," Spartacus Educational, August 2014. http://spartacus-educational.com/USAwealthT.htm. Accessed September 12, 2016.

Weaver, Robert Clifton

Robert Weaver, one of the most influential African Americans in the **New Deal**, was born on December 29, 1907, in Washington, D.C. He earned a bachelor's degree from Harvard in 1929 and then a master's degree and a Ph.D. in 1931 and 1934, respectively. Secretary of the Interior Harold Ickes used Weaver as an adviser on minority affairs, and as such, Weaver became a member of the so-called black cabinet. In 1937 Weaver was named special assistant for the U.S. Housing Authority, a position he kept until 1940. Weaver later had a distinguished academic career at Columbia University and New York University, writing such well-received books as *Negro Labor: A National Problem* (1946) and *The Negro Ghetto* (1948). In 1954 he became deputy commissioner of the New York State Division of Housing. Between 1955 and 1959, he served as rent administrator for the state of New York before joining the Ford Foundation.

In 1961, President John F. Kennedy named him head of the Federal Housing and Home Finance Agency, and in 1966, Weaver became the first African American in history to serve in a presidential cabinet when Lyndon B. Johnson named him secretary of housing and urban development. Weaver served there for eight years, and in 1969 he left public service to become president of Bernard Baruch College. Robert Weaver died on July 17, 1997.

Further Reading

Greenberg, Cheryl Lynn. 2009. *To Ask for an Equal Chance: African Americans in the Great Depression*, Lanham, MD: Rowman & Littlefield; Pritchett, Wendell E. 2008. *Robert Clifton Weaver and the American City: The Life and Times of an Urban Reformer*, Chicago: University of Chicago Press.

West Coast Hotel Co. v. Parrish (1937)

The U.S. Supreme Court decided the *West Coast Hotel Co. v. Parrish* case on March 29, 1937. The case revolved around a minimum wage law for women that the state legislature of Washington had passed. The law generated opposition from businessmen who did not want to pay a minimum wage and from feminist groups convinced that such gender labor restrictions only increased discrimination against women by resting on a belief in female inequality. In 1923, in *Adkins v. Children's Hospital*, the Court had overturned a minimum wage law for children, and opponents of the law felt that *West Coast Hotel* was a similar legal situation.

But the legal climate of opinion had changed dramatically between 1923 and 1937. President **Franklin D. Roosevelt** had launched his attack on the conservative Court by proposing his **court-packing scheme**. Although the attempt to reorganize the judiciary failed, it did prompt an ideological shift on the Court, and *West Coast v. Parrish* was the first example of the change. The judges overturned *Adkins* by a narrow 5 to 4 margin. The principle of freedom of contract, Chief Justice Charles Evans Hughes wrote, was not unlimited, and government had the right to regulate the economy in the interests of the larger community. The chief justice also argued that the judiciary, except in the most extraordinary circumstances, ought to defer to the legislative branch in such matters. Justice Owen Josephus Roberts, who usually could be counted on to vote with the conservative bloc, voted to uphold the minimum wage law. In doing so, he gave liberals an upper hand on the Court and made President Roosevelt's court-packing scheme moot. Journalists dubbed Roberts's decision the "switch in time that saved nine."

See also: Court-Packing Scheme

Further Reading

Hall, Kermit L., and James W. Ely Jr. 2009. *The Oxford Guide to United States Supreme Court Decisions*, 2nd ed., New York: Oxford University Press; Shesol, Jeff. 2011. *Supreme Power: Franklin Roosevelt vs. the Supreme Court*, New York: W. W. Norton & Company.

White, Walter Francis

Walter Francis White was born on July 1, 1893, in Atlanta, Georgia. He enjoyed a mixed racial ancestry, and although he could have passed as a white man, he lived as a proud African American. In 1916, White graduated from Atlanta University and found a job with the Atlanta Insurance Company. He also established an Atlanta chapter of the **National Association for the Advancement of Colored People** (NAACP). In 1918, he moved to New York to work as assistant secretary of the national NAACP. White succeeded James Weldon Johnson in 1931 as secretary of the NAACP, and he remained at the post until his death in 1955.

During the 1930s, White invested most of his energies in promoting a Federal Anti-Lynching Bill in Congress. Senators Edward Costigan of Colorado and **Robert Wagner** of New York sponsored the legislation, which NAACP lawyers had drafted, but it never passed. Opposition from southern Democrats was too strong. Several of the NAACP's legal battles,

Walter White served the cause of African Americans as assistant and executive secretary of the National Association for the Advancement of Colored People (NAACP) from the 1920s through the 1950s. White, of such mixed racial ancestry that he was often mistaken for a white man, came to be the most devoted fighter in the effort to stamp out lynching in the United States after World War I. (Library of Congress)

however, like the fight to save the **Scottsboro boys**, succeeded. White was outspoken in his demands for black voting rights, an end to Jim Crow segregation, a ban on poll taxes, and desegregation of the armed forces and public schools. The greatest factor limiting White's work, beyond the entrenched racism in white America, was the Great Depression's impact on NAACP finances. With its coffers badly depleted, White's opportunities to challenge racist institutions were quite limited. He kept the faith, however, and lived long enough to see the beginning of the Supreme Court's assault on Jim Crow. Walter White died on March 21, 1955.

See also: National Association for the Advancement of Colored People; Scottsboro Boys

Further Reading

Dyja, Tom. 2008. *Walter White: The Dilemma of Black Identity in America*, Chicago: Ivan R. Dee; Janken, Kenneth Robert. 2003. *White: The Biography of Walter White, Mr. NAACP*, New York: New Press.

Williams, Aubrey Willis

Aubrey Williams was born into poverty in rural Springville, Alabama, in 1890. As a child he had to go into the cotton fields to earn money to supplement the family's poverty-level income, and the experience gave him a lifelong appreciation for the plight of poor people and the challenge of being black in the South. Although he was not an African American, he witnessed firsthand the numbing effects of racism and discrimination, and instead of incorporating the racism as part of himself, as did so many white southerners, Williams became committed to the idea of the social gospel and the need to treat poor people in general and black people in particular with respect.

During World War I, Williams worked for the Red Cross and fought for the French Foreign Legion, and that experience also gave him an appreciation for people of color. In 1922 he became executive secretary of the Wisconsin Conference of Social Work and committed himself to the battle against poverty, disease, and child abuse. He became convinced that the battle had to be fought on several fronts—the law, the state house, Congress, and in the public mind, where understanding of the causes of poverty in America seemed so limited. Williams was also a firm believer that the only effective form of public assistance was work relief, in which the indigent labored for their weekly stipend. Only then, he was convinced, could they retain a sense of dignity.

In 1932 and 1933, Williams worked for the **Reconstruction Finance Corporation** (RFC) in Alabama and Mississippi after the **Emergency Relief and Construction Act** gave the RFC a relief mission. After the inauguration of **Franklin D. Roosevelt**, Williams became deputy to Federal Emergency Relief administrator **Harry Hopkins**. Williams became a key figure in the **Federal Emergency Relief Administration** and the **Civil Works Administration**, and he worked diligently to make sure that black people received a share of the work relief programs. In 1935, Williams was appointed executive director of the **National Youth Administration** (NYA) and deputy director of the **Works Progress Administration** (WPA). He hired black staff members at the WPA and NYA and refused to segregate blacks in agency operations in the South. Williams's attitudes, of course, cost him political support among powerful southern congressmen, but he simply refused to let his principles become compromised by political concerns. He remained at the helm of the NYA until its demise in 1943.

Williams spent much of the rest of his life denouncing the Red Scare tactics of right-wing Republicans and southern Democrats and speaking in favor of civil rights for African Americans. He had a nobility about him that left a legacy of respect among those who knew him and knew of his influence. Aubrey Williams died in 1965.

Further Reading

Greenberg, Cheryl Lynn. 2009. *To Ask for an Equal Chance: African Americans in the Great Depression*, Lanham, MD: Rowman & Littlefield; Rose, Nancy E. 2009. *Put to Work: The WPA and Public Employment in the Great Depression*, 2nd ed., New York: Monthly Review Press.

Willkie, Wendell Lewis

Wendell Lewis Willkie was born on February 18, 1892, in Elwood, Indiana. In 1913 he graduated from Indiana University and then earned a law degree there in 1916. He became a corporate attorney for Firestone Tire and Rubber Company in Akron, Ohio. Willkie also became active in local Democratic Party politics, where he displayed conservative but certainly not ideological attitudes. Willkie supported President Woodrow Wilson's attempt to get the United States in the League of Nations, and he condemned Ku Klux Klan influence in the Democratic Party during the 1920s. Willkie moved to New York in 1929 and became a partner in the law firm of Weadock and Willkie. His firm handled the account of the billion-dollar utility empire of Commonwealth and Southern Corporation, and in 1933, Willkie became president of the company.

Willkie was a leader in the business community opposition to many **New Deal** programs, especially the **Tennessee Valley Authority** and the **Public Utility Holding Company Act of 1935**. Although Willkie did not oppose government breakup of monopolies or regulation of companies to prevent abuses, he felt the New Deal had gone too far in actually breaking up efficient, well-run companies. He also spoke out against deficit spending, confiscatory taxes, and bureaucratic waste, all of which he thought the New Deal excelled in. In 1936, Willkie switched political allegiances and voted for Alf Landon. **Franklin D. Roosevelt** and the New Deal had simply gone too far beyond the reach of Willkie's Wilsonian progressivism.

In 1940, a coalition of anti-Roosevelt Democrats, Wall Street investors, and anti–New Deal journalists began pushing Willkie's candidacy for the Republican presidential nomination. He won the nomination on the sixth ballot at the Republican National Convention, and he selected Senator Charles McNary of Oregon as his running mate. Willkie built his campaign around a theme that accused President Roosevelt of vastly expanding the federal bureaucracy without ever really solving the Depression and with letting the country's military defenses lapse into a state of unreadiness. He also hoped that the third-term issue might derail Roosevelt. No president had ever sought a third term in office, and Republicans anticipated victory.

The criticisms were certainly justified, but the Willkie-McNary ticket could not deal with the deteriorating international situation. The outbreak of World War II in Europe in 1939 had led to increased purchases of war goods in the United States, and millions of new jobs were being created. Most Americans could see the Great Depression slipping into the past.

At the same time, Americans became loathe to switch leaders when war seemed on the horizon. Franklin D. Roosevelt had become almost a father figure to tens of millions of people, and Willkie could not compete with that image. When the votes were counted, FDR defeated Willkie 27,307,819 to 22,321,018, with 499 electoral votes to Willkie's 82. Wendell Willkie died on October 2, 1944.

Further Reading

Dunn, Susan. 2013. *1940: FDR, Willkie, Lindbergh, Hitler—The Election amid the Storm*, New Haven, CT: Yale University Press; Peters, Charles. 2005. *Five Days in Philadelphia*, New York: Public Affairs.

Winchell, Walter

Walter Winchell was born in New York City on April 7, 1897. He quit school after the sixth grade and, with Jack Weiner and George Jessell, went to work at the Imperial Theater. The three friends formed a group of singing ushers and soon worked the local vaudeville circuit. Winchell joined the U.S. Navy during World War I, and after the war, he returned to vaudeville. In 1922, with no training in writing or journalism, Winchell became a reporter for the *Vaudeville News*, where he did theater reviews. Winchell moved to the *New York Graphic* in 1924, and five years later, he had his own syndicated column with the *New York Daily Mirror*.

To come up with celebrity gossip, Winchell at first spent a great deal of time in New York nightclubs, but he soon developed a system of contacts and sources that became the envy of journalism. He claimed the Stork Club as his unofficial office. Beginning in May 1930, Winchell had a daily evening **radio** show that trafficked in crime stories, celebrity gossip, and politics. Winchell's rapid-fire, staccato voice became his trademark, and because he was absolutely fearless, with millions of listeners, he became quite powerful. Despite his fractured syntax and penchant for making up words or changing the meaning of words, Winchell became the most popular journalist in the country. He regularly pilloried members of Congress but could not heap enough praise on President **Franklin D. Roosevelt**. Late in the 1930s, Winchell took on Adolf Hitler and the "Ratsies" (Nazis), and during the 1950s, he was an outspoken backer of Senator Joseph McCarthy. Winchell remained on radio until 1955. Historians now look back on Walter Winchell as the father of broadcast celebrity gossip. Winchell died on February 20, 1972.

See also: Radio

Further Reading

Gabler, Neal. 1995. *Winchell: Gossip, Power and the Culture of Celebrity*, New York: Vintage Books; Weinraub, Bernard. November 18, 1998. "He Turned Gossip into Tawdry Power; Walter Winchell, Who Climbed High and Fell Far, Still Scintillates," *New York Times*, http://www.nytimes.com/1998/11/18/arts/he-turned-gossip-into-tawdry-power-walter-winchell-who-climbed-high-fell-far.html?_r=0. Accessed September 9, 2016.

Woodward, Ellen Sullivan

Ellen Woodward was born in Oxford, Mississippi, on July 11, 1887. Her father, William Amberg Sullivan, had been a congressman and U.S. senator, and she acquired an interest in public affairs from him. She married Albert Young Woodward, an attorney and state legislator, but after his sudden death in 1925, she was appointed to complete his unfulfilled term in the state legislature. From 1926 to 1933, Woodward served as a member, and then as director, of the Mississippi State Board of Development, where she gained critical experience administering a variety of state public works, industrial, agricultural, and educational programs. Competent, efficient, charming, and politically connected, Woodward became one of the most influential women in the state.

In August 1933, **Harry Hopkins** named Woodward to head the women's division of the **Federal Emergency Relief Administration**. Her close relationship with Hopkins brought her into contact with First Lady **Eleanor Roosevelt**, and the two women developed a close friendship. Woodward eventually succeeded to similar duties in the **Civil Works Administration** and the **Works Progress Administration** (WPA). At the WPA, she supervised the

Ellen Sullivan Woodward, head of women's public works projects during the New Deal. (Library of Congress)

work of more than 500,000 women relief workers who were employed in such activities as household training, gardening, public health extension, canning, and rural library development. When Harry Hopkins left the WPA in December 1938, Woodward left as well and was appointed to the three-member Social Security Board, where she served until 1946. During those years, she crusaded for the extension of **unemployment** compensation and Social Security coverage to women workers and benefits for widows and dependent children.

From 1946 to 1953, Woodward headed the Office of Inter-Agency and International Relations of the Federal Security Agency. When she retired in 1953, she was widely regarded as one of the most influential women in the **Roosevelt** administrations, third behind Secretary of Labor Frances Perkins and First Lady Eleanor Roosevelt. Ellen Woodward died on September 23, 1971.

Further Reading

Miller Center of Public Affairs, University of Virginia. "Franklin D. Roosevelt: The American Franchise," http://millercenter.org/president/biography/fdroosevelt-the-american-franchise. Accessed September 9, 2016; Swain, Martha H. 1995. *Ellen S. Woodward: New Deal Advocate for Women* (Twentieth-Century America Series), Jackson: University Press of Mississippi.

Works Progress Administration

The greatest challenge facing public policymakers during the years of the Great Depression was **unemployment**. During the **Hoover** administration and the early years of the **Roosevelt** administration, a variety of relief measures were implemented. The **Federal Emergency Relief Administration** (FERA) was the first **New Deal** relief agency, but critics charged that it was little more than a "dole" because recipients did not have to work for what they received. According to many Americans, a dole, or a welfare check, robbed people of their individual dignity and their incentive to work. More successful, as far as most Americans were concerned, were government relief projects that required recipients to work for the money they received. Such programs included the **Public Works Administration**, the **Civil Works Administration**, the Civilian Conservation Corps, and the Works Progress Administration (WPA).

The WPA was by far the largest and most extensive of the New Deal's work relief agencies. President Franklin D. Roosevelt established the WPA by executive order on May 6, 1935, to implement the dictates of the Emergency Relief Appropriation Act. The legislation appropriated nearly

$5 billion, of which $1.4 billion went to the WPA. The WPA had a specific mission from the president to get out of the "relief business" and to help solve the unemployment problem through legitimate, useful government work programs. With the advent of the WPA, the FERA ceased operation. **Harry Hopkins** headed the WPA, with **Aubrey Williams** as his assistant and **Ellen Woodward** in charge of the WPA's women's division.

Under Hopkins's direction, the WPA engaged in a great variety of work projects. It had two basic divisions. The nonconstruction division, Federal Project Number One ("Federal One"), consisted of the WPA's professional and artistic programs: the **Federal Music Project**, which hired unemployed musicians to teach music in schools and community centers and to perform at public concerts; the **Federal Theatre Project**, which hired unemployed actors, directors, and stage professionals to tour the country putting on plays and musicals; the **Federal Dance Project**, which hired unemployed dancers and choreographers to teach dance and to stage dance productions; the **Federal Art Project**, which hired unemployed artists as teachers and to paint murals on public buildings; the **Federal Writers' Project**, which hired unemployed teachers, librarians, and writers to conduct research, write oral histories, and serve as state and regional travel and business guides; and the Historical Records Survey. WPA workers also served in libraries, community centers, schools, and health clinics. Eventually, more than 40,000 people were employed in the federal theater, music, art, dance, and writing projects. A total of 500,000 women were employed in such relief activities as household training, public and preventative health education, public gardening, school lunch preparation, canning, and child care.

The WPA construction division operated on a massive scale, and between 1935 and 1943, it constructed or improved 2,500 hospitals, 5,900 school buildings, 3,000 storage dams, 78,000 bridges, 1,000 airports, more than 10,000 public parks, and 650,000 miles of rural roads, sidewalks, park trails, and urban streets. At its peak, the WPA had 3.3 million people on the payroll.

Critics had a field day with the WPA. Businessmen complained that the WPA provided unfair competition with them. Conservatives criticized the WPA for being a bureaucratic nightmare and ridiculed its activities as "boondoggling." Some even said that its acronym stood for "We Piddle Around." Other conservatives complained that the WPA projects for writers, artists, actors, dancers, and musicians were too liberal and promoted social protest. Labor union leaders complained that the average WPA wage of $50 per month eroded wage levels in the economy at large.

In 1939, as part of the **Reorganization Act**, the WPA was renamed the Works Projects Administration and transferred to the newly created

Federal Works Agency. When World War II erupted in Europe, the WPA quickly changed its focus to national defense projects, but rapidly rising employment in the private sector soon rendered its mission moot. In June 1943 the WPA was eliminated.

See also: Federal Art Project; Federal Dance Project; Federal Music Project; Federal Theatre Project; Federal Works Agency; Federal Writers' Project; Unemployment

Further Reading

Library of Congress. "By the People, For the People: Posters from the WPA, 1936–1943," American Memory, http://memory.loc.gov/ammem/wpaposters/wpahome.html. Accessed September 3, 2016; Rose, Nancy E. 2009. *Put to Work: The WPA and Public Employment in the Great Depression*, 2nd ed., New York: Monthly Review Press; Taylor, Nick. 2008. *American-Made, The Enduring Legacy of the WPA: When FDR Put the Nation to Work*, New York: Random House.

Primary Documents

Rugged Individualism
Herbert Hoover's "Principles and Ideals of the United States Government"
October 22, 1928

Introduction

Herbert Hoover embraced a philosophy of government that he defined as Americanism, and he held to it so firmly that it did not allow for very much compromise or flexibility in practical governance. The tenets of his doctrine included individualism, equal opportunity, class mobility, and material progress through free enterprise capitalism. In 1920 he published an essay, "American Individualism," explaining a philosophy from which he was determined not to stray. He associated these ideas with the success and strength of the United States, whose attributes he considered superior to all other nations. Any significant deviation from that American tradition, he predicted, would result in disaster. His 1928 campaign speech, "Rugged Individualism," draws heavily from the earlier essay. His firm commitment to principles reflects a good deal of light on his policies and behavior during his presidency.

In "American Individualism" he rejected selfish, unrestrained individualism, insisting on an individualism that also embraced civic responsibility in a society that protected equal opportunity. Individual self-interest was the motive force of leadership, without which a society could not prosper. In his own version of Darwinism, he argued that individualism well rewarded in "the free-running mills of competition" will select leaders from the masses. "Democracy arises out of individualism and prospers through it alone." The great mistake of European and other governments was their tendency to apply one form or another of collective solutions to modern problems. The result was disaster. The proper role of government is to protect responsible individualism and equal opportunity. Beyond measures that maintain order and protect individualism, there is little for the government to do in a democratic society. Too much government activism, especially in business affairs, would destroy individualism and ultimately democracy itself. In the years that followed the publication of "American Individualism," Hoover held firm to his ideas.

In "Rugged Individualism" Hoover began a standard campaign speech by recognizing the accomplishments and prosperity of the nation during the two Republican administrations of Warren-Harding and Calvin Coolidge. He attributed this success to Republican policies, which steadfastly held to an individualist philosophy. The speech then echoed the earlier essay, listing the elements of what he called the American "system." These included rejection of European collectivism, support for individual initiative, national policies that let a free capitalism reign, and avoiding doles, which weakened the moral fiber of a people—all of which were consistent with limited government. He cleverly invoked the memory of labor leader Samuel Gompers, who once remarked that more government was a danger to freedom. Gompers, of course, lived in an era when government action was often hostile to organized labor.

The speech was delivered at a time when the United States seemed to be riding the crest of prosperity and the future held the promise of more. How Hoover's rigid adherence to the political philosophy he outlined here served him in dealing with hard times during the Great Depression has been a matter of great interest to historians.

This campaign now draws near to a close. The platforms of the two parties defining principles and offering solutions of various national problems have been presented and are being earnestly considered by our people.

After four months' debate it is not the Republican Party which finds reason for abandonment of any of the principles it has laid down or of the views it has expressed for solution of the problems before the country. The principles to which it adheres are rooted deeply in the foundations of our national life and the solutions which it proposed are based on experience with government and a consciousness that it may have the responsibility for placing those solutions into action.

* * *

It detracts nothing from the character and energy of the American people; it minimizes in no degree the quality of their accomplishments to say that the policies of the Republican Party have played a large part in the building of this progress of these last seven and one-half years. I can say with emphasis that without the wise policies which the Republican

Party has brought into action in this period, no such progress would have been possible.

The first responsibility of the Republican Administration was to renew the march of progress from its collapse by the war. That task involved the restoration of confidence in the future and the liberation and stimulation of the constructive energies of our people. It is not my purpose to enter upon a detailed recitation of the history of the great constructive measures of the past seven and a half years.

It is sufficient to remind you of the restoration of employment to the millions who walked your streets in idleness, to remind you of the creation of the budget system; **the reduction of six billions of national debt** which gave the impulse of that vast sum returned to industry and commerce; the four sequent reductions of taxes and thereby the lift to the living of every family; the enactment of an adequate protective tariff and immigration laws which have raised and safeguarded our wages from floods of goods or labor from foreign countries; the creation of credit facilities and many aids to agriculture; the building up of foreign trade; the care of veterans, the development of aviation, of radio, of our inland waterways, our highways; the expansion of scientific research, of welfare activities, safer highways, safer mines, outdoor recreation, in better homes, in public health and the care of children. . . .

But in addition to this great record of contributions of the Republican Party to progress, there has been a further fundamental contribution—a contribution perhaps more important than all the others—and that is the resistance of the Republican Party to every attempt to inject the Government into business in competition with its citizens.

After the war, when the Republican Party assumed administration of the country, we were faced with the problem of determination of the very nature of our national life. During 150 years we have built up a form of self-government and we had built up a social system which is peculiarly our own. It differs fundamentally from all others in the world. It is the American system. It is just as definite and positive a political and social system as has ever been developed on earth. It is founded upon the conception that self-government can be preserved only by decentralization of Government in the State and by fixing local responsibility; but further than this, it is founded upon the social conception that only through ordered liberty, freedom and equal opportunity to the individual will his initiative and enterprise drive the march of progress.

During the war we necessarily turned to the Government to solve every difficult economic problem; the Government having absorbed every energy of our people to war, there was no other solution. **For the preservation of the State the Government became a centralized despotism** which undertook responsibilities, assumed powers, exercised rights, and took over the business of citizens. To large degree we regimented our whole people temporarily into a socialistic state. However justified it was in time of war if continued in peace time it would destroy not only our system but progress and freedom in our own country and throughout the world. When the war closed the most vital of all issues was whether Governments should continue war ownership and operation of many instrumentalities of production and distribution. **We were challenged with the choice of the American system "rugged individualism" or the choice of a European system of diametrically opposed doctrines—doctrines of paternalism and state socialism.** The acceptance of these ideas meant the destruction of self-government through centralization of government; it meant the undermining of initiative and enterprise upon which our people have grown to unparalleled greatness.

The Democratic administration cooperated with the Republican Party to demobilize many of her activities, and the Republican Party from the beginning of its period of power resolutely turned its face away from these ideas and these war practices, back to our fundamental conception of the state and the rights and responsibilities of the individual. Thereby it restored confidence and hope in the American people, it freed and stimulated enterprise, **it restored the Government to its position as an umpire instead of a player in the economic game.** For these reasons the American people have gone forward in progress while the rest of the world is halting and some countries have even gone backwards. If anyone will study the causes which retarded recuperation of Europe, he will find much of it due to the stifling of private initiative on one hand, and overloading of the Government with business on the other.

I regret, however, to say that there has been revived in this campaign a proposal which would be a long step to the abandonment of our American system, to turn to the idea of government in business. Because the country is faced with difficulty and doubt over certain national problems—that is prohibition, farm relief and electrical power—**our opponents propose that we must to some degree thrust government into these businesses and in effect adopt state socialism as a solution.**

There is, therefore, submitted to the American people the question— Shall we depart from the American system and start upon a new road. And I wish to emphasize this question on this occasion. I wish to make clear my position on the principles involved for they go to the very roots of American life in every act of our Government. I should like to state to you the effect of the extension of government into business upon our system of self-government and our economic system. But even more important is the effect upon the average man. **That is the effect on the very basis of liberty and freedom not only to those left outside the fold of expanded bureaucracy but to those embraced within it.**

When the Federal Government undertakes a business, the state governments are at once deprived of control and taxation of that business; when the state government undertakes a business it at once deprived the municipalities of taxation and control of that business. Business requires centralization; self-government requires decentralization. Our government to succeed in business must become in effect a despotism. There is thus at once an insidious destruction of self-government.

Moreover there is a limit to human capacity in administration. Particularly is there a limit to the capacity of legislative bodies to supervise governmental activities. Every time the Federal Government goes into business 530 Senators and Congressmen become the Board of Directors of that business. Every time a state government goes into business 100 or 200 state senators and assemblymen become directors of that business. Even if they were supermen, no bodies of such numbers can competently direct that type of human activities which requires instant decision and action. No such body can deal adequately with all sections of the country. And yet if we would preserve government by the people we must preserve the authority of our legislators over the activities of our Government. We have trouble enough with log rolling in legislative bodies today. It originates naturally from desires of citizens to advance their particular section or to secure some necessary service. It would be multiplied a thousand-fold were the Federal and state governments in these businesses. The effect upon our economic progress would be even worse. Business progressiveness is dependent on competition. New methods and new ideas are the outgrowth of the spirit of adventure of individual initiative and of individual enterprise. Without adventure there is no progress. No government administration can rightly speculate and take risks with taxpayers' money. But even more important than this—leadership in business must be through the sheer rise of ability and character. That rise can take place only in the free atmosphere of competition. Competition is closed by bureaucracy. Certainly political choice is a feeble basis for choice of leaders to conduct a business. . . .

But we can examine this question from the point of view of the person who gets a Government job and is admitted into the new bureaucracy. Upon that subject let me quote from a speech of that great leader of labor, **Samuel Gompers**, delivered in Montreal in 1920, a few years before his death. He said:

"I believe there is no man to whom I would take second position in my loyalty to the Republic of the United States, and yet I would not give it more power over the individual citizenship of our country.

"It is a question of whether it shall be Government ownership or private ownership under control. . . . If I were in the minority of one in this convention, I would want to cast my vote so that the men of labor shall not willingly enslave themselves to Government authority in their industrial effort for freedom. . . ."

I would amplify Mr. Gompers' statement. These great bodies of Government employees would either comprise political machines at the disposal of the party in power, or alternatively to prevent this, the Government, by stringent civil-service rules, must debar its employees from their full rights as free men. If it would keep employees out of politics, its rules must strip them of all right to expression of opinion. It is easy to conceive that they might become so large a body as by their votes to dictate to the Government and their political rights need be further reduced. It must strip them of the liberty to bargain for their own wages, for no Government employee can strike against his Government and thus the whole people. It makes a legislative body with all its political currents their final employer. That bargaining does not rest upon economic need or economic strength but on political potency.

But what of those who are outside the bureaucracy? What is the effect upon their lives of the Government on business and these hundreds of thousands more officials?

At once their opportunities in life are limited because a large area of activities is removed from their participation. Further the Government does not tolerate amongst its customers the freedom of competitive reprisals to which private corporations are subject. Bureaucracy does not spread the spirit of independence; it spreads the spirit of submission into our daily life, penetrates the temper of our people; not with the habit of powerful resistance to wrong, but with the habit of timid acceptance of the irresistible might.

Bureaucracy is ever desirous of spreading its influence and its power. You cannot give to a government the mastery of the daily working life of a people without at the same time giving it mastery of the peoples' souls and thoughts. Every expansion of government means that government in order to protect itself from political consequences of its errors and wrongs is driven onward and onward without peace to greater and greater control of the country's press and platform. Free speech does not live many hours after free industry and free commerce die.

It is false liberalism that interprets itself into the Government operation of business. The bureaucratization of our country would poison the very roots of liberalism that is free speech, free assembly, free press, political equality and equality of opportunity. It is the road, not to more liberty, but to less liberty. Liberalism should be found not striving to spread bureaucracy, but striving to set bounds to it. True liberalism seeks freedom first in the confident belief that without freedom the pursuit of all other blessings and benefits is vain. That belief is the foundation of all American progress, political as well as economic.

Liberalism is a force truly of the spirit, a force proceeding from the deep realization that economic freedom cannot be sacrificed if political freedom is to be preserved. Even if governmental conduct of business could give us more efficiency instead of giving us decreased efficiency, the fundamental objection to it would remain unaltered and unabated. It would destroy political equality. It would cramp and cripple mental and spiritual energies of our people. It would dry up the spirit of liberty and progress. It would extinguish equality of opportunity, and for these reasons fundamentally and primarily it must be resisted. For a hundred and fifty years liberalism has found its true spirit in the American system, not in the European systems.

I do not wish to be misunderstood in this statement. I am defining a general policy! It does not mean that our government is to part with one iota of its national resources without complete protection to the public interest. **I have already stated that where the government is engaged in public works for purposes of flood control, of navigation, of irrigation, of scientific research or national defense, or in pioneering a new art, it will at times necessarily produce power or commodities as a by-product.** But they must be by-products, not the major purpose. . . .

Our people have the right to know whether we can continue to solve our great problems without abandonment of our American system. I know we can. We have demonstrated that our system is responsive enough to meet any new and intricate development in our economic and business life. We have demonstrated that we can maintain our democracy as master in its own house and that we can preserve equality of opportunity and individual freedom.

In the last fifty years we have discovered that mass production will produce articles for us at half the cost that obtained previously. We have seen the resultant growth of large units of production and distribution. This is big business. Business must be bigger for our tools are bigger, our country is bigger. We build a single dynamo of a hundred thousand horsepower. Even fifteen years ago that would have been a big business all by itself. Yet today advance in production requires that we set ten of these units together.

Our great problem is to make certain that while we maintain the fullest use of the large units of business yet that they shall be held subordinate to the public interest. The American people from bitter experience have a rightful fear that these great units might be used to dominate our industrial life and by illegal and unethical practices destroy equality of opportunity. . . .

One of the great problems of government is to determine to what extent the Government itself shall interfere with commerce and industry and how much it shall leave to individual exertion. It is just as important that business keep out of government as that government keep out of business. No system is perfect. We have had abuses in the conduct of business that every good citizen resents. But I insist that the results show our system [is] better than any other and retains the essentials of freedom. . . .

By adherence to the principles of decentralization, self-government, ordered liberty, and opportunity and freedom to the individual our American experiment has yielded a degree of well-being unparalleled in all the world. It has come nearer to the abolition of poverty, to the abolition of fear of want that humanity has ever reached before. Progress of the past seven years is the proof of it. It furnishes an answer to those who would ask us to abandon the system by which this has been accomplished. . . .

In this country we have developed a higher sense of cooperation than has ever been known before. This has come partly as the result of stimulation during the war, partly from the impulses of industry itself. We have ten thousand examples of this cooperative tendency in the enormous growth of the associational activities during recent years. Chambers of commerce, trade associations, professional associations, labor unions, trade councils, civic associations, farm cooperatives—these are all so embracing that there is scarcely an individual in our country who does not belong to one or more of them. They represent every phase of our national life both on the economic and the welfare side. They represent a vast ferment toward conscious cooperation. While some of them are selfish and narrow, the majority of them recognize a responsibility to the public as well as to their own interest.

The government, in its obligation to the public, can through skilled specialists cooperate with these various associations for the accomplishment of high public purposes. And this cooperation can take two distinct directions. The first is in the promotion of constructive projects of public interest, such as the elimination of waste in industry, the stabilization of business and development of scientific research. It can contribute to reducing unemployment and seasonal employment. It can by organized cooperation assist and promote great movements for better homes, for child welfare and for recreation.

The second form that this cooperation can take is in the cure of abuses and the establishment of a higher code of ethics and a more strict standard in its conduct of business. One test of our economic and social system is its capacity to cure its own abuses. New abuses and new relationships to the public interest will occur as long as we continue to progress. If we are to be wholly dependent upon government to cure every evil we shall by this very method have created an enlarged and deadening abuse through the extension of bureaucracy and the clumsy and incapable handling of delicate economic forces. And much abuse has been and can be cured by inspiration and cooperation, rather than by regulation of the government. . . .

All this is possible because of the cooperative spirit and ability at team play in the American people. There is here a fundamental relief from the necessity of extension of the government into every avenue of business and welfare and therefore a powerful implement for the promotion of progress. . . .

Source: Herbert Hoover, "Principles and Ideals of the United States Government," speech given October 22, 1928. Available at http://millercenter.org/president/speeches/detail/6000.

Muscle Shoals Veto Message
Herbert Hoover's Veto of the Muscle Shoals Resolution
March 3, 1931

Introduction

The Muscle Shoals dam project had lain dormant since the end of World War I. The government had begun the project during the war, aiming to use electricity generated from water power to produce explosive nitrates for the war effort. Plans to sell the facility to private investors failed, and Senator George Norris of Nebraska struggled during the 1920s to turn Muscle Shoals into a government-operated venture to provide low-cost electricity and agricultural fertilizer for the people of the Tennessee Valley. While he succeeded in persuading Congress to pass the necessary legislation, the bill hit a roadblock with President Hoover. As a matter of principle, Hoover rejected the idea of increasing the role of the federal government, especially in the economic life of the nation. As he noted in his message, Hoover had supported federal dam projects too costly for local governments, but even if the production of electricity resulted from these projects, distribution of the power should not be in competition with private capital. In the Norris design, the government was to be the producer and seller of the electricity. Hoover consistently identified the very nature of American civilization with free enterprise based on the investment of private capital. Government involvement was not necessary or desirable. Neither the increasing unemployment and hard times of the intensifying Great Depression nor the broad support for the Norris project in the region could undermine the president's ideological resistance to such government activism.

Senator Norris never gave up on his idea for the development of Muscle Shoals. He tried again and succeeded in the early days of the Roosevelt administration, with the passage and presidential approval of the Tennessee Valley Act.

President Herbert Hoover

To the Senate:

I return herewith, without my approval, Senate Joint Resolution 49, to provide for the national defense by the creation of a corporation for the operation of the Government properties at and near Muscle Shoals in the State of Alabama; to authorize the letting of Muscle Shoals properties under certain conditions; and for other purposes.

This bill proposes the transformation of the war plant at Muscle Shoals, together with important expansions, into a permanently operated Government institution for the production and distribution of power and the manufacture of fertilizers. . . .

General Considerations

I am firmly opposed to the Government entering into any business the major purpose of which is competition with our citizens. There are national emergencies which require that the Government should temporarily enter the field of business, but they must be emergency actions and in matters where the cost of the project is secondary to much higher considerations. **There are many localities where the Federal Government is justified in the construction of great dams and reservoirs, where navigation, flood control, reclamation, or stream regulation are of dominant importance, and where they are beyond capacity or purpose of private or local government capital to construct**. In these cases power is often a by-product and should be disposed of by contract or lease. But for the Federal Government deliberately to go out to build up and expand such an occasion to the major purpose of a power and manufacturing business is to break down the initiative and enterprise of the American people; it is the negation of the ideals upon which our civilization has been based.

This bill raises one of the important issues confronting our people. That is squarely the issue of Federal Government ownership and operation of power and manufacturing business not as a minor by-product but as a major purpose. Involved in this question is the agitation against the conduct of the power industry. The power problem is not to be solved by the Federal Government going into the power business, nor is it to be solved by the project in this bill. The remedy for abuses in the conduct of that industry lies upon the business itself. I have recommended to the Congress on various occasions that action should be taken to establish Federal regulation of interstate power in cooperation with State authorities. This bill would launch the Federal Government upon a policy of ownership and operation of power utilities upon a basis of competition instead of by the proper Government function of regulation for the protection of all the people. I hesitate to contemplate the future of our institutions, of our Government, and of our country if the preoccupation of its officials is to be no longer the promotion of justice and equal opportunity but is to be devoted to barter in the markets. That is not liberalism, it is degeneration.

This proposal can be effectively opposed upon other and perhaps narrower grounds. The establishment of a Federal-operated power business and fertilizer factory in the Tennessee Valley means Federal control from Washington with all the vicissitudes of national politics and the tyrannies of remote bureaucracy imposed upon the people of that valley without voice by them in their own resources, the overriding of State and local government, the undermining of State and local responsibility. The very history of this project over the past 10 years should be a complete demonstration of the ineptness of the Federal Government to administer such enterprise and of the penalties which the local communities suffer under it.

This bill distinctly proposes to enter the field of powers reserved to the States. It would deprive the adjacent States of the right to control rates for this power and would deprive them of taxes on property within their borders, and would invade and weaken the authority of local government.

Aside from the wider issues involved, the immediate effect of this legislation would be that no other development of power could take place on the Tennessee River with the Government in the field. That river contains two or three millions of potential horsepower, but the threat of the subjection of that area to a competition which under this bill carries no responsibility to earn interest on the investment or taxes will either destroy the possibility of private development of the great resources of the river or alternately impose the extension of this development upon the Federal Government. It would appear that this latter is the course desired by many proponents of this bill. There are many other objections which can be raised to this bill, of lesser importance but in themselves a warranty for its disapproval.

It must be understood that these criticisms are directed to the project set up in this bill; they are not directed to the possibilities of a project denuded of uneconomic and unsound provisions, nor is it a reflection upon the value of these resources.

I sympathize greatly with the desire of the people of Tennessee and Alabama to see this great asset turned to practical use. It can be so turned and to their benefit. I am loath to leave a subject of this character without a suggestion for solution. Congress has been thwarted for 10 years in finding a solution by rivalry of private interests and by the determination of certain groups to commit Federal Government to Government ownership and operation of power. The real development of the resources and the industries of the Tennessee Valley can only be accomplished by the people in that valley themselves. Muscle Shoals can only be administered by the people upon the ground, responsible to their own communities, directing them solely for the benefit of their communities and not for purposes of pursuit of social theories or national politics. Any other course deprives them of liberty.

I would therefore suggest that the States of Alabama and Tennessee, who are the ones primarily concerned, should set up a commission of their own representatives, together with a representative from the national farm organizations and the Corps of Army Engineers; that there be vested in that commission full authority to lease the plants at Muscle Shoals in the interest of the local community and agriculture generally. It could lease the nitrate plants to the advantage of agriculture. The power plant to-day is earning a margin over operating expenses. Such a commission could increase the margin without further capital outlay and should be required to use all such margins for the benefit of agriculture.

The Federal Government should, as in the case of **Boulder Canyon**, construct Cove Creek Dam as a regulatory measure for the flood protection of the Tennessee Valley and the development of its water resources, but on the same bases as those imposed at Boulder Canyon; that is, that construction should be undertaken at such time as the proposed commission is able to secure contracts for use of the increased water supply to power users or the lease of the power produced as a by-product from such a dam on term that will return to the Government interest upon its outlay with amortization. On this basis the Federal Government will have cooperated to place the question into the hands of the people primarily concerned. They can lease as their wisdom dictates and for the industries that they deem best in their own interest. It would get a war relic out of politics and into the realm of service.

Source: Herbert Hoover, "Veto of the Muscle Shoals Resolution," March 3, 1931, in *Public Papers of the Presidents: Herbert Hoover: Volume 3, 1931* (Washington, DC: Government Printing Office, 1976), 120.

Protest at the Bank of the United States Image of a Bank Run, 1931

Introduction

Embracing theories of unlimited free enterprise left the American economic system with few checks against the greed and gambling instincts of big business, especially the banking industry. Without oversight or regulation, the nation's banks, large and small, speculated with other people's money for great profits. When the market bubble burst, high-risk ventures failed,

In this picture we see panicked depositors protesting outside the closed doors of the Bank of the United States, among the largest banks to collapse during the Great Depression. The official-sounding name of this private bank offered no comfort to angry depositors. Some lucky ones had managed to draw out their money before the bank closed on December 11, 1930. Others were not so fortunate. Even small banks faced "runs" by frightened depositors. The Frank Capra film *It's a Wonderful Life*, starring Jimmy Stewart, captures such a moment.

and thousands of banks across the country collapsed. Depositors who had trusted their life savings to these banks now found the doors closed and their money gone.

Source: Library of Congress.

The Philosophy of Government
Franklin D. Roosevelt's Speech to the Commonwealth Club of San Francisco
September 23, 1932

Introduction

The Commonwealth Club of San Francisco was founded in 1903 as a forum for the discussion of public affairs. A long list of important political figures speaking on public issues brought great prestige to the club, and an invitation to a presidential candidate delivered instant national attention. By 1932

American politics had reached a point when candidates for high office more frequently relied on staff for help in drafting speeches. At the Commonwealth Club Roosevelt worked with a draft that had been prepared by Adolf Berle, one of his key campaign advisers. The sentiments expressed were consistent with his admiration for the challenge to big business made by his kinsman, Theodore Roosevelt; with the development of his political ideas as a Wilsonian progressive; and with the spirit of the New Deal to come.

Knowing that the occasion would draw national press attention, Roosevelt took advantage of the invitation to outline a philosophy of government that he hoped people could applaud and identify with. He placed himself squarely in the tradition of Thomas Jefferson but with important adjustments for modern economic realities. An America transformed by the Industrial Revolution required a new and more active role for government than Jefferson's much smaller and more agrarian nation. Industrialists, he pointed out, were eager enough to lobby for government subsidies and trade protection, but they scorned any effort at the regulation of business practices for the common good. Roosevelt saw a danger to individual freedom and to democracy in concentrated economic power in private hands without the restraint of public oversight. The candidate used the address to forecast his intention to lead an activist government capable of challenging the economic power of capital and shaping the nation's economic well-being.

Political campaigns can sometimes muddy the issues in seeking the broadest appeal, and the 1932 campaign was no exception. But the Commonwealth Club Address provided a sharp contrast between the governing philosophies of Franklin Roosevelt and Herbert Hoover. Better than any other single speech, the address embodied the ideological underpinnings of the New Deal struggle to adjust the relationship of government to American capitalism.

I count it a privilege to be invited to address the Commonwealth Club. It has stood in the life of this city and state, and it is perhaps accurate to add, the nation, as a group of citizen leaders interested in fundamental problems of government, and chiefly concerned with achievement of progress in government through non-partisan means. The privilege of addressing you, therefore, in the heat of a political campaign, is great. I want to respond to your courtesy in terms consistent with your policy.

I want to speak not of politics but of government. I want to speak not of parties, but of universal principles. They are not political, except in that larger sense in which a great American once expressed a definition of politics, that nothing in all of human life is foreign to the science of politics. . . .

The issue of government has always been whether individual men and women will have to serve some system of government of economics, or whether a system of government and economics exists to serve individual men and women. This question has persistently dominated the discussion of government for many generations. On questions relating to these things men have differed, and for time immemorial it is probable that honest men will continue to differ.

The final word belongs to no man; yet we can still believe in change and in progress. Democracy, as a dear old friend of mine in Indiana, **Meredith Nicholson,** has called it, is a quest, a never-ending seeking for better things, and in the seeking for these things and the striving for better things, and in the seeking for these things and the striving for them, there are many roads to follow. But, if we map the course of these roads, we find that there are only two general directions.

When we look about us, we are likely to forget how hard people have worked to win the privilege of government. The growth of the national governments of Europe was a struggle for the development of a centralized force in the nation, strong enough to impose peace upon ruling barons. In many instances the victory of the central government, the creation of a strong central government, was a haven of refuge to the individual. The people preferred the master far away to the exploitation and cruelty of the smaller master near at hand.

But the creators of national government were perforce ruthless men. They were often cruel in their methods, but they did strive steadily toward something that society needed and very much wanted, a strong central state, able to keep the peace, to stamp out civil war, to put the unruly nobleman in his place, and to permit the bulk of individuals to live safely. The man of ruthless force had his place in developing a pioneer country, just as he did in fixing the power of the central government in the development of nations. Society paid him well for his services and its development. When the development among the nations of Europe, however, has been completed, ambition, and ruthlessness, having served its term tended to overstep its mark.

There came a growing feeling that government was conducted for the benefit of a few who thrived unduly at the expense of all. The people sought a balancing—a limiting force. There came gradually, through town councils, trade guilds, national parliaments, by constitution and by popular participation and control, limitations on arbitrary power.

Another factor that tended to limit the power of those who ruled was the rise of the ethical conception that a ruler bore a responsibility for the welfare of his subjects.

The American colonies were born in this struggle. The American Revolution was a turning point in it. After the revolution the struggle continued and shaped itself in the public life of the country. There were those who because they had seen the confusion which attended the years of war for American independence surrendered to the belief that popular government was essentially dangerous and essentially unworkable. They were honest people, my friends, and we cannot deny that their experience had warranted some measure of fear. **The most brilliant, honest and able exponent of this point of view was Hamilton. He was too impatient of slow moving methods**. Fundamentally he believed that the safety of the republic lay in the autocratic strength of its government, that the destiny of individuals was to serve that government, and that fundamentally a great and strong group of central institutions, guided by a small group of able and public spirited citizens could best direct all government.

But Mr. Jefferson, in the summer of 1776, after drafting the Declaration of Independence turned his mind to the same problem and took a different view. He did not deceive himself with outward forms. Government to him was a means to an end, not an end in itself; it might be either a refuge and a help or a threat and a danger, depending on the circumstances. We find him carefully analyzing the society for which he was to organize a government. "We have no paupers. The great mass of our population is of laborers, our rich who cannot live without labor, either manual or professional, being few and of moderate wealth. Most of the laboring class possess property, cultivate their own lands, have families and from the demand for their labor, are enabled to exact from the rich and the competent such prices as enable them to feed abundantly, clothe above mere decency, to labor moderately and raise their families."

These people, he considered, had two sets of rights, those of "personal competency" and those involved in acquiring and possessing property. By "personal competency" he meant the right of free thinking, freedom of forming and expressing opinions, and freedom of personal living each man according to his own lights. To insure the first set of rights, a government must so order its functions as not to interfere with the individual. But even Jefferson realized that the exercise of the property rights might so interfere with the rights of the individual that the government, without whose assistance the property rights could not exist, must intervene, not to destroy individualism but to protect it.

You are familiar with the great political duel which followed, and how Hamilton, and his friends, building towards a dominant centralized power were at length defeated in the great election of 1800, by Mr. Jefferson's party. **Out of that duel came the two parties, Republican and Democratic, as we know them today**.

So began, in American political life, the new day, the day of the individual against the system, the day in which individualism was made the great watchword of American life. The happiest of economic conditions made that day long and splendid. On the Western frontier, land was substantially free. No one, who did not shirk the task of earning a living, was entirely without opportunity to do so. **Depressions could, and did, come and go; but they could not alter the fundamental fact that most of the people lived partly by selling their labor and partly by extracting their livelihood from the soil, so that starvation and dislocation were practically impossible.** At the very worst there was always the possibility of climbing into a covered wagon and moving west where the untilled prairies afforded a haven for men to whom the East did not provide a place. So great were our natural resources that we could offer this relief not only to our own people, but to the distressed of all the world; we could invite immigration from Europe, and welcome it with open arms. Traditionally, when a depression came, a new section of land was opened in the West; and even our temporary misfortune served our manifest destiny.

It was the middle of the 19th century that a new force was released and a new dream created. The force was what is called the industrial revolution, the advance of steam and machinery and the rise of the forerunners of the modern industrial plant. The dream was the dream of an economic machine, able to raise the standard of living for everyone; to bring luxury within the reach of the humblest; to annihilate distance by steam power and later by electricity, and to release everyone from the drudgery of the heaviest manual toil. It was to be expected that this would necessarily affect government. Heretofore, government had merely been called upon to produce conditions within which people could live happily, labor peacefully, and rest secure. Now it was called upon to aid in the consummation of this new dream. There was, however, a shadow over the dream. To be made real, it required use of the talents of men of tremendous will, and tremendous ambition, since by no other force could the problems of financing and engineering and new developments be brought to a consummation.

So manifest were the advantages of the machine age, however, that the United States fearlessly, cheerfully, and, I think, rightly, accepted the bitter with the sweet. It was thought that no price was too high to pay for the advantages which we could draw from a finished industrial system. The history of the last half century is accordingly in large measure a history of a group of financial Titans, whose methods were not scrutinized with too much care, and who were honored in proportion as they produced the results, irrespective of the means they used. The financiers who pushed the railroads to the Pacific were always ruthless, we have them today. **It has been estimated that the American investor paid for the American railway system more than three times over in the process; but despite that**

fact the net advantage was to the United States. As long as we had free land; as long as population was growing by leaps and bounds; as long as our industrial plants were insufficient to supply our needs, society chose to give the ambitious man free play and unlimited reward provided only that he produced the economic plant so much desired.

During this period of expansion, there was equal opportunity for all and the business of government was not to interfere but to assist in the development of industry. This was done at the request of businessmen themselves. The tariff was originally imposed for the purpose of "fostering our infant industry," a phrase I think the older among you will remember as a political issue not so long ago. The railroads were subsidized, sometimes by grants of money, oftener by grants of land; some of the most valuable oil lands in the United States were granted to assist the financing of the railroad which pushed through the Southwest. A nascent merchant marine was assisted by grants of money, or by mail subsidies, so that our steam shipping might ply the seven seas. Some of my friends tell me that they do not want the Government in business. With this I agree; but I wonder whether they realize the implications of the past. For while it has been American doctrine that the government must not go into business in competition with private enterprises, still it has been traditional particularly in Republican administrations for business urgently to ask the government to put at private disposal all kinds of government assistance.

The same man who tells you that he does not want to see the government interfere in business—and he means it, and has plenty of good reasons for saying so—is the first to go to Washington and ask the government for a prohibitory tariff on his product. **When things get just bad enough—as they did two years ago—he will go with equal speed to the United States government and ask for a loan; and the Reconstruction Finance Corporation is the outcome of it.** Each group has sought protection from the government for its own special interest, without realizing that the function of government must be to favor no small group at the expense of its duty to protect the rights of personal freedom and of private property of all its citizens.

In retrospect we can now see that the turn of the tide came with the turn of the century. We were reaching our last frontier; there was no more free land and our industrial combinations had become great uncontrolled and irresponsible units of power within the state. Clear-sighted men saw with fear the danger that opportunity would no longer be equal; that the growing corporation, like the feudal baron of old, might threaten the economic freedom of individuals to earn a living. In that hour, our antitrust laws were born. The cry was raised against the great corporations. **Theodore Roosevelt**, the first great Republican progressive, fought a Presidential campaign on the issue of "trust busting" and talked freely about malefactors of great wealth. If the government had a policy it was rather to turn the clock back, to destroy the large combinations and to return to the time when every man owned his individual small business.

This was impossible; Theodore Roosevelt, abandoning the idea of "trust busting," was forced to work out a difference between "good" trusts and "bad" trusts. The Supreme Court set forth the famous "rule of reason" by which it seems to have meant that a concentration of industrial power was permissible if the method by which it got its power, and the use it made of that power, was reasonable.

Woodrow Wilson, elected in 1912, saw the situation more clearly. Where Jefferson had feared the encroachment of political power on the lives of individuals, Wilson knew that the new power was financial. He say, in the highly centralized economic system, the depot of the twentieth century, on whom great masses of individuals relied for their safety and their livelihood, and whose irresponsibility and greed (if it were not controlled) would reduce them to starvation and penury. **The concentration of financial power had not proceeded so far in 1912 as it has today; but it had grown far enough for Mr. Wilson to realize fully its implications. It is interesting, now, to read his speeches**.

What is called "radical" today (and I have reason to know whereof I speak) is mild compared to the campaign of Mr. Wilson. "No man can deny," he said, "that the lines of endeavor have more and more narrowed and stiffened; no man who knows anything about the development of industry in this country can have failed to observe that the larger kinds of credit are more and more difficult to obtain unless you obtain them upon terms of uniting your efforts with those who already control the industry of the country, and nobody can fail to observe that every man who tries to set himself up in competition with any process of manufacture which has taken place under the control of large combinations of capital will presently find himself either squeezed out or obliged to sell and allow himself to be absorbed."

Had there been no World War—had Mr. Wilson been able to devote eight years to domestic instead of to international affairs—we might have had a wholly different situation at the present time. **However, the then distant roar of European cannon, growing ever louder, forced him to abandon the study of this issue**. The problem he saw so clearly is left with us as a legacy; and no one of us on either side of the political controversy can deny that it is a matter of grave concern to the government.

A glance at the situation today only too clearly indicates that equality of opportunity as we have known it no longer exists. Our industrial plant is built; the problem just now is whether under existing conditions it is not overbuilt. Our last frontier has long since been reached, and there is practically no more free land. More than half of our people do not live on the farms or on lands and cannot derive a living by cultivating their own property. There is no safety valve in the form of a Western prairie to which those thrown out of work by the Eastern economic machines can go for a new start. We are not able to invite the immigration from Europe to share our endless plenty. We are now providing a drab living for our own people.

Our system of constantly rising tariffs has at last reacted against us to the point of closing our Canadian frontier on the north, our European markets on the east, many of our Latin American markets to the south, and a goodly proportion of our Pacific markets on the west, through the retaliatory tariffs of those countries. It has forced many of our great industrial institutions who exported their surplus production to such countries, to establish plants in such countries within the tariff walls. This has resulted in the reduction of the operation of their American plants, and opportunity for employment.

Just as freedom to farm has ceased, so also the opportunity in business has narrowed. It still is true that men can start small enterprises, trusting to native shrewdness and ability to keep abreast of competitors; but area after area has been preempted altogether by the great corporations, and even in the fields which still have no great concerns, the small man starts with a handicap. The unfeeling statistics of the past three decades show that the independent business man is running a losing race. Perhaps he is forced to the wall; perhaps he cannot command credit; perhaps he is "squeezed out," in Mr. Wilson's words, by highly organized corporate competitors, as your corner grocery man can tell you.

Recently a careful study was made of the concentration of business in the United States. It showed that our economic life was dominated by some six hundred odd corporations who controlled two-thirds of American industry. **Ten million small business men divided the other third. More striking still, it appeared that if the process of concentration goes on at the same rate, at the end of another century we shall have all American industry controlled by a dozen corporations, and run by perhaps a hundred men. Put plainly, we are steering a steady course toward economic oligarchy, if we are not there already**.

Clearly, all this calls for a re-appraisal of values. A mere builder of more industrial plants, a creator of more railroad systems, and organizer of more corporations, is as likely to be a danger as a help. The day of the great promoter or the financial titan, to whom we granted anything if only he would build, or develop, is over. Our task now is not discovery or exploitation of natural resources, or necessarily producing more goods. It is the soberer, less dramatic business of administering resources and plants already in hand, of seeking to reestablish foreign markets for our surplus production, of meeting the problem of under consumption, of adjusting production to consumption, of distributing wealth and products more equitably, of adapting existing economic organizations to the service of the people. The day of enlightened administration has come.

Just as in older times the central government was first a haven of refuge, and then a threat, so now in a closer economic system the central and ambitious financial unit is no longer a servant of national desire, but a danger. I would draw the parallel one step farther. We did not think because national government had become a threat in the 18th century that therefore we should abandon the principle of national government. Nor today should we abandon the principle of strong economic units called corporations, merely because their power is susceptible of easy abuse. In other times we dealt with the problem of an unduly ambitious central government by modifying it gradually into a constitutional democratic government. So today we are modifying and controlling our economic units.

As I see it, the task of government in its relation to business is to assist the development of an economic declaration of rights, an economic constitutional order. This is the common task of statesman and business man. It is the minimum requirement of a more permanently safe order of things.

Every man has a right to life; and this means that he has also a right to make a comfortable living. He may by sloth or crime decline to exercise that right; but it may not be denied him. We have no actual famine or death; our industrial and agricultural mechanism can produce enough and to spare. Our government formal and informal, political and economic, owes to everyone an avenue to possess himself of a portion of that plenty sufficient for his needs, through his own work.

Every man has a right to his own property; which means a right to be assured, to the fullest extent attainable, in the safety of his savings. By no other means can men carry the burdens of those parts of life which, in the nature of things afford no chance of labor; childhood, sickness, old age. In all thought of property, this right is paramount; all other property rights must yield to it. If, in accord with this principle, we must restrict the operations of the speculator, the manipulator, even the financier, I believe we must accept the restriction as needful, not to hamper individualism but to protect it.

These two requirements must be satisfied, in the main, by the individuals who claim and hold control of the great industrial and financial combinations which dominate so large a part of our industrial life. They have undertaken to be, not business men, but princes—princes of property. I am not prepared to say that the system which produces them is wrong. I am very clear that they must fearlessly and competently assume the responsibility which goes with the power. So many enlightened business men know this that the statement would be little more than a platitude, were it not for an added implication.

This implication is, briefly, that the responsible heads of finance and industry instead of acting each for himself, must work together to achieve the common end. They must, where necessary, sacrifice this or that private advantage; and in reciprocal self-denial must seek a general advantage. It is here that formal government—political government, if you choose, comes in. Whenever in the pursuit of this objective the lone wolf, the unethical competitor, the reckless promoter, the Ishmael or Insull whose hand is against every man's, declines to join in achieving and end recognized as being for the public welfare, and threatens to drag the industry back to a state of anarchy, the government may properly be asked to apply restraint. Likewise, should the group ever use its collective power contrary to public welfare, the government must be swift to enter and protect the public interest.

The government should assume the function of economic regulation only as a last resort, to be tried only when private initiative, inspired by high responsibility, with such assistance and balance as government can give, has finally failed. As yet there has been no final failure, because there has been no attempt, and I decline to assume that this nation is unable to meet the situation.

The final term of the high contract was for liberty and the pursuit of happiness. We have learnt a great deal of both in the past century. We know that individual liberty and individual happiness mean nothing unless both are ordered in the sense that one man's meat is not another man's poison. We know that the old "rights of personal competency"—the right to read, to think, to speak to choose and live a mode of life, must be respected at all hazards. We know that liberty to do anything which deprives others of those elemental rights is outside the protection of any compact; and that government in this regard is the maintenance of a balance, within which every individual may have a place if he will take it; in which every individual may find safety if he wishes it; in which every individual may attain such power as his ability permits, consistent with his assuming the accompanying responsibility. . . .

Faith in America, faith in our tradition of personal responsibility, faith in our institutions, faith in ourselves demands that we recognize the new terms of the old social contract. We shall fulfill them, as we fulfilled the obligation of the apparent Utopia which Jefferson imagined for us in 1776, and which Jefferson, Roosevelt and Wilson sought to bring to realization. We must do so, lest a rising tide of misery engendered by our common failure, engulf us all. But failure is not an American habit; and in the strength of great hope we must all shoulder our common load.

―――――

Source: Franklin D. Roosevelt. Speech given September 23, 1932, to the Commonwealth Club of San Francisco. Franklin D. Roosevelt, "The Great Communicator," The Master Speech Files, 1898, 1910–1945. Series 1: Franklin D. Roosevelt's Political Ascension. FDR Library and Archives. Available at http://www.ucs.louisiana.edu/~ras2777/conlaw/fdr.html.

The Banking Crisis
Franklin D. Roosevelt's First Fireside Chat, March 12, 1933

Introduction

By March 1932 American banks had lost so much volume of their assets that they no longer had adequate liquidity to function safely. This meant they did not have sufficient sums of money on deposit to satisfy demand should customers ask for their money. The system was clearly broken. "Panic stricken" would not be an inappropriate description of the leading American bankers, who had little to offer as a solution to the crisis. The president's declaration of a banking holiday on Monday, March 6, provided a three-day window to find a solution.

Those three days were filled with intense, not to say frantic, brainstorming and finally decisive action to save the day. Officers of the Federal Reserve Board, bankers, and treasury officials proposed legislation to check gold hoarding and export and authorized the Federal Reserve to issue notes in sufficient amounts to provide liquidity to the economy. They also established a review process to determine which banks were sound enough to reopen and which had to be kept closed. On Wednesday President Roosevelt received a draft of the bill and immediately summoned a bipartisan group from the House and Senate for an evening briefing to push for swift passage. At this moment of high crisis, the speedy action proved not to be a radical overhaul of the key institutions of capitalism but a basically conservative shoring up of the banking system. The aim was to restore enough public confidence in the financial system to keep the economy from total collapse. The purpose was achieved.

The nation's banks were kept closed through the week and were scheduled to reopen on Monday. The hope, of course, was that people would not mob their banks demanding their cash and render the reforms useless. On Sunday night, March 12, President Roosevelt went on national radio for a "fireside chat" with the American people. Roosevelt worked well with radio. In a voice that communicated calm and confidence, he explained what the banking act meant in language that all could understand. Avoiding technicalities, he assured his audience that the banks allowed to reopen would be sound. The core message insisted that their money would be safer in the reopened banks than "under the mattress." The people listened and believed him. On Monday morning banks reopened without serious incident, money and gold returned to the banks for deposit, and the immediate crisis passed. For the moment even the president's enemies grudgingly applauded. Within days more than twelve thousand banks reopened, and that number more than doubled within a few weeks. Some eleven hundred banks were not allowed to reopen.

It is generally conceded that Roosevelt's broadcast to the nation had much to do with restoring confidence sufficient for a smooth reopening of the country's banks. This was to be the first of many such fireside chats at key moments during the New Deal. The president's voice was made for the airwaves. His talks were drafted in language geared to a mass audience, and he had an instinctive actor's skill in communicating clearly to an audience that sensed his confidence and trusted his sincerity. Radio proved a useful tool in boosting support for New Deal programs and was no small help at election time.

I want to talk for a few minutes with the people of the United States about banking—with the comparatively few who understand the mechanics of banking but more particularly with the overwhelming majority who use banks for the making of deposits and the drawing of checks. I want to tell you what has been done in the last few days, why it was done, and what the next steps are going to be. I recognize that the many proclamations from State capitols and from Washington, the legislation, the Treasury regulations, etc., couched for the most part in banking and legal terms, should be explained for the benefit of the average citizen. I owe this in particular because of the fortitude and good temper with which everybody has accepted the inconvenience and hardships of the banking holiday. I know that when you understand what we in Washington have been about I shall continue to have your cooperation as fully as I have had your sympathy and help during the past week.

First of all, let me state the simple fact that when you deposit money in a bank the bank does not put the money into a safe deposit vault. It invests your money in many different forms of credit—bonds, commercial paper, mortgages and many other kinds of loans. **In other words, the bank puts your money to work to keep the wheels of industry and of agriculture turning around. A comparatively small part of the money you put into the bank is kept in currency—an amount which in normal times is wholly sufficient to cover the cash needs of the average citizen. In other** words, the total amount of all the currency in the country is only a small fraction of the total deposits in all of the banks.

What, then, happened during the last few days of February and the first few days of March? Because of undermined confidence on the part of the public, there was a general rush by a large portion of our population to turn bank deposits into currency or gold—a rush so great that the soundest banks could not get enough currency to meet the demand. The reason for this was that on the spur of the moment it was, of course, impossible to sell perfectly sound assets of a bank and convert them into cash except at panic prices far below their real value.

By the afternoon of March 3d scarcely a bank in the country was open to do business. Proclamations temporarily closing them in whole or in part had been issued by the Governors in almost all the States.

It was then that I issued the proclamation providing for the nationwide bank holiday, and this was the first step in the Government's reconstruction of our financial and economic fabric.

The second step was the legislation promptly and patriotically passed by the Congress confirming my proclamation and broadening my powers so that it became possible in view of the requirement of time to extend the holiday and lift the ban of that holiday gradually. This law also gave authority to develop a program of rehabilitation of our banking facilities. I want to tell our citizens in every part of the Nation that the national Congress—Republicans and Democrats alike—showed by this action a devotion to public welfare and a realization of the emergency and the necessity for speed that it is difficult to match in our history.

The third stage has been the series of regulations permitting the banks to continue their functions to take care of the distribution of food and household necessities and the payment of payrolls.

This bank holiday, while resulting in many cases in great inconvenience, is affording us the opportunity to supply the currency necessary to meet the situation. No sound bank is a dollar worse off than it was when it closed its doors last Monday. Neither is any bank which may turn out not to be in a position for immediate opening. The new law allows the twelve Federal Reserve Banks to issue additional currency on good assets and thus the banks which reopen will be able to meet every legitimate call. The new currency is being sent out by the Bureau of Engraving and Printing in large volume to every part of the country. It is sound currency because it is backed by actual, good assets.

A question you will ask is this: why are all the banks not to be reopened at the same time? The answer is simple. Your Government does not intend that the history of the past few years shall be repeated. We do not want and will not have another epidemic of bank failures.

As a result, we start tomorrow, Monday, with the opening of banks in the twelve Federal Reserve Bank cities—those banks which on first examination by the Treasury have already been found to be all right. This will be followed on Tuesday by the resumption of all their functions by banks already found to be sound in cities where there are recognized clearing houses. That means about 250 cities of the United States.

On Wednesday and succeeding days banks in smaller places all through the country will resume business, subject, of course, to the Government's physical ability to complete its survey. It is necessary that the reopening of banks be extended over a period in order to permit the banks to make applications for necessary loans, to obtain currency needed to meet their requirements and to enable the Government to make common sense checkups.

Let me make it clear to you that if your bank does not open the first day you are by no means justified in believing that it will not open. A bank that opens on one of the subsequent days is in exactly the same status as the bank that opens tomorrow.

I know that many people are worrying about State banks not members of the Federal Reserve System. These banks can and will receive assistance from member banks and from the Reconstruction Finance Corporation. These State banks are following the same course as the National banks except that they get their licenses to resume business from the State authorities, and these authorities have been asked by the Secretary of the Treasury to permit their good banks to open up on the same schedule as the national banks. I am confident that the State Banking Departments will be as careful as the national Government in the policy relating to the opening of banks and will follow the same broad policy.

It is possible that when the banks resume a very few people who have not recovered from their fear may again begin withdrawals. Let me make it clear that the banks will take care of all needs—and it is my belief that hoarding during the past week has become an exceedingly unfashionable pastime. It needs no prophet to tell you that when the people find that they can get their money—that they can get it when they want it for all legitimate purposes—the phantom of fear will soon be laid. People will again be glad to have their money where it will be safely taken care of and where they can use it conveniently at any time. I can assure you that it is safer to keep your money in a reopened bank than under the mattress.

The success of our whole great national program depends, of course, upon the cooperation of the public—on its intelligent support and use of a reliable system. . . .

One more point before I close. There will be, of course, some banks unable to reopen without being reorganized. The new law allows the Government to assist in making these reorganizations quickly and effectively and even allows the Government to subscribe to at least a part of new capital which may be required.

I hope you can see from this elemental recital of what your Government is doing that there is nothing complex, or radical, in the process.

We had a bad banking situation. Some of our bankers had shown themselves either incompetent or dishonest in their handling of the people's funds. They had used the money entrusted to them in speculations and unwise loans. This was, of course, not true in the vast majority of our banks, but it was true in enough of them to shock the people for a time into a sense of insecurity and to put them into a frame of mind where they did not differentiate, but seemed to assume that the acts of a comparative few had tainted them all. It was the Government's job to straighten out this situation and do it as quickly as possible. And the job is being performed.

I do not promise you that every bank will be reopened or that individual losses will not be suffered, but there will be no losses that possibly could be avoided; and there would have been more and greater losses had we continued to drift. I can even promise you salvation for some at least of the sorely pressed banks. We shall be engaged not merely in reopening sound banks but in the creation of sound banks through reorganization.

It has been wonderful to me to catch the note of confidence from all over the country. I can never be sufficiently grateful to the people for the loyal support they have given me in their acceptance of the judgment that has dictated our course, even though all our processes may not have seemed clear to them.

After all, there is an element in the readjustment of our financial system more important than currency, more important than gold, and that is the confidence of the people. Confidence and courage are the essentials of success in carrying out our plan. You people must have faith; you must not be stampeded by rumors or guesses. Let us unite in banishing fear. We have provided the machinery to restore our financial system; it is up to you to support and make it work.

It is your problem no less than it is mine. Together we cannot fail.

Source: "The First 'Fireside Chat'—An Intimate Talk with the People of the United States on Banking," March 12, 1933, in *The Public Papers and Addresses of Franklin D. Roosevelt, Volume 2, The Year of Crisis, 1933* (New York: Random House, 1938), 61.

Helping the American Farmer
Agricultural Adjustment Act
May 12, 1933

Introduction

Before the New Deal began, the American farmer had been suffering from low prices for a decade. Many families lost their land to foreclosure, and hundreds of thousands left the countryside looking for work in the cities. Farmers were the ironic victims of their own efficiency and success. Hard work, mechanization, and expanded acreage under cultivation made a fabulously productive combination. In short, the American farmer produced much more food and fiber than could be consumed at home or exported. The effect on prices and income was calamitous, forcing farmers to sell their crops for less than it cost to grow them. To make matters worse, drought struck vast areas of the Great Plains in 1930 and continued for several years. By 1933 "desperate" was an apt term for the condition of millions of American farmers. Getting some help to the nation's farmers was one of the urgent tasks of the first hundred days of the new administration. Roosevelt underscored that sense of urgency in a message to Congress when he wrote, "The proposed legislation is necessary now for the simple reason that the spring crops will soon be planted and if we wait for another month or six weeks the effect on the prices of this year's crops will be wholly lost."

The first move was the passage of the Agricultural Adjustment Act. One strategy adopted by the law limited production so that farm prices might rise enough to keep farmers solvent. Limits on production of basic commodities, which included cotton, tobacco, dairy products, rice, hogs, corn, and wheat, were to be supervised by the Agricultural Adjustment Administration (AAA). Farmers would be paid to take some land out of cultivation, and some surplus production was to be bought by the government. In one of the tragic ironies of the Great Depression years, some crops and a great numbers of hogs were destroyed to keep them off the market while millions went hungry. The objective of the law was to raise prices to a level of parity with the purchasing power of farmers in the good times of years past.

Conflicts and tensions inevitably developed in the administration of such a massive program. Some critics argued that the AAA benefited large producers more than small farmers. The idea of reducing production and destroying crops did not sit well with farmers or consumers. But the program was generally popular and did achieve its goals. Farm prices steadily increased, and farm income grew by 50 percent by 1936. Foreclosures on farm properties dropped sharply.

To bolster the inflationary effect of the legislation, Senator Elmer Thomas of Oklahoma succeeded in attaching an amendment on monetary policy to the AAA. The Thomas Amendment gave the president power to reduce the gold backing of the dollar and to issue paper money backed by silver. Though reluctant to do this, Roosevelt acceded to the idea in preference to more demanding and compulsory inflationary proposals circulating in Congress.

As was the case with other important New Deal legislation, the Agricultural Adjustment Act had trouble in the conservative courts. In 1936 the Supreme Court struck down a crucial provision of the law in the case of Butler v. United States. *The action of the government to tax processors as a means of funding the work of the AAA was declared unconstitutional by a 6 to 3 majority. This forced the Roosevelt administration to seek other means to achieve its goals.*

An Act

To relieve the existing national economic emergency by increasing agricultural purchasing power, to raise revenue for extraordinary expenses incurred by reason of such emergency, to provide emergency relief with respect to agricultural indebtedness, to provide for the orderly liquidation of joint-stock land banks, and for other purposes.

Be it enacted by the Senate and House of Representatives of the United States of America in Congress assembled,

Title I—Agricultural Adjustment
Declaration of Emergency

That the present acute economic emergency being in part the consequence of a severe and increasing disparity between the prices of agricultural and other commodities, which disparity has largely destroyed the purchasing power of farmers for industrial products, has broken down the orderly exchange of commodities, and has seriously impaired the agricultural assets supporting the national credit structure, it is hereby declared that these conditions in the basic industry of agriculture have affected transactions in agricultural commodities with a national public interest, have burdened and obstructed the normal currents of commerce in such commodities, and render imperative the immediate enactment of title I of this Act.

Declaration of Policy

Sec. 2. It is hereby declared to be the policy of Congress—

(1) To establish and maintain such balance between the production and consumption of agricultural commodities, and such

marketing conditions therefor, as will reestablish prices to farmers at a level that will give agricultural commodities a purchasing power with respect to articles that farmers buy, equivalent to the purchasing power of agricultural commodities in the base period. **The base period in the case of all agricultural commodities except tobacco shall be the prewar period, August 1909–July 1914. In the case of tobacco, the base period shall be the postwar period, August 1919–July 1929.**

(2) To approach such equality of purchasing power by gradual correction of the present inequalities therein at as rapid a rate as is deemed feasible in view of the current consumptive demand in domestic and foreign markets.

(3) To protect the consumers' interest by readjusting farm production at such level as will not increase the percentage of the consumers' retail expenditures for agricultural commodities, or products derived therefrom, which is returned to the farmer, above the percentage which was returned to the farmer in the prewar period, August 1909–July 1914.

* * *

Sec. 6. (a) The Secretary of Agriculture is hereby authorized to enter into option contracts with the producers of cotton to sell to any such producer an amount of cotton to be agreed upon not in excess of the amount of reduction in production of cotton by such producer below the amount produced by him in the preceding crop year, in all cases where such producer agrees in writing to reduce the amount of cotton produced by him in 1933, below his production in the previous year, by not less than 30 per centum, without increase in commercial fertilization per acre.

(b) To any such producer so agreeing to reduce production the Secretary of Agriculture shall deliver a nontransferable-option contract agreeing to sell to said producer an amount, equivalent to the amount of his agreed reduction, of the cotton in the possession and control of the Secretary. . . .

Part 2—Commodity Benefits

General Powers

Sec. 8. In order to effectuate the declared policy, the Secretary of Agriculture shall have power—

(1) To provide for reduction in the acreage or reduction in the production for market, or both, of any basic agricultural commodity, through agreements with producers or by other voluntary

methods, and to provide for rental or benefit payments in connection therewith or upon that part of the production of any basic agricultural commodity required for domestic consumption, in such amounts as the Secretary deems fair and reasonable, to be paid out of any moneys available for such payments. Under regulations of the Secretary of Agriculture requiring adequate facilities for the storage of any non-perishable agricultural commodity on the farm, inspection and measurement of any such commodity so stored, and the locking and sealing thereof, and such other regulations as may be prescribed by the Secretary of Agriculture for the protection of such commodity and for the marketing thereof, a reasonable percentage of any benefit payment may be advanced on any such commodity so stored. In any such case, such deduction may be made from the amount of the benefit payment as the Secretary of Agriculture determines will reasonably compensate for the cost of inspection and sealing, but no deduction may be made for interest.

(2) To enter into marketing agreements with processors, associations of producers, and others engaged in the handling, in the current of interstate or foreign commerce of any agricultural commodity or product thereof, after due notice and opportunity for hearing to interested parties. The making of any such agreement shall not be held to be in violation of any of the antitrust laws of the United States, and any such agreement shall be deemed to be lawful. . . .

(3) To issue licenses permitting processors, associations of producers, and others to engage in the handling, in the current of interstate or foreign commerce, of any agricultural commodity or product thereof, or any competing commodity or product thereof. Such licenses shall be subject to such terms and conditions, not in conflict with existing Acts of Congress or regulations pursuant thereto, as may be necessary to eliminate unfair practices or charges that prevent or tend to prevent the effectuation of the declared policy and the restoration of normal economic conditions in the marketing of such commodities or products and the financing thereof. The Secretary of Agriculture may suspend or revoke any such license, after due notice and opportunity for hearing, for violations of the terms or conditions thereof. . . .

Processing Tax

Sec. 9 (a) **To obtain revenue for extraordinary expenses incurred by reason of the national economic emergency, there shall be levied processing**

taxes as hereinafter provided. When the Secretary of Agriculture determines that rental or benefit payments are to be made with respect to any basic agricultural commodity, he shall proclaim such determination, and a processing tax shall be in effect with respect to such commodity from the beginning of the marketing year therefor next following the date of such proclamation. The processing tax shall be levied, assessed, and collected upon the first domestic processing of the commodity, whether of domestic production or imported, and shall be paid by the processor. The rate of tax shall conform to the requirements of subsection (b). Such rate shall be determined by the Secretary of Agriculture as of the date the tax first takes effect, and the rate so determined shall, at such intervals as the Secretary finds necessary to effectuate the declared policy, be adjusted by him to conform to such requirements. . . .

(b) The processing tax shall be at such rate as equals the difference between the current average farm price for the commodity and the fair exchange value of the commodity; except that if the Secretary has reason to believe that the tax at such rate will cause such reduction in the quantity of the commodity or products thereof domestically consumed as to result in the accumulation of surplus stocks of the commodity or products thereof or in the depression of the farm price of the commodity, then he shall cause an appropriate investigation to be made and afford due notice and opportunity for hearing to interested parties. If thereupon the Secretary finds that such result will occur, then the processing tax shall be at such rate as will prevent such accumulation of surplus stocks and depression of the farm price of the commodity. . . .

(d) As used in part 2 of this title—

(1) In case of wheat, rice, and corn, the term "processing" means the milling or other processing (except cleaning and drying) of wheat, rice, or corn for market, including custom milling for toll as well as commercial milling, but shall not include the grinding or cracking thereof not in the form of flour for feed purposes only.
(2) In case of cotton, the term "processing" means the spinning, manufacturing, or other processing (except ginning) of cotton; and the term "cotton" shall not include cotton linters.
(3) In case of tobacco, the term "processing" means the manufacturing or other processing (except drying or converting into insecticides and fertilizers) of tobacco.
(4) In case of hogs, the term "processing" means the slaughter of hogs for market.

* * *

Appropriation

Sec. 12. (a) There is hereby appropriated, out of any money in the Treasury not otherwise appropriated, the sum of $100,000,000 to be available to the Secretary of Agriculture for administrative expenses under this title and for rental and benefit payments made with respect to reduction in acreage or reduction in production for market under part 2 of this title. Such sum shall remain available until expended.

* * *

Title III—Financing—and Exercising Power Conferred by Section 8 of Article I of the Constitution: To Coin Money and to Regulate the Value Thereof

Sec. 43. Whenever the President finds, upon investigation, that (1) the foreign commerce of the United States is adversely affected by reason of the depreciation in the value of the currency of any other government or governments in relation to the Present standard value of gold, or (2) action under this section is necessary in order to regulate and maintain the parity of currency issues of the United States, or (3) an economic emergency requires an expansion of credit, or (4) an expansion of credit is necessary to secure by international agreement a stabilization at proper levels of the currencies of various governments, the President is authorized, in his discretion—

(a) To direct the Secretary of the Treasury to enter into agreements with the several Federal Reserve banks and with the Federal Reserve Board whereby the Federal Reserve Board will, and it is hereby authorized to, notwithstanding any provisions of law or rules and regulations to the contrary, permit such reserve banks to agree that they will, (1) conduct, pursuant to existing law, throughout specified periods, open market operations in obligations of the United States Government or corporations in which the United States is the majority stockholder, and (2) purchase directly and hold in portfolio for an agreed period or periods of time Treasury bills or other obligations of the United States Government in an aggregate sum of $3,000,000,000 in addition to those they may then hold, unless prior to the termination of such period or periods the Secretary shall consent to their sale. . . .

(b) If the Secretary, when directed by the President, is unable to secure the assent of the several Federal Reserve banks and the Federal Reserve Board to the agreements authorized in this section, or if operations under the above provisions prove to be inadequate to meet the purposes of this section, or if for any other reason additional measures are required in the judgment of the President to meet such purpose, then the President is authorized—

(1) To direct the Secretary of the Treasury to cause to be issued in such amount or amounts as he may from time to time order, United States notes, as provided in the Act entitled "An Act to authorize the issue of United States notes and for the redemption of funding thereof and for funding the floating debt of the United States," approved February 25, 1862, and Acts supplementary thereto and amendatory thereof, in the same size and of similar color to the Federal Reserve notes heretofore issued and in denominations of $1, $5, $10, $20, $50, $100, $500, $1,000, and $10,000; but notes issued under this subsection shall be issued only for the purpose of meeting maturing Federal obligations to repay sums borrowed by the United States and for purchasing United States bonds and other interest-bearing obligations of the United States: Provided, That when any such notes are used for such purpose the bond or other obligation so acquired or taken up shall be retired and canceled. Such notes shall be issued at such times and in such amounts as the President may approve but the aggregate amount of such notes outstanding at any time shall not exceed $3,000,000,000. . . .

(2) By proclamation to fix the weight of the gold dollar in grains nine tenths fine and also to fix the weight of the silver dollar in grains nine tenths fine at a definite fixed ratio in relation to the gold dollar at such amounts as he finds necessary from his investigation to stabilize domestic prices or to protect the foreign commerce against the adverse effect of depreciated foreign currencies, and to provide for the unlimited coinage of such gold and silver at the ratio so fixed, or in case the Government of the United States enters into an agreement with any government or governments under the terms of which the ratio between the value of gold and other currency issued by the United States and by any such government or governments is established, the President may fix the weight of the gold dollar in accordance with the ratio so agreed upon, and such gold dollar, the weight of which is so fixed, shall be the standard unit of value, and all forms of money issued or coined by the United States shall be maintained at a parity with this standard and it shall be the duty of the Secretary of the Treasury to maintain such parity, but in no event shall the weight of the gold dollar be fixed so as to reduce its present weight by more than 50 per centum. . . .

Sec. 45. (a) The President is authorized, for a period of six months from the date of the passage of this Act, to accept silver in payment of the whole or any part of the principal or interest now due, or to become due within six months after such date, from any foreign government or governments on account of any indebtedness to the United States, such silver to be accepted at not to exceed the price of 50 cents an ounce in United States currency. The aggregate value of the silver accepted under this section shall not exceed $200,000,000. . . .

(d) The Secretary of the Treasury shall cause silver certificates to be issued in such denominations as he deems advisable to the total number of dollars for which such silver was accepted in payment of debts. Such silver certificates shall be used by the Treasurer of the United States in payment of any obligations of the United States.

Source: Pub. L. No. 73-10, 48 Stat. 31 (1933).

"The Teacher Faces the Depression" Eunice Langdon, *Nation Magazine* August 16, 1933

Introduction

Farmers and industrial workers suffered much in the Great Depression, but so too did Americans in other sectors of economic life. The hard times also hit the highly educated, the talented, and professionals in many fields. Projects funded by the Works Progress Administration (WPA) helped artists, writers, and musicians who could not find work. Highly skilled college graduates with professional training in fields like engineering, science, and business administration were also idle. The following essay illuminates the plight of one such group—teachers—who suffered pay cuts and payless paydays, sometimes extending for months. Others could find no positions at all. The "Dawes" referred to in the article was Charles G. Dawes, former vice president of the United States, once head of the Reconstruction Finance Corporation, and at this point president of City National Bank in Chicago. City teachers descended on the bank on April 24 demanding to be paid and shouting Dawes's name. He appeared and tried to calm the crowd but failed, and the protests continued.

On April 27, according to the New York *Times*, Paul Schneider, aged forty-four, a sick and crippled Chicago school teacher, shot himself to death. His widow, left with three children, stated that he had not been paid for eight months, that his property had depreciated, groceries which his family needed could be bought only on wage assignment, and worry had aggravated his illness. Less than a month after Paul Schneider's discouragement drove him to suicide, the militant action of the Chicago teachers—patient no longer—in invading the banks and refusing to be distracted or amused by the picturesque profanity of Mr. [Charles G.] Dawes resulted in the payment of $12,000,000 due them for the last months of 1932. Their pay for the five months of 1933 is still owed them. Four hundred of them are reported to be in asylums and sanitariums as a result of the strain, and are possibly beyond help by this very belated and partial payment. Replies to a questionnaire reveal, according to William G. Carr, director of the Research Division of the National Education Association, that 2,278 teachers in 263 schools have been unable to meet payments on $7,800,567 of life insurance, and 759 have been unable to meet payments on their homes. Large numbers of teachers have borrowed to the limit of their insurance policies and in some cases from loan sharks at exorbitant rates of interest. More than 500, only a part of those who applied, have been assisted by one teachers' charitable foundation. In short, all the horrors of prolonged *unemployment* are incidents of employment in the public-school system of the second largest city in the country, which is conducting a "Century of Progress" exposition.

But the situation of the Chicago teachers, distressing as it is, is far from unique. Because of certain incongruous and sensational angles in the situation which habitually make Chicago "news," the plight of Chicago's teachers has received a relatively large amount of publicity, whereas the equally desperate, perhaps more hopeless condition of teachers in rural schools throughout the South and in many sections of the West and Middle West has gone almost unnoticed. Public education is threatened with something little short of an absolute breakdown in vast areas of the country. Alabama owes its teachers $7,000,000. Eighty-five per cent of its elementary and secondary schools were reported as closed in April of this year and the rest as running on part time. Many schools, according to a statement made by Dr. A. F. Harmon, State Superintendent of Education, closed before January 1 of this year not to open again until October if they do then. Some counties have gone back to a three months' term such as was maintained thirty years ago. Few teachers of elementary, high-school, or college rank in State institutions have been paid their full salaries, and most of them are from three to eight months behind. Even these unpaid salaries had previously been cut from 10 to 40 per cent, as they have in other States. Where they have been paid, it has been only partly in cash and partly in scrip, which merchants in some places are no longer willing to accept. In Georgia, teachers in rural counties have gone unpaid for months and in many places their credit is exhausted. Some of them have met the situation by camping in schoolhouses, cooking their meals in the domestic-science rooms. In some rural communities farmers have helped by taking turns in boarding teachers, but in many instances this has proved too great a burden for the impoverished families. These statements, like many official reports, investigations, and surveys, apply almost wholly to white teachers in white schools. But it is a safe assumption that in those States and counties which normally spend from three to sixty times as much on their white as on their colored schools, the sufferings of the Negro school teachers and of the Negro school population have been proportionately heavier. Here as elsewhere complete breakdown has been averted largely by the devotion of the teachers, who have not only gone on working without pay, but have often out of their depleted means helped needy school children.

And as if this crippled condition of the schools were not sufficiently serious, in every locality cries for further retrenchment from taxpayers' committees, citizens' budget commissions, the bankers, the power interests, the merchants' associations, and the real-estate associations are being heard To a large extent these have already been heeded, and at time when unprecedentedly heavy demands are being made on our public schools they have been forced almost everywhere to run on reduced budgets, to cut teachers' salaries, to increase the size of classes, and to drop such "fads and frills" as the teaching of music, child-guidance work, playground work, school gardens, vacation schools—in short, all the myriad developments of the school system which are intelligent responses to the complex needs of the community, the very features which make the public-school system, with all its weaknesses and shortcomings, an asset to democracy.

And what are the results? In Michigan, says George E. Carrothers of the University of Michigan, "a 7 per cent increase in the number of students in Michigan high school' has been accompanied by a 3 per cent decrease in the number of teachers, salary cuts of from 10 to 40 per cent, and the elimination of courses, which is putting an unparalleled burden on teachers and school systems to keep State educational standards up to normal." Detroit has cut its night-school service in half, increased the size of classes, and eliminated free summer schools; Indianapolis has eliminated its department of curriculum revision, eliminated night schools, summer schools, and teachers' colleges, and greatly reduced its appropriations for kindergartens. In Chicago nearly all evening schools have been closed, summer schools have been discontinued, community centers abolished, playgrounds reduced. To quote again from William Carr's recent summary of the situation in the New York *Herald Tribune*:

One or more phases of school service have been eliminated or curtailed in more than half of the city school systems of the nation. Conservative estimates indicate that by the end of the school year kindergartens will be reduced or eliminated in at least 170 cities, night schools in 120 cities, schools for handicapped children in 170 cities, art instruction in 100 cities, music instruction in 160 cities, school nurses in 135 cities, home economics or manual training or both in 145 cities, and physical education in 160 cities.

A short-sighted "economy" has insisted in all these cases on the elimination or the curtailment especially of those services which even in normal times are the strongest forces against disintegration, demoralization, and gangsterism, and which become acutely necessary in the face of the problems raised by the depression. Professor Paul Mort, of Teachers College in New York, announced last winter after a nationwide survey of educational financing that approximately 9,500,000 American boys and girls were being deprived of their educational birthright because of the depression. As large portions of the survey on which this conclusion was based dealt exclusively with white teachers and white schools it seems safe to regard these figures as highly conservative.

"Education is not sacred," said Mayor [Joseph V.] McKee at a meeting of the New York City Board of Estimate last October. For this and similar courtesies some 200,000 voters wrote in his name on their ballots in November and many more were prevented from expressing their appreciation only by the "fixing" of Tammany's voting machines. McKee's soul, however, goes marching on. According to an analysis by the Public Education Association, the educational budget in New York City for 1933 suffered the following reductions: First, the budget presented by the Board of Education in 1933 was $2,800,000 less than that for 1932. And since there is normally an annual increase in the budget of $5,000,000 on account of the increased number of pupils, the budget request for 1933 was lower than it normally would have been by approximately $7,800,000. This reduction was accomplished in the main by increasing the size of classes, restricting the number of sessions of evening schools, suspending the summer schools and other summer activities, reducing personnel, using substitutes instead of regular teachers to fill vacancies, and making large cuts in supplies and equipment. . . .

As Dr. Abraham Lefkowitz of the Teachers' Union recently pointed out in his pamphlet, "Teachers and the Economic Situation," teachers who were public employees were among the last to profit by rising wages in the boom years following 1914. Their salaries were established by law and could not readily be adjusted. The maximum salary for high-school teachers in New York at that time was $2,650, and this was reached only after fourteen years of service. (Again a comparison of the service rendered the community by the teachers and their remuneration with that of some of the members of the Citizens' Budget Commission is suggestive.) With rising prices, however, the purchasing power of the dollar shrank so rapidly that by June, 1920, with the price index at 216.5, the purchasing power of this maximum salary was $1,219. In August 1920, as a result of an active campaign by the teachers, the Legislature of the State of New York raised salaries so that the maximum reached $3,700. But the purchasing power of even this maximum was still below that of the maximum of 1913.

In 1928–29 a further adjustment raised the maximum salary to $4,500, at which level it remained until the salary cut passed by the extraordinary session of the legislature this winter. In the face of rising prices, however, even the teacher obtaining the present maximum salary may soon find himself worse off than he was before his salary was raised—and this even without further wage cuts. The suggested moratorium on increments, while not affecting holders of these maximum salaries would hit all those on the lower salary levels—in itself a very gross injustice.

These are the conditions facing teachers fortunate enough to be employed. What of the unemployed? Their number in New York City alone has been variously estimated at from 5,000 to 15,000. The Teachers' Union, which gives the lower figure, makes a distinction between those actually on eligible lists and those who for some reason have failed or had no opportunity to take the regular license examinations.) The Unemployment Relief Committee was recently said to be supporting 954 of them. Probably very few of the others have had the good luck to reach the stage of destitution at which they will be eligible for relief from the Home Relief Bureau or will be given "made work" by the Emergency Work Bureau. Many are known to have applied unsuccessfully to these and similar organizations. One such teacher, a young girl, according to a letter in the possession of the Unemployed Teachers Association was ineligible because in her family of five people, one, a brother, was working and making $17 a week. . . .

Members of the New York Board of Education and of such boards throughout the country face no easy task. The pressure on them to reduce expenses, even by such disastrous economies as those described above, from all the reactionary elements in the community has been tremendous and is still going on. It is unfortunate that such boards are usually composed of people who are primarily politicians rather than educators and hence over-responsive to pressure of this kind. In the present emergency, moreover, there has been added to the usual reactionary business interests, the voice of the bewildered and overburdened small taxpayer, who may actually be bearing a disproportionate share of the cost of education. The equalization of the tax burden by a form of taxation placing this load where it belongs, State and federal aid to education throughout the nation, the strengthening of teachers' associations everywhere, and determined action against false "economies" by all who realize what is at stake will be needed if the schools and the teaching profession are to be saved from disaster.

Source: Eunice Langdon, "The Teacher Faces the Depression," *The Nation*, August 16, 1933, Vol. 137, No. 3554, p. 182.

Legacy of the New Deal
The Social Security Act
August 14, 1935

Introduction

The most enduring legacy of Franklin D. Roosevelt and the New Deal is the Social Security System. The president saw it as his greatest peacetime accomplishment. The first hundred days and the first two years of the Roosevelt presidency were occupied with the immediate problems of the economic collapse: deflation, business stagnation, and massive unemployment. In 1935 the president added to his agenda a broad campaign for economic and social justice. This new agenda is sometimes referred to as the Second New Deal. Its aim was not merely a recovery from hard times but also the creation of a permanent structure of security measures to protect Americans against the often harsh realities of an urbanizing industrial society in good times and bad.

The Social Security Act was the keystone of that structure. It was an ambitious plan for a national system of compulsory old-age insurance and aid to the widowed, dependent children, and the disabled. For the old and indigent who did not qualify under the employment provisions of the act, a cooperative element of federal and state aid would apply. For those younger than the specified retirement age of sixty-five, the law established a program of federal and state unemployment insurance. This idea resonated especially with the millions of victims of Great Depression joblessness.

Secretary of Labor Frances Perkins headed a White House committee to draft a legislative plan that would win the president's approval. In January 1935 Roosevelt sent the draft to Congress. Liberal warhorse Robert Wagner of New York took charge of the bill in the Senate, guided it to passage, and added another chapter to his record of service to the New Deal.

Critics on the right attacked the proposed legislation as something that would weaken the self-reliance and personal responsibility of Americans. Those to the left of Roosevelt protested that the regressive payroll tax to fund the program would be a burden on workers. The president dismissed both arguments. In his message to Congress Roosevelt struck a blend of idealism and realism: "We can never insure one hundred percent of the population against one hundred percent of the hazards and vicissitudes of life, but we have tried to frame a law which will give some measure of protection to the average citizen and to his family against the loss of a job and against poverty-ridden old age."

Providing a safety net for the aged, the poor, and the disabled was entirely consistent with his long-standing progressive philosophy and his religious commitment to social justice. This was a kind of social insurance program some form of which already existed in most industrial countries and which mainstream American political leaders had advocated at least as far back as Theodore Roosevelt. The president insisted that workers make tax contributions to the system, investing them with a moral right to its benefits so that "no damn politician can ever scrap my social security program." Although the Supreme Court struck down a number of important New Deal laws, the Social Security Act survived Court scrutiny. The constitutionality of the act was affirmed in Steward Machine Company v. Davis, *301 U.S. 548 (1937), and* Helvering v. Davis, *301 U.S. 619 (1937).*

There were some temporary drawbacks to the legislation. Building financial reserves for the system drew needed monies out of circulation in the economy, and the Social Security payroll tax was a cost to wage earners in what were still hard times. The law at first also left out large categories of workers, including farmers, service workers, and the self-employed. The passage of time soon eased the burden of the reserves and the payroll tax, and later amendments extended Social Security coverage to millions more people. After more than seventy-five years, the Social Security System still stands as the most important monument to Franklin Roosevelt's New Deal.

Social Security—
An act to provide for the general welfare by establishing a system of Federal old-age benefits, and by enabling the several States to make more adequate provision for aged persons, blind persons, dependent and crippled children, maternal and child welfare, public health, and the administration of their unemployment compensation laws; to establish a Social Security Board; to raise revenue; and for other purposes.

Be it enacted by the Senate and House of Representatives of the United States of America in Congress assembled,

Title I—Grants to States for Old-Age Assistance

Sec. 1. For the purpose of enabling each State to furnish financial assistance, as far as practicable under the conditions in such State, to aged needy individuals, there is hereby authorized to be appropriated for the fiscal year ended June 30, 1936, the sum of $49,750,000, and there is hereby authorized to be appropriated for each fiscal year thereafter a sum sufficient to carry out the purposes of this title. . . .

State Old-Age Assistance Plans

Sec. 2. (a) A State plan for old-age assistance must

(1) provide that it shall be in effect in all political subdivisions of the State, and, if administered by them, be mandatory upon them;

(2) provide for financial participation by the State;
(3) either provide for the establishment or designation of a single State agency to administer the plan, or provide for the establishment or designation of a single State agency to supervise the administration of the plan;
(4) provide for granting to any individual, whose claim for old-age assistance is denied, an opportunity for a fair hearing before such State agency.

* * *

Title II—Federal Old-Age Benefits
Old-Age Reserve Account

Sec. 201. (a) There is hereby created an account in the Treasury of the United States to be known as the Old-Age Reserve Account hereinafter in this title called the Account. There is hereby authorized to be appropriated to the Account for each fiscal year, beginning with the fiscal year ending June 30, 1937, an amount sufficient as an annual premium to provide for the payments required under this title, such amount to be determined on a reserve basis in accordance with accepted actuarial principles, and based upon such tables of mortality as the Secretary of the Treasury shall from time to time adopt, and upon an interest rate of 3 per centum per annum compounded annually. The Secretary of the Treasury shall submit annually to the Bureau of the Budget an estimate of the appropriations to be made to the Account.

(b) It shall be the duty of the Secretary of the Treasury to invest such portion of the amounts credited to the Account as is not, in his judgment, required to meet current withdrawals. Such investment may be made only in interest-bearing obligations of the United States or in obligations guaranteed as to both principal and interest by the United States. . . .

Old-Age Benefit Payments

Sec. 202. (a) **Every qualified individual (as defined in section 210) shall be entitled to receive, with respect to the period beginning on the date he attains the age of sixty-five, or on January 1, 1942, whichever is the later, and ending on the date of his death, an old-age benefit (payable as nearly as practicable in equal monthly installments) as follows:**

(1) If the total wages (as defined in section 210) determined by the Board to have been paid to him, with respect to employment (as defined in section 210) after December 31, 1936, and before

he attained the age of sixty-five, were not more than $3,000, the old-age benefit shall be at a monthly rate of one-half of 1 per centum of such total wages;
(2) If such total wages were more than $3,000, the old-age benefit shall be at a monthly rate equal to the sum of the following:

(A) One-half of 1 per centum of $3,000; plus
(B) One-twelfth of 1 per centum of the amount by which such total wages exceeded $3,000 and did not exceed $45,000; plus
(C) One-twenty-fourth of 1 per centum of the amount by which such total wages exceeded $45,000.

(b) In no case shall the monthly rate computed under subsection (a) exceed $85.
(c) If the Board finds at any time that more or less than the correct amount has theretofore been paid to any individual under this section, then, under regulations made by the Board, proper adjustments shall be made in connection with subsequent payments under this section to the same individual.
(d) Whenever the Board finds that any qualified individual has received wages with respect to regular employment after he attained the age of sixty-five, the old-age benefit payable to such individual shall be reduced, for each calendar month in any part of which such regular employment occurred, by an amount equal to one months benefit. Such reduction shall be made, under regulations prescribed by the Board, by deductions from one or more payments of old-age benefit to such individual.

Payments Upon Death

Sec. 203. (a) If any individual dies before attaining the age of sixty-five, there shall be paid to his estate an amount equal to 3 per centum of the total wages determined by the Board to have been paid to him, with respect to employment after December 31, 1936.

(b) If the Board finds that the correct amount of the old-age benefit payable to a qualified individual during his life under section 202 was less than 3 per centum of the total wages by which such old-age benefit was measurable, then there shall be paid to his estate a sum equal to the amount, if any, by which such 3 per centum exceeds the amount (whether more or less than the correct amount) paid to him during his life as old-age benefit.

(c) If the Board finds that the total amount paid to a qualified individual under an old-age benefit during his life was less than the correct amount to which he was entitled under section 202, and that the correct amount of such old-age benefit was 3 per centum or more of the total wages by which such old-age benefit was measurable, then there shall be paid to his estate a sum equal to the amount, if any, by which the correct amount of the old-age benefit exceeds the amount which was so paid to him during his life.

* * *

Title III—Grants to States for Unemployment Compensation Administration Appropriation

Sec. 301. For the purpose of assisting the States in the administration of their unemployment compensation laws, there is hereby authorized to be appropriated, for the fiscal year ending June 30, 1936, the sum of $4,000,000, and for each fiscal year thereafter the sum of $49,000,000, to be used as hereinafter provided. . . .

State Plans for Aid to Dependent Children

Sec. 402. (a) A State plan for aid to dependent children must

(1) provide that it shall be in effect in all political subdivisions of the State, and, if administered by them, be mandatory upon them;
(2) provide for financial participation by the State;
(3) either provide for the establishment or designation of a single State agency to administer the plan, or provide for the establishment or designation of a single State agency to supervise the administration of the plan;
(4) provide for granting to any individual, whose claim with respect to aid to a dependent child is denied, an opportunity for a fair hearing before such State agency;

* * *

Title V—Grants to States for Maternal and Child Welfare

Part 1—Maternal and Child Health Services

Appropriation

Sec. 501. For the purpose of enabling each State to extend and improve, as far as practicable under the conditions in such State, services for promoting the health of mothers and children, especially in rural areas and in areas suffering from severe economic distress, there is hereby authorized to be appropriated for each fiscal year, beginning with the fiscal year ending June 30, 1936, the sum of $3,800,000. The sums made available under this section shall be used for making payments to States which have submitted, and had approved by the Chief of the Children's Bureau, State plans for such services.

* * *

Part 2—Services for Crippled Children Appropriation

Sec. 511. For the purpose of enabling each State to extend and improve (especially in rural areas and in areas suffering from severe economic distress), as far as practicable under the conditions in such State, services for locating crippled children and for providing medical, surgical, corrective, and other services and care, and facilities for diagnosis, hospitalization, and aftercare, for children who are crippled or who are suffering from conditions which lead to crippling, there is hereby authorized to be appropriated for each fiscal year beginning with the fiscal year ending June 30, 1936, the sum of $2,850,000. The sums made available under this section shall be used for making payments to States which have submitted, and had approved by the Chief of the Childrens Bureau, State plans for such services.

* * *

Part 3—Child Welfare Services

Sec. 521. (a) For the purpose of enabling the United States, through the Childrens Bureau, to cooperate with State public-welfare agencies establishing, extending, and strengthening, especially in predominantly rural areas, public-welfare services (hereinafter in this section referred to as child-welfare services) for the protection and care of homeless, dependent, and neglected children, and children in danger of becoming delinquent, there is hereby authorized to be appropriated for each fiscal year, beginning with the year ending June 30, 1936, the sum of $1,500,000. Such amount shall be allotted by the Secretary of Labor for use by cooperating State public-welfare agencies on the basis of plans developed jointly by the State agency and the Childrens Bureau, to each State, $10,000, and the remainder to each State on the basis of such plans, not to exceed such part of the remainder as the rural population of such State bears to the total rural population of the United States. The amount so allotted shall be expended for payment of part of the cost of district, county or other local child-welfare services in areas predominantly rural, and for developing State services for the encouragement and assistance of adequate methods of community child-welfare organization in areas predominantly rural and other areas of special need.

* * *

Title VI—Public Health Work Appropriation

Sec. 601. For the purpose of assisting States, counties, health districts, and other political subdivisions of the States in establishing and maintaining adequate public-health services, including the training of personnel for State and local health work, there is hereby authorized to be appropriated for each fiscal year, beginning with the fiscal year ending June 30, 1936, the sum of $8,000,000 to be used as hereinafter provided.

State and Local Public Health Services

Sec. 602. (a) The Surgeon General of the Public Health Service, with the approval of the Secretary of the Treasury, shall, at the beginning of each fiscal year, allot to the States the total of (1) the amount appropriated for such year pursuant to section 601; and (2) the amounts of the allotments under this section for the preceding fiscal year remaining unpaid to the States at the end of such fiscal year. The amounts of such allotments shall be determined on the basis of (1) the population; (2) the special health problems; and (3) the financial needs; of the respective States. Upon making such allotments the Surgeon General of the Public Health Service shall certify the amounts thereof to the Secretary of the Treasury.

* * *

Title VIII—Taxes With Respect to Employment

Income Tax on Employees

Sec. 801. **In addition to other taxes, there shall be levied, collected, and paid upon the income of every individual a tax equal to the following percentages of the wages (as defined in section 811) received by him after December 31, 1936, with respect to employment (as defined in section 811) after such date:**

> (1) With respect to employment during the calendar years 1937, 1938, and 1939, the rate shall be 1 per centum.

(2) With respect to employment during the calendar years 1940, 1941, and 1942, the rate shall 1 per centum.
(3) With respect to employment during the calendar years 1943, 1944, and 1945, the rate shall be 2 per centum.
(4) With respect to employment during the calendar years 1946, 1947, and 1948, the rate shall be 2 per centum.
(5) With respect to employment after December 31, 1948, the rate shall be 3 per centum.

Deduction of Tax From Wages

Sec. 802. (a) The tax imposed by section 801 shall be collected by the employer of the taxpayer by deducting the amount of the tax from the wages as and when paid. Every employer required so to deduct the tax is hereby made liable for the payment of such tax, and is hereby indemnified against the claims and demands of any person for the amount of any such payment made by such employer. . . .

Excise Tax on Employers

Sec. 804. In addition to other taxes, every employer shall pay an excise tax, with respect to having individuals in his employ, equal to the following percentages of the wages (as defined in section 811) paid by him after December 31, 1936, with respect to employment (as defined in section 811) after such date:

(1) With respect to employment during the calendar years 1937, 1938, and 1939, the rate shall be 1 per centum.
(2) With respect to employment during the calendar years 1940, 1941, and 1942, the rate shall be 1 per centum.
(3) With respect to employment during the calendar years 1943, 1944, and 1945, the rate shall be 2 per centum.
(4) With respect to employment during the calendar years 1946, 1947, and 1948, the rate shall be 2 per centum.
(5) With respect to employment after December 31, 1948, the rate shall be 3 per centum.

* * *

Unemployment Trust Fund

Sec. 904. (a) There is hereby established in the Treasury of the United States a trust fund to be known as the Unemployment Trust Fund, hereinafter in this title called the Fund. The Secretary of the Treasury is authorized and directed to receive and hold in the Fund all moneys deposited therein by a State agency from a State unemployment fund. Such deposit may be made directly with the Secretary of the Treasury or with any Federal reserve bank or member bank of the Federal Reserve System designated by him for such purpose.

(b) It shall be the duty of the Secretary of the Treasury to invest such portion of the Fund as is not, in his judgment, required to meet current withdrawals. Such investment may be made only in interest-bearing obligations of the United States or in obligations guaranteed as to both principal and interest by the United States. . . .

(f) The Secretary of the Treasury is authorized and directed to pay out of the Fund to any State agency such amount as it may duly requisition, not exceeding the amount standing to the account of such State agency at the time of such payment.

Title X—Grants to States for Aid to the Blind Appropriation

Sec. 1001. For the purpose of enabling each State to furnish financial assistance, as far as practicable under the conditions in such State, to needy individuals who are blind, there is hereby authorized to be appropriated for the fiscal year ending June 30, 1936, the sum of $3,000,000, and there is hereby authorized to be appropriated for each fiscal year thereafter a sum sufficient to carry out the purposes of this title. The sums made available under this section shall be used for making payments to States which have submitted, and had approved by the Social Security Board, State plans for aid to the blind.

State Plans for Aid to the Blind

Sec. 1002. (a) A State plan for aid to the blind must

(1) provide that it shall be in effect in all political subdivisions of the State, and, if administered by them, be mandatory upon them;
(2) provide for financial participation by the State;
(3) either provide for the establishment or designation of a single State agency to administer the plan, or provide for the establishment or designation of a single State agency to supervise the administration of the plan;
(4) provide for granting to any individual, whose claim for aid is denied, an opportunity for a fair hearing before such State agency.

Source: Social Security Act, Pub. L. No. 74-271, U.S. Stat. 49 (1935), 620.

WPA Workers in Alabama
Image of Honest Work Done through the Works Progress Administration
June 2, 1936

Introduction

The WPA (Works Progress Administration) was one of the most popular and productive New Deal programs. It was directed by President Roosevelt's closest adviser, Harry Hopkins, who oversaw this massive program that expended over $11 billion in projects from 1935 to 1941. The WPA offered employment to millions across lines of race and gender. Its beneficiaries included skilled and unskilled workers, as well as scientists, artists, musicians, and writers. Its projects benefited virtually every city, town, and county in the United States.

Source: Library of Congress.

A team of once-unemployed men toil with hand tools on a typical WPA project laying a water main. This was not a "make-work" detail for a welfare payment but provided a useful benefit to the community and rewarded honest work. Thousands of such projects across the country improved the infrastructure of the United States, ranging from water and sewer systems to highways, airports, and public buildings. These men were engaged in ditch digging, but it was digging with dignity, honest work when none other was available, paid work when families were in need.

Moving toward Racial Equality
Executive Order 8802
June 25, 1941

Introduction

While the Fourteenth Amendment affirming equality of citizenship had long since been passed and ratified, racial discrimination continued to plague the United States during the years of the Roosevelt administration. New Deal programs from the Civilian Conservation Corps and the WPA to the Social Security Act clearly benefited African Americans. However, the solid, one-party Democratic South persisted in thoroughgoing social, political, and economic discrimination against African Americans. The president needed the votes of southern senators and congressmen to pass his New Deal legislation, and the administration offered little direct or dramatic action on civil rights. Eleanor Roosevelt spoke publicly and often in behalf of black causes and urged the president to do more. The sympathetic president was walking a political tightrope. He had often spoken optimistically about progress in race relations; now black leaders pressed for action.

When the first peacetime draft of men into the armed forces began in late 1940, black leaders protested the severe racial discrimination practiced by the military establishment. Discrimination against African Americans ran through every service. In the U.S. Army there were only five black officers, and three of those were chaplains. The Marines and the Army Air Corps permitted no blacks to enter. The Navy confined black enlistees to kitchen, laundry, and other servant duties. One of the most outspoken of the African American protesters was A. Philip Randolph, head of the Brotherhood of Sleeping Car Porters, an important black union. Randolph was one of the most highly regarded black leaders in the country. He met with Roosevelt in September 1940 to press for desegregation in the military. When inaction and what seemed to be backtracking followed that meeting, Randolph struck on the idea of a march on Washington to press the issue. Encouraged by the response of other black leaders and the rank and file, he set July 1 as the date of the march and organized a march committee with branches in cities across the country. The White House was not pleased and urged Randolph not to go ahead with the plan. The showdown came at another meeting with Roosevelt in June 1941, just days before the scheduled march. Both sides made concessions, and they reached a key agreement.

Randolph agreed to cancel the march when the president committed himself to Executive Order 8802, which commanded an end to discrimination in employment in defense industries and set up a Fair Employment Practices Committee to police the order. In defense industries, as in the military, well-qualified African Americans were routinely assigned to menial *tasks with little chance for advancement. The order did not desegregate the armed forces, nor did it attack systematic racial discrimination in the country. Roosevelt's executive order was, however, the first real effort of the federal government since the early years of Reconstruction after the Civil War to actively support an important move toward racial equality. It certainly encouraged Randolph and other leaders to engage in renewed activism for black civil rights, and it turned an important corner in the long struggle for racial equality. It is an interesting note on the times that Randolph and other black leaders applied directly to the president for an executive order. No legislation to check racial discrimination could have passed Congress in 1941.*

WHEREAS it is the policy of the United States to encourage full participation in the national defense program by all citizens of the United States, regardless of race, creed, color, or national origin, in the firm belief that the democratic way of life within the Nation can be defended successfully only with the help and support of all groups within its borders; and

WHEREAS there is evidence that available and needed workers have been barred from employment in industries engaged in defense production solely because of considerations of race, creed, color, or national origin, to the detriment of workers' morale and of national unity:

NOW, THEREFORE, by virtue of the authority vested in me by the Constitution and the statutes, and as a prerequisite to the successful conduct of our national defense production effort, I do hereby reaffirm the policy of the United States that there shall be no discrimination in the employment of workers in defense industries or government because of race, creed, color, or national origin, and I do hereby declare that it is the duty of employers and of labor organizations, in furtherance of said policy and of this order, to provide for the full and equitable participation of all workers in defense industries, without discrimination because of race, creed, color, or national origin;

And it is hereby ordered as follows:

1. All departments and agencies of the Government of the United States concerned with vocational and training programs for defense production shall take special measures appropriate to assure that such programs are administered without discrimination because of race, creed, color, or national origin;
2. All contracting agencies of the Government of the United States shall include in all defense contracts hereafter negotiated by them a provision obligating the contractor not to discriminate against any worker because of race, creed, color, or national origin;
3. There is established in the **Office of Production Management**

A Committee on Fair Employment Practice, which shall consist of a chairman and four other members to be appointed by the President. The Chairman and members of the Committee shall serve as such without compensation but shall be entitled to actual and necessary transportation, subsistence and other expenses incidental to performance of their duties. The Committee shall receive and investigate complaints of discrimination in violation of the provisions of this order and shall take appropriate steps to redress grievances which it finds to be valid. The Committee shall also recommend to the several departments and agencies of the Government of the United States and to the President all measures which may be deemed by it necessary or proper to effectuate the provisions of this order.

Franklin D. Roosevelt
The White House,
June 25, 1941

Source: Executive Order 8802, June 25, 1941. General Records of the United States Government, Record Group 11, National Archives.

Sample Document-Based Essay Question (DBQ)

Question

Compare and contrast the ways Herbert Hoover and Franklin Delano Roosevelt responded to the Great Depression, incorporating their individual conceptions of what falls within the purview of the presidential office and what the responsibilities of the federal government should be. Include discussion of specific programs, events, and pieces of legislation, as well as national responses. Draw on the following seven primary documents and factual evidence from your study of the event to support your answer.

Document 1: Rugged Individualism

Herbert Hoover's "Principles and Ideals of the United States Government" (October 22, 1928)

Document Information

Herbert Hoover's campaign speech outlining the philosophy of "rugged individualism," which promoted equal opportunity, civic responsibility, class mobility, and material progress through free enterprise capitalism. Hoover argued that individual self-interest gave rise to the type of leadership that allowed a democratic society to prosper and that the rightful role of government was to protect responsible individualism and equal opportunity—and then get out of the way.

Document Inference

"Rugged Individualism" represents the American way of life and its proud legacy of individual achievement.

Entries Related to the Document

Emergency Relief and Construction Act of 1932; Hoover, Herbert Clark; Revenue Act of 1932; Stock Market Crash

Document 2: Muscle Shoals Veto Message

Herbert Hoover's Veto of the Muscle Shoals Resolution (March 3, 1931)

Document Information

Hoover blocked an initiative for the federal government to take over the stalled Muscle Shoals dam project, which would have provided low-cost electricity and agricultural fertilizer for Tennessee Valley residents. Hoover had supported dam projects in the past, but was reluctant to nationalize any project that would have created competition for private capital, despite the nation's worsening economic state.

Document Inferences

Hoover believes so strongly in free enterprise and the investment of private capital as the backbone of American civilization that he defers to it even at the expense of immediate economic relief for poor citizens.

Entries Related to the Document

Ashwander v. Tennessee Valley Authority (1936); Hoover, Herbert Clark; Tennessee Valley Authority

Document 3: Philosophy of Government

Franklin D. Roosevelt's Speech to the Commonwealth Club of San Francisco (September 23, 1932)

Document Information

In a highly publicized campaign speech, Roosevelt argued for an activist government, rooting the security of American democracy in public oversight and regulation of big business.

Document Inferences

The speech embodies the ideology of the New Deal struggle to adjust the relationship of government to American capitalism.

Entries Related to the Document
Banking Act of 1935; Federal Reserve Board; First 100 Days; Glass-Steagall Act; New Deal; Roosevelt, Franklin Delano

Document 4: The Banking Crisis
Franklin D. Roosevelt's First Fireside Chat (March 12, 1933)

Document Information
Roosevelt's first radio address to the American people—delivered in his calm, clear, trustworthy manner—explained his approach to resolving the banking crisis and achieved his aim of getting the public to trust the banks again and redeposit their money and gold bars.

Document Inferences
Reflects Roosevelt's belief that restoring the nation's hope would go a long way toward restoring the economy and the capitalist system. Demonstrates the effectiveness of radio in creating a national response to the crisis.

Entries Related to the Document
Banking Crisis; Fireside Chats; First 100 Days; Radio; Roosevelt, Franklin Delano

Document 5: Legacy of the New Deal
The Social Security Act (August 14, 1935)

Document Information
Roosevelt's signing of the Social Security Act provided insurance and aid to the elderly and disabled.

Document Inferences
One of the most controversial and enduring legacies of the New Deal, the establishment of the Social Security system moves past the emergency

measures of the early New Deal and reflects Roosevelt's goal of a permanent economic security for all Americans.

Entries Related to the Document

Committee on Economic Security; Second New Deal; Social Security Act of 1935; Townsend, Francis Everett; Wagner, Robert Ferdinand

Top Tips for Answering Document-Based Essay Questions

Reading the Question

First, read the question several times and underline its various parts to make sure you fully understand what the question is asking. Most document-based essay questions have multiple parts to them and one of the most common mistakes students made is to answer only a portion of the question. It is important to spend some time going over each part of the question to make sure your essay will answer the question in full.

Once you have understood the question, noting its key terms and date parameters, it is helpful to make a list of your outside knowledge and facts that you are going to draw on in your essay.

Developing a Thesis Statement

One test for assessing the strength of your thesis statement is to imagine that it is the only sentence in your essay. If your thesis had to stand on its own, would it provide an answer to the question?

It can be helpful to develop a thesis statement after you have read the question and jotted down a list of your outside knowledge, *but before* you examine the documents.

Writing a thesis statement first and then examining the documents can make it easier to see how the documents can be used to support your thesis. Of course, once you examine the documents, they may spark a new idea, which will make it necessary to edit your thesis.

Analyzing the Documents

Ask yourself whose point of view is being expressed in the document and consider the document's origins and the context in which it was created. You should also consider who the intended audience was and what the document's original purpose may have been. It may be helpful to make notes on the documents as you examine them.

Using the Documents

Your interpretation of the documents should be incorporated into your essay as *evidence* in support of your thesis. Your essay should not simply offer a description or assessment of the documents.

There is no need to cite the documents in the order they were presented in the exam, and though you should refer to a majority of the documents in your essay, it is not absolutely necessary to cite each one.

Conclusion

A good conclusion will reiterate your thesis statement from the introductory paragraph and tie together your supporting evidence.

Appendix A: Chronology of the Great Depression in America

1928

March 4   Republican candidate Herbert Hoover is sworn in as president, promising "a chicken in every pot" and "a car in every garage."

1929

October   The stock market crashes.

October 24   Stocks plummet on "Black Thursday."

October 29   On "Black Tuesday," stocks collapse and banks call in loans.

November   By mid-November, 50 percent of all asset values are wiped out.

1930

    More than 40 percent of homes in America own a radio.

March   Unemployment exceeds 3.2 million. President Herbert Hoover announces that the effects of the crash will be over within sixty days.

June 17   Congress passes the Hawley-Smoot Tariff, raising U.S. tariffs on raw materials.

December 11   The Bank of the United States closes, one of many bank failures nationwide. With over $200 million in deposits lost, it is the largest bank failure in U.S. history. By year's end, 744 banks will fail.

1931

Unemployment rises to almost 16 percent.

March 31　Nine African American teenagers, who became known in the press as the Scottsboro Boys, are falsely accused of raping two white women on a train in Alabama. The case becomes representative of racial injustice in the southern legal system.

May　The Federal Reserve's federal funds rate hits a record low of 1.5 percent.

1932

The GNP drops a record 13.4 percent. Unemployment hits 23.6 percent. Over 13 million Americans are out of work.

January 22　Hoover signs the Reconstruction Finance Corporation Act, which establishes the Reconstruction Finance Corporation (RFC). The RFC can loan money to troubled banks, insurance companies, credit unions, building and loan associations, and railroads.

January 23　Franklin Delano Roosevelt, the Democratic governor of New York, begins his run for president.

May　A "bonus army" of over 17,000 veterans march on Washington to demand their compensation for service in World War I.

July 21　President Hoover signs the Emergency Relief and Construction Act. The legislation issues bonds to state and local governments for relief efforts and public construction projects like roads, bridges, and water and sewer systems. It is too modest to have much impact and only reinforces the negative public impression of Hoover.

July 22　Congress passes the Federal Home Loan Bank Act, making more funds available to institutions to grant discounted home loans.

November 8　Franklin D. Roosevelt is elected president, defeating incumbent Herbert Hoover in a landslide victory.

December　Prices fall for livestock and cash crops. Corn sells for 13 cents per bushel, down from $1.07 per bushel in 1925.

1933

Almost 95 percent of U.S. banks are in danger of closing. Depositors have lost $140 billion to bank failures. Unemployment reaches 25 percent.

January	Over 15 million Americans are unemployed.
March 4	Franklin D. Roosevelt is sworn in as the 32nd president of the United States. In his inauguration speech, Roosevelt tells Americans that "the only thing we have to fear is fear itself." The first 100 days of Roosevelt's presidency launch the New Deal, the most prolific period of legislation in U.S. history.
March 6	Roosevelt declares a bank holiday—a moratorium on all banking operations in the United States.
March 9	Congress passes the Emergency Banking Act, allowing the government to reopen all solvent banks and provide aid to banks in need.
March 12	Roosevelt delivers his first "fireside chat" national radio address, explaining the banking crisis and his plans for resolving it to the American people.
March 20	Roosevelt signs the Economy Act to appease conservative Democrats who urged a balanced budget and spending cuts. The act reduces government salaries and veterans' allowances, and cut departmental spending for a total of $243 million in budget cuts.
March 21	Congress establishes the Civilian Conservation Corps (CCC), to employ young men and promote conservation work.
April 19	The Emergency Banking Act takes the United States off the gold standard.
May 12	The Federal Emergency Relief Act establishes the Federal Emergency Relief Administration (FERA).
May 12	Congress passes the Agricultural Adjustment Act (AAA), to achieve parity for farmers.
May 18	Congress establishes the Tennessee Valley Authority (TVA), to generate lower-cost hydroelectric power in needy areas.
June 6	Congress passes the Home Owners Refinancing Act to provide mortgage assistance and help prevent foreclosures.
June 13	Congress passes the Emergency Railroad Transportation Act to restore financial stability to the railroad industry. The act creates an organized management system to oversee the industry, cut costs, and eliminate waste and duplication of services.
June 16	The National Industrial Recovery Act is passed, creating the National Recovery Administration (NRA) and establishing

the Public Works Administration (PWA), which puts people to work doing construction and public works projects.

 June 16 Congress passes the Glass-Steagall Act, creating the Federal Deposit Insurance Corporation (FDIC) and preventing commercial banks from participating in investment banking.

 November 9 Congress creates the Civil Works Administration, allowing for temporary jobs building bridges, schools, airports, hospitals, and parks, and constructing new highways and roads.

December 5 Congress repeals the Eighteenth Amendment, ending Prohibition.

1934

 Dust Bowl storms begin. Drought, combined with soil erosion, results in a series of catastrophic dust storms in the Midwest. Farming families begin migrating west, looking for work.

 Unemployment is down to 22 percent.

 January Dr. Francis Townsend, a retiree, calls for the creation of a government program whereby all senior citizens over the age of sixty will receive a monthly pension of $200.

 February 2 Roosevelt establishes the Export-Import Bank for the purpose of stimulating foreign trade.

 April 21 Congress passes the Bankhead Cotton Control Act to promote farmer participation in AAA programs, which were designed to reduce cotton production in the United States so that prices would rise and give farmers a living wage.

 June 6 Congress establishes the Securities and Exchange Commission.

June 19 Congress creates the Federal Communications Commission (FCC) to regulate radio communications.

June 28 Congress passes the National Housing Act, establishing the Federal Housing Administration (FHA).

 On June 28, Congress passes the Federal Farm Bankruptcy Act (also known as the Frazier-Lemke Farm Bankruptcy Act) to assist farmers whose debts greatly exceed their assets. Farmers can declare bankruptcy and have their debts scaled down. The Supreme Court will eventually declare the act unconstitutional.

| August | Republicans and conservative Democrats (including Al Smith) form the Liberty League to oppose Roosevelt's policies. | |

1935

January 4	In President Roosevelt's State of the Union address, he rolls out a list of social reforms that come to be known as the Second New Deal, focusing on antitrust activity and Keynesian deficit spending.	
April	The Resettlement Administration relocates farming families to more favorable lands.	
May 6	Congress creates the Works Progress Administration, putting more than 8.5 million people to work building highways, roads, bridges, and airports, and creating jobs for artists and musicians.	
May 7	Congress establishes the Rural Electrification Administration (REA) to bring electricity to rural areas.	
May 27	In *Schechter Poultry Corp v. United States*, the Supreme Court declares the NRA unconstitutional.	
June	Congress creates the National Youth Administration, providing work and education programs for teenagers and young adults.	
July 5	Congress passes the National Labor Relations Act, supporting union rights.	
August 14	Congress passes the Social Security Act, providing federal-state unemployment insurance and security for the elderly.	
August 23	President Roosevelt signs the Banking Act of 1935 into law, making the Federal Deposit Insurance Corporation (FDIC) a permanent institution and reorganizing the Federal Reserve System.	
November 9	John L. Lewis founds the Committee for Industrial Organization (CIO).	
December	By year's end, unemployment is down to 20 percent.	

1936

| January 6 | The Agricultural Adjustment Act is struck down by the Supreme Court in *United States v. Butler*. | |

February 17 — In *Ashwander v. Tennessee Valley Authority*, the Supreme Court upholds the Tennessee Valley Authority, helping legitimize a new role for the federal government in national economic affairs.

March — FSA Photographer Dorothea Lange takes the *Migrant Mother* series during her work with migrant farmers in California.

June 20 — President Roosevelt signs the Federal Anti-Price Discrimination Act, prohibiting price discrimination by manufacturers in favor of large chain stores. Discounts, rebates, and high selling allowances are prohibited as well. The Federal Trade Commission (FTC) is authorized to investigate any price discrimination that reduces competition.

June — Roosevelt becomes the Democratic presidential nominee for the 1936 presidential election.

October 31 — A *Literary Digest* poll predicts a victory for Republican nominee Alf Landon in the presidential election of 1936. The magazine loses credibility when Franklin D. Roosevelt is elected by a landslide.

November 3 — Franklin D. Roosevelt easily wins the 1936 presidential election, with 523 electoral votes to Alf Landon's 8.

November 12 — General Motors workers begin their sit-down strike at the GM plant in Flint, Michigan. Strikes against major plants continue into 1937, when GM signs a contract with the United Auto Workers on February 11.

December — By year's end, unemployment is down to 15 percent.

1937

January 20 — Franklin D. Roosevelt is inaugurated, beginning his second term as president.

February 5 — President Roosevelt announces the Judicial Procedures Reform Bill (commonly known as the "court-packing plan"). The bill will allow him to add one additional justice to the court for each member over the age of seventy. The bill is defeated by Congress and is widely criticized.

March 2 — The CIO wins union recognition at Carnegie Steel in Pittsburgh.

April 12 — In *National Labor Relations Board v. Jones & Laughlin Steel Corporation*, the Supreme Court upholds the

	National Labor Relations Act of 1935 (The Wagner Act). It is one of several pieces of New Deal legislation that the Court upholds in the later years of the crisis.	
May	The U.S. economy goes into a sharp recession that lasts through much of 1938. Known as the "Roosevelt Recession," it is partly sparked by Roosevelt's shift away from direct relief efforts and decrease in spending.	
May 24	In *Helvering v. Davis*, the Supreme Court upholds the Social Security Act of 1935.	
July 22	Congress passes the Bankhead-Jones Farm Tenancy Act, authorizing the government to acquire and develop damaged lands. It also grants credit to tenant farmers to purchase land.	
September 1	Congress passes the Wagner-Steagall Housing Act. It creates the U.S. Housing Authority to grant loans to states and communities to promote low-cost home construction, curbing the spread of slums and increasing levels of home-ownership.	

1938

February 16	The Federal Crop Insurance Act establishes the Federal Crop Insurance Corporation (FCIC), creating federal crop insurance to protect farmers from natural disasters.	
June 22	Congress passes the Bankruptcy Act (the Chandler Act), amending federal bankruptcy law and protecting the interests of small investors in corporations.	
June 25	Congress passes the Fair Labor Standards Act, establishing minimum wage, overtime pay, and child labor laws.	
June 25	Congress passes the Food, Drug, and Cosmetic Act. It expands the Pure Food and Drug Act of 1906, allowing the FDA to bring charges against drug manufactures who mislabel products or make unsubstantiated claims about a drug's effectiveness. Food manufacturers must also list ingredients on labels.	
September 30	At the Munich Conference, Great Britain, France, and Italy agree to allow Hitler to annex the Sudetenland in Czechoslovakia.	
November 8	For the first time since the start of the Depression, Democrats lose seats to Republicans in both the House and the Senate in the midterm elections.	

1939

January 12 — In response to the escalating military action in Europe, Roosevelt asks Congress for a two-year increase to the defense budget.

January 16 — Roosevelt recommends the expansion of Social Security benefits, especially for women and children.

March 15 — Hitler's forces invade and occupy Czechoslovakia.

April 14 — John Steinbeck's novel *The Grapes of Wrath* is published, dramatizing the plight of tenant farming families during the Dust Bowl.

September 1 — Hitler invades Poland, beginning World War II in Europe.

November 4 — The Neutrality Act of 1939 repealing the arms embargo instituted in 1935. U.S. manufacturing increases, strengthening the economy.

1940

January 4 — Roosevelt's annual budget request to Congress includes $1.8 billion in defense spending. The new demand for arms and equipment increases spending, production, and employment.

November 5 — Franklin Roosevelt is elected to an unprecedented third term, the only president in U.S. history to do so. He beats Republican candidate Wendell Willkie with 449 electoral votes to Willkie's 82.

1941

December 7 — Japan bombs the American naval base at Pearl Harbor near Honolulu, Hawaii. The United States enters World War II. The United States will emerge from the war as an economic superpower.

Appendix B: Period Learning Objectives for Students

A review of the initiatives, events, people, programs, and social responses highlighted in this book should help enhance students' knowledge of the Great Depression that took place in the United States in the 1930s. An in-depth understanding of period details, combined with a broader analysis of emergent themes, can help students trace historical patterns to arrive at a greater understanding of current responses and events, and engage thoughtfully with the material at hand.

Students should be able to do the following:

- Explain the ways in which cycles of credit and market fluctuation in the early 1930s prompted demands for stronger financial regulation.
- Compare and contrast the responses of different presidential administrations to national crises, tracing the evolution of modern liberalism from FDR's expanded use of government power.
- Analyze issues of determining constitutionality within the three branches of government, explaining how the Roosevelt administration worked within the Supreme Court's restrictions to implement unprecedented New Deal programs.
- Explain how patterns of exchange, markets, and private enterprise have developed, and analyze ways that governments have responded to economic issues.
- Explain how new forms of mass media, such as radio and film, both reflected a national culture and helped to create one, and shaped the nation's response to the crisis.
- Explain how the New Deal's legacy of reforms and regulations helped to realign the political affiliations of many ethnic and minority groups, as well as working-class voters, with the Democratic Party.

Appendix C: Listing of Biographical Entries

Arnold, Thurman
Berle, Adolf
Caldwell, Erskine
Cohen, Benjamin
Corcoran, Thomas
Coughlin, Charles Edward
Dewson, Mary
Dos Passos, John
Eccles, Marriner
Evans, Walker
Fischer, Irving
Henderson, Leon
Hickok, Lorena
Hoover, Herbert Clark
Hopkins, Harry Lloyd
Howe, Louis
Johnson, Hugh Samuel
Jones, Jesse
Keynes, John Maynard
Lange, Dorothea
Lemke, William
Lewis, John Llewellyn
Long, Huey
Lorentz, Pare

Morgan, John Pierpont, Jr.
Peek, George Nelson
Reno, Milo
Roosevelt, Anna Eleanor
Roosevelt, Franklin Delano
Scottsboro Boys
Shahn, Benjamin
Simpson, John A.
Steinbeck, John Ernst
Thomas, Elmer
Townsend, Francis Everett
Tugwell, Rexford Guy
Vann, Robert Lee
Wagner, Robert Ferdinand
Wallace, Henry Agard
Warburg, James
Warren, George Frederick
Weaver, Robert Clifton
White, Walter Francis
Williams, Aubrey Willis
Willkie, Wendell Lewis
Winchell, Walter
Woodward, Ellen Sullivan

Appendix D: Listing of Entries Related to Supreme Court Cases and Acts of Congress

Supreme Court Cases

Ashwander v. Tennessee Valley Authority (1936)
Carter v. Carter Coal Company (1936)
Helvering v. Davis (1937)
Panama Refining Company v. Ryan (1935)
Railroad Retirement Board et al. v. Alton Railroad Company et al. (1935)
Schechter Poultry Corporation v. United States (1935)
United States v. Butler (1936)
West Coast Hotel Co. v. Parrish (1937)

Acts of Congress

Bankhead Cotton Control Act of 1934
Bankhead-Jones Farm Tenancy Act of 1937
Banking Act of 1935
Chandler Act of 1938
Economy Act of 1933
Emergency Railroad Transportation Act of 1933
Emergency Relief and Construction Act of 1932
Fair Labor Standards Act of 1938
Federal Anti-Price Discrimination Act of 1936
Federal Crop Insurance Act of 1938
Federal Farm Bankruptcy Act of 1934
Federal Home Loan Bank Act of 1932
Food, Drug, and Cosmetic Act of 1938
Glass-Steagall Act of 1933
Hawley-Smoot Tariff of 1930
Investment Company Act of 1940

Kerr-Smith Tobacco Control Act of 1934
Motor Carrier Act of 1935
Municipal Bankruptcy Act of 1934
National Housing Act of 1934
Public Utility Holding Company Act of 1935
Reciprocal Trade Agreements Act of 1934
Reorganization Act of 1939
Revenue Act of 1932
Securities Act of 1933
Silver Purchase Act of 1934
Social Security Act of 1935
Soil Conservation Act of 1935
Soil Conservation and Domestic Allotment Act of 1936
Taylor Grazing Act of 1934
Transportation Act of 1940
Wagner-Peyser Act of 1933
Wagner-Steagall Housing Act of 1937
Walsh-Healey Public Contracts Act of 1936
Warren Potato Control Act of 1935
Wealth Tax Act of 1935

BIBLIOGRAPHY

Agriculture

Agee, James, and Walker Evans. 2001. *Let Us Now Praise Famous Men*. Reprint. New York: Mariner.

Barnard, Rita. 1995. *The Great Depression and the Culture of Abundance*. Cambridge, UK: Cambridge University Press.

Biles, Roger. 2006. *The South and the New Deal*. Lexington: University Press of Kentucky.

Burns, Ken. 2012. *The Dust Bowl: A Film by Ken Burns*, DVD, 240 min., PBS.

Egan, Timothy. 2006. *The Worst Hard Time: The Untold Story of Those Who Survived the Great American Dust Bowl*. New York: Mariner.

Gilbert, Jess. 2015. *Planning Democracy: Agrarian Intellectuals and the Intended New Deal*. New Haven, CT: Yale University Press.

Grubbs, Donald H. 2000. *Cry from the Cotton: The Southern Tenant Farmers' Union and the New Deal*. Fayetteville: University of Arkansas Press.

Hamilton, David E. 1991. *From New Day to New Deal: American Farm Policy from Hoover to Roosevelt, 1928–1933*. Chapel Hill: University of North Carolina Press.

Hurt, Douglas. 1994. *American Agriculture: A Brief History*. Ames: Iowa State University Press.

Meltzer, Milton. 2000. *Driven from the Land: The Story of the Dust Bowl*. New York: Benchmark Books.

Meyer, Carrie A. 2007. *Days on the Family Farm: From the Golden Age through the Great Depression*. Minneapolis: University of Minnesota Press.

Roberts, Charles Kenneth. 2015. *The Farm Security Administration and Rural Rehabilitation in the South*. Knoxville: University of Tennessee Press.

Rutland, Robert A. 1997. *A Boyhood in the Dust Bowl, 1926–1934*. Niwot: University Press of Colorado.

Shindo, Charles J. 1997. *Dust Bowl Migrants in the American Imagination.* Lawrence: University Press of Kansas.

Truelsen, Stewart R. 2009. *Forward Farm Bureau: Ninety Year History of the American Farm Bureau Federation.* Washington, DC: American Farm Bureau Federation.

Voice of Agriculture. *Our History, Our Time: A Documentary on the History of American Farming and the American Farm Bureau from 1919 to the Present,* video, 22:05 min., American Farm Bureau Federation, http://fbvideos.org/about-us/our-history-our-time/2212092510001. Accessed September 1, 2016.

Volanto, Keith J. 2004. *Texas, Cotton, and the New Deal.* College Station: Texas A&M University Press.

Wessels Living History Farm. 2003. "Farming in the 1930s." http://livinghistoryfarm.org/farminginthe30s/farminginthe1930s.html. Accessed September 3, 2016.

White, Ann Folino. 2014. *Plowed Under: Food Policy Protests and Performance in New Deal America.* Bloomington: Indiana University Press.

Arts and Culture

A&E Home Video. 2004. *John Steinbeck: An American Writer* (Biography series), DVD, 50 min.

Agee, James, and Walker Evans. 2001. *Let Us Now Praise Famous Men.* Reprint. New York: Mariner.

Carr, Virginia Spencer. 2004. *Dos Passos: A Life.* Evanston, IL: Northwestern University Press.

Carter, Ennis. 2008. *Posters for the People: Art of the WPA.* Philadelphia: Quirk Books.

Cohen, Stu. 2008. *The Likes of Us: Photography and the Farm Security Administration.* Boston: David R. Godine.

Dickstein, Morris. 2010. *Dancing in the Dark: A Cultural History of the Great Depression.* New York: W. W. Norton & Company.

Douglas, Susan J. 2004. *Listening In: Radio and the American Imagination.* Minneapolis: University of Minnesota Press.

Egan, Timothy. 2008. *The Photographs of Ben Shahn* (Library of Congress: Fields of Vision). London: Giles.

Franko, Mark. 2002. *The Work of Dance: Labor, Movement, and Identity in the 1930s.* Middletown, CT: Wesleyan University Press.

Gough, Peter. 2015. *Sounds of the New Deal: The Federal Music Project in the West.* Champaign: University of Illinois Press.

Grieve, Victoria. 2009. *The Federal Art Project and the Creation of Middlebrow Culture.* Champaign: University of Illinois Press.

Hapke, Laura. 2008. *Labor's Canvas: American Working-Class History and the WPA Art of the 1930s*. Newcastle, UK: Cambridge Scholars Publishing.

Hirsch, Jerrold. 2003. *Portrait of America: A Cultural History of the Federal Writers' Project*. Chapel Hill: University of North Carolina Press.

Jewell, Richard. 2007. *The Golden Age of Cinema: Hollywood, 1929–1945*. Oxford, UK: Blackwell Publishing.

Lange, Dorothea. 2015. *Dorothea Lange: 500 FSA Photographs*. Mark Rochkind, compiler. CreateSpace Independent Publishing Platform.

Library of Congress. "American Life Histories: Manuscripts from the Federal Writers' Project, 1936–1940." American Memory. http://memory.loc.gov/ammem/wpaintro/wpahome.html. Accessed September 3, 2016.

Library of Congress. "By the People, For the People: Posters from the WPA, 1936–1943." American Memory. http://memory.loc.gov/ammem/wpaposters/wpahome.html. Accessed September 3, 2016.

Library of Congress: American Memory. "America from the Great Depression to World War II: Photographs from the FSA-OWI, 1935–1945." http://memory.loc.gov/ammem/fsowhome.html. Accessed September 22, 2016.

Stewart, Catherine A. 2016. *Long Past Slavery: Representing Race in the Federal Writers' Project*. Chapel Hill: University of North Carolina Press.

Taylor, David A. 2009. *Soul of a People: The WPA Writers' Project Discovers Depression America*. Hoboken, NJ: Wiley.

Thompson, Jerry L. 2012. *The Story of a Photograph: Walker Evans, Ellie Mae Burroughs, and the Great Depression*. Kindle ed. Now and Then Reader.

University of Washington University Libraries Digital Collections. "Civil Works Administration Photographs." http://content.lib.washington.edu/civilworksweb/index.html. Accessed September 1, 2016.

Young, William H., and Nancy K. Young. 2005. *Music of the Great Depression*. Westport, CT: Greenwood.

Young, William H., and Nancy K. Young. 2007. *The Great Depression in America: A Cultural Encyclopedia*. Westport, CT: Greenwood.

Business and Industry

Berle, Adolf A., and Gardiner C. Means. 1991. *The Modern Corporation and Private Property*. Reprint ed. Livingston, NJ: Transaction Publishers.

Folsom, Burton W. "The First Government Bailouts: The Story of the RFC." Foundation for Economic Education (FEE), November 30, 2011. https://fee.org/articles/the-first-government-bailouts-the-story-of-the-rfc/. Accessed September 1, 2016.

Howard, Vicki. 2015. *From Main Street to Mall: The Rise and Fall of the American Department Store*. Philadelphia: University of Pennsylvania Press.

Hyman, Leonard S., Andrew S. Hyman, and Robert C. Hyman. 2005. *America's Electric Utilities: Past, Present, and Future.* 8th ed. Arlington, VA: Public Utilities Reports.

Lumley, Darwyn H. 2009. *Breaking the Banks in Motor City: The Auto Industry, the 1933 Detroit Banking Crisis, and the Start of the New Deal.* Jefferson, NC: McFarland.

PBS. "Regulation: Public vs. Private Power: From FDR to Today." *Frontline.* http://www.pbs.org/wgbh/pages/frontline/shows/blackout/regulation/timeline.html. Accessed September 9, 2016.

Phillips-Fein, Kim. 2010. *Invisible Hands: The Businessmen's Crusade against the New Deal.* New York: W. W. Norton & Company.

Skeel, David. 2006. *Icarus in the Boardroom: The Fundamental Flaws in Corporate America and Where They Came From.* New York: Oxford University Press.

Communication and Media

Brinkley, Alan. 1983. *Voices of Protest: Huey Long, Father Coughlin, and the Great Depression.* New York: Vintage.

Douglas, Susan J. 2004. *Listening In: Radio and the American Imagination.* Minneapolis: University of Minnesota Press.

Gabler, Neal. 1995. *Winchell: Gossip, Power and the Culture of Celebrity.* New York: Vintage.

Kiewe, Amos. 2007. *FDR's First Fireside Chat: Public Confidence and the Banking Crisis.* College Station: Texas A&M University Press.

Smith, Stephen. "Radio: The Internet of the 1930s." American RadioWorks. November 10, 2014. http://www.americanradioworks.org/segments/radio-the-internet-of-the-1930s/. Accessed September 9, 2016.

Daily Life

Barnard, Rita. 1995. *The Great Depression and the Culture of Abundance.* Cambridge, UK: Cambridge University Press.

Meyer, Carrie A. 2007. *Days on the Family Farm: From the Golden Age through the Great Depression.* Minneapolis: University of Minnesota Press.

Rees, Jonathan, and Jonathan Z. S. Pollack. 2004. *The Voice of the People: Primary Sources on the History of American Labor, Industrial Relations, and Working-Class Culture.* Hoboken, NJ: Wiley-Blackwell.

Roth, Benjamin. 2010. *The Great Depression: A Diary.* James Ledbetter and Daniel B. Roth, eds. New York: PublicAffairs.

Terkel, Studs. 1970. *Hard Times: An Oral History of the Great Depression.* New York: Pantheon Books.

Ziegelman, Jane, and Andrew Coe. *A Square Meal: A Culinary History of the Great Depression.* New York: HarperCollins.

General

Alter, Jonathan. 2007. *The Defining Moment: FDR's Hundred Days and the Triumph of Hope.* New York: Simon & Schuster.

Badger, Anthony J. 2002. *The New Deal: The Depression Years.* Chicago: Ivan R. Dee.

Badger, Anthony J. 2009. *FDR: The First Hundred Days.* New York: Farrar, Straus and Giroux.

Beasley, Maurine. 2010. *Eleanor Roosevelt: Transformative First Lady.* Wichita: University Press of Kansas.

Beasley, Maurine H., Holly C. Shulman, and Henry R. Beasley. 2001. *The Eleanor Roosevelt Encyclopedia.* Westport, CT: Greenwood.

Burns, Ken. *The Roosevelts: An Intimate History*, Blu-ray, 7 discs, 840 min., PBS.

Cohen, Adam. 2010. *Nothing to Fear: FDR's Inner Circle and the Hundred Days That Created Modern America.* New York: Penguin Books.

Columbian College of Arts and Sciences. "Eleanor Roosevelt Papers Project." https://erpapers.columbian.gwu.edu/. Accessed September 12, 2016.

Franklin Delano Roosevelt Library. http://www.fdrlibrary.marist.edu.

Golay, Michael. 2016. *America 1933: The Great Depression, Lorena Hickok, Eleanor Roosevelt, and the Shaping of the New Deal.* New York: Simon & Schuster.

Herbert Hoover Presidential Library and Museum. "Gallery Six: The Great Depression." http://hoover.archives.gov/exhibits/Hooverstory/gallery06/. Accessed September 1, 2016.

Hiltzik, Michael. 2011. *The New Deal: A Modern History.* New York: Simon & Schuster.

Kennedy, David M. 2003. *The American People in the Great Depression: Freedom from Fear, Part I* (Oxford History of the United States). New York: Oxford University Press.

Leuchtenburg, William E. 2009. *Franklin D. Roosevelt and the New Deal: 1932–1940.* New York: Harper Perennial.

Peters, Gerhard, and John T. Wooley. "The American Presidency Project." http://www.presidency.ucsb.edu/index.php. Accessed September 1, 2016.

Rauchway, Eric. 2008. *The Great Depression and the New Deal: A Very Short Introduction.* New York: Oxford University Press.

Smith, Jason Scott. 2014. *A Concise History of the New Deal.* Cambridge: Cambridge University Press.

Smith, Jean Edward. 2007. *FDR.* New York: Random House.

Stern, Mark, and June Axinn. 2011. *Social Welfare: A History of the American Response to Need.* 8th ed. Upper Saddle River, NJ: Pearson.

Thompson, Kathleen, and Hilary MacAustin, eds. 2001. *Children of the Depression.* Bloomington: Indiana University Press.

Time. "The Legacy of FDR." http://content.time.com/time/specials/packages/0,28757,1906802,00.html. Accessed September 9, 2016.

Watkins, T. H. 2000. *The Hungry Years: A Narrative History of the Great Depression in America*. New York: Henry Holt and Company.

Government Programs

Altman, Nancy J. 2005. *The Battle for Social Security: From FDR's Vision to Bush's Gamble*. Hoboken, NJ: Wiley.

Clawson, Marion. 2011. *New Deal Planning: The National Resources Planning Board* (RFF Natural Resource Management Set). Washington, DC: RFF Press.

Glaser, Leah S. 2009. *Electrifying the Rural American West: Stories of Power, People, and Place*. Lincoln: University of Nebraska Press

Himmelberg, Robert. 2000. *The Origins of the National Recovery Administration*. 2nd ed. New York: Fordham University Press.

Maher, Neil M. 2009. *Nature's New Deal: The Civilian Conservation Corps and the Roots of the American Environmental Movement*. New York: Oxford University Press.

Ray, Ruth, and Toni Calasanti. 2011. *Nobody's Burden: Lessons from the Great Depression on the Struggle for Old-Age Security*. Lanham, MD: Lexington Books.

Reagan, Patrick D. 2000. *Designing a New America: The Origins of New Deal Planning, 1890–1943*. Amherst: University of Massachusetts Press.

Roberts, Charles Kenneth. 2015. *The Farm Security Administration and Rural Rehabilitation in the South*. Knoxville: University of Tennessee Press.

Rose, Nancy E. 2009. *Put to Work: The WPA and Public Employment in the Great Depression*. 2nd ed. New York: Monthly Review Press.

Stone, Robert, dir. 2010. *American Experience: Civilian Conservation Corps*, DVD, 60 min., PBS.

Taylor, Nick. 2008. *American-Made, The Enduring Legacy of the WPA: When FDR Put the Nation to Work*. New York: Random House.

Legislation

Badger, Anthony J. "The Hundred Days and Beyond: What Did the New Deal Accomplish?" *History Now: The Journal of the Gilder Lehrman Institute*. https://www.gilderlehrman.org/history-by-era/new-deal/essays/hundred-days-and-beyond-what-did-new-deal-accomplish. Accessed September 2, 2016.

Biles, Roger. 2006. *The South and the New Deal*. Lexington: University Press of Kentucky.

Brinkley, Alan. 1995. *The End of Reform: New Deal Liberalism in Recession and War*. New York: Vintage Books.

Clawson, Marion. 2011. *New Deal Planning: The National Resources Planning Board* (RFF Natural Resource Management Set). Washington, DC: RFF Press.

Dyja, Tom. 2008. *Walter White: The Dilemma of Black Identity in America*. Chicago: Ivan R. Dee.

Economist. "The Battle of Smoot-Hawley." December 18, 2008. http://www.economist.com/node/12798595. Accessed September 5, 2016.

Gilbert, Jess. 2015. *Planning Democracy: Agrarian Intellectuals and the Intended New Deal*. New Haven, CT: Yale University Press.

Irwin, Douglas A. 2011. *Peddling Protectionism: Smoot-Hawley and the Great Depression*. Princeton: Princeton University Press.

Peters, Gerhard, and John T. Wooley. "Executive Orders in the APP Collection." The American Presidency Project. http://www.presidency.ucsb.edu/executive_orders.php?year=1933. Accessed September 3, 2016.

Money and Banking

Atack, Jeremy, and Peter Passell. *A New Economic View of America History: From Colonial Times to 1940*. 2nd ed. New York: W. W. Norton & Company.

Bagehot, Alexander. "Episode 1: Show No Signs of Panic." The Bankster Podcast. http://www.thebanksterpodcast.com/home/2016/4/18/episode-1-show-no-signs-of-panic. Accessed September 1, 2016.

Bagehot, Alexander. "Episode 3: The Committee, Part I." The Bankster Podcast. http://www.thebanksterpodcast.com/home/2016/5/6/episode-3-the-committee-part-i. Accessed September 1, 2016.

Barnard, Rita. 1995. *The Great Depression and the Culture of Abundance*. Cambridge, UK: Cambridge University Press.

Bernanke, Ben. "Chairman Ben S. Bernanke Lecture Series Part I." 2012. USTREAM. Internet Archive Wayback Machine. https://web.archive.org/web/20120327042254/http://www.ustream.tv/recorded/21242022. Accessed September 5, 2016.

Bernanke, Ben. 2000. *Essays on the Great Depression*. Princeton: Princeton University Press.

Bernanke, Ben. 2013. *The Federal Reserve and the Financial Crisis*. Princeton: Princeton University Press.

Economist. "The Battle of Smoot-Hawley." December 18, 2008. http://www.economist.com/node/12798595. Accessed September 5, 2016.

Eichengreen, Barry. 1996. *Golden Fetters: The Gold Standard and the Great Depression, 1919–1939*. New York: Oxford University Press.

Federal Reserve History. http://www.federalreservehistory.org.

Kennedy, Susan Estabrook. 2014. *The Banking Crisis of 1933*. Reprint ed. Lexington: University Press of Kentucky.

Kiewe, Amos. 2007. *FDR's First Fireside Chat: Public Confidence and the Banking Crisis* (Library of Presidential Rhetoric). College Station: Texas A&M University Press.

Lind, Michael. 2013. *Land of Promise: An Economic History of the United States.* New York: HarperCollins.

Meltzer, Allan H. 2004. *A History of the Federal Reserve, Volume 1: 1913–1951.* Chicago: University of Chicago Press.

Morris, Charles R. 2006. *The Tycoons: How Andrew Carnegie, John D. Rockefeller, Jay Gould, and J. P. Morgan Invented the American Supereconomy.* New York: Owl Books.

Northrup, Cynthia Clark. 2003. *The American Economy: A Historical Encyclopedia.* Santa Barbara, CA: ABC-CLIO.

Olson, James S., and Abraham O. Mendoza. 2015. *American Economic History: A Dictionary and Chronology.* Santa Barbara, CA: ABC-CLIO.

Parker, Selwyn. 2008. *The Great Crash: How the Stock Market Crash of 1929 Plunged the World into Depression.* London: Piatkus.

Payne, Phillip G. 2015. *Crash! How the Economic Boom and Bust of the 1920s Worked.* Baltimore: Johns Hopkins.

PBS. *American Experience: The Crash of 1929*, DVD, 60 min.

Rauchway, Eric. 2015. *The Money Makers: How Roosevelt and Keynes Ended the Depression, Defeated Fascism and Secured a Prosperous Peace.* New York: Basic Books.

Ravallion, Martin. 2016. *The Economics of Poverty: History, Measurement, and Policy.* New York: Oxford University Press.

Rothbard, Murray N. 2002. *A History of Money and Banking in the United States: The Colonial Era to World War II.* Auburn, AL: Mises Institute.

Securities and Exchange Commission Historical Society. http://www.sechistorical.org/.

Seligman, Joel. 2003. *The Transformation of Wall Street: A History of the Securities and Exchange Commission and Modern Corporate Finance.* 3rd ed. New York: Aspen Publishers.

Organized Labor

Grubbs, Donald H. 2000. *Cry from the Cotton: The Southern Tenant Farmers' Union and the New Deal.* Fayetteville: University of Arkansas Press.

Rees, Jonathan, and Jonathan Z. S. Pollack. 2004. *The Voice of the People: Primary Sources on the History of American Labor, Industrial Relations, and Working-Class Culture.* Hoboken, NJ: Wiley-Blackwell.

White, Ahmed. 2016. *The Last Great Strike: Little Steel, the CIO, and the Struggle for Labor Rights in New Deal America.* Oakland: University of California Press.

Politics

Brinkley, Alan. 1983. *Voices of Protest: Huey Long, Father Coughlin, and the Great Depression.* New York: Vintage.

Brinkley, Alan. 1995. *The End of Reform: New Deal Liberalism in Recession and War*. New York: Vintage Books.

Dunn, Susan. 2013. *1940: FDR, Willkie, Lindbergh, Hitler—The Election amid the Storm*. New Haven, CT: Yale University Press.

Gordon, Collin. 1994. *New Deals: Business, Labor, and Politics in America, 1920–1935*. Cambridge, UK: Cambridge University Press.

McKean, David. *Peddling Influence: Thomas "Tommy the Cork" Corcoran and the Birth of Modern Lobbying*. Hanover, NH: Steerforth Press.

Presidency

Armstrong Economics. "Roosevelt's Brains Trust." https://www.armstrongeconomics.com/research/economic-thought/economics/roosevelts-brains-trust/. Accessed September 1, 2016.

Calabresi, Stephen G., and Christopher S. Yoo. 2008. *The Unitary Executive: Presidential Power from Washington to Bush*. New Haven, CT: Yale University Press.

Dickinson, Matthew. 1997. *Bitter Harvest: FDR, Presidential Power, and the Growth of the Presidential Branch*. Cambridge, MA: Cambridge University Press, 1999.

Miller Center. "American President: Presidential Speech Archive." http://millercenter.org/president/speeches#fdroosevelt. Accessed September 12, 2016.

Rappleye, Charles. 2016. *Herbert Hoover in the White House: The Ordeal of the Presidency*. New York: Simon and Schuster.

Race Relations

Greenberg, Cheryl Lynn. 2009. *To Ask for an Equal Chance: African Americans in the Great Depression*. Lanham, MD: Rowman & Littlefield.

Janken, Kenneth Robert. 2003. *White: The Biography of Walter White, Mr. NAACP*. New York: New Press.

PBS. *Scottsboro: An American Tragedy. American Experience*, DVD, 90 min.

Sklaroff, Lauren Rebecca. 2009. *Black Culture and the New Deal: The Quest for Civil Rights in the Roosevelt Era*. Chapel Hill: University of North Carolina Press.

Stewart, Catherine A. 2016. *Long Past Slavery: Representing Race in the Federal Writers' Project*. Chapel Hill: University of North Carolina Press.

Sullivan, Patricia. 1996. *Days of Hope: Race and Diversity in the New Deal Era*. Chapel Hill: University of North Carolina Press.

Trotter, Joe W. 2004. "African Americans, Impact of the Great Depression on." *Encyclopedia of the Great Depression*. Vol. 1. Robert S. McElvaine, ed. New York: Macmillan Reference USA. Gale: *U.S. History in Context*. http://ic.galegroup.com/ic/uhic/ReferenceDetailsPage/DocumentToolsPortletWindow?displayGroupName=Reference&jsid=7812016b5ea4d6684ea4837e2c6ef921&action=2&catId=&documentId=GALE%7CCCX3404500017&u=sand55832&zid=b57acc008e359910d5c24de390bb447b. Accessed September 3, 2016.

Supreme Court

Leuchtenburg, William E. 1995. *The Supreme Court Reborn: Constitutional Revolution in the Age of Roosevelt*. Oxford: Oxford University Press.

Leuchtenburg, William E. "When Franklin Roosevelt Clashed with the Supreme Court and Lost." *Smithsonian* magazine. May 2005. http://www.smithsonianmag.com/history/when-franklin-roosevelt-clashed-with-the-supreme-court-and-lost-78497994/?no-ist. Accessed September 9, 2016.

Shesol, Jeff. 2011. *Supreme Power: Franklin Roosevelt vs. the Supreme Court*. New York: W. W. Norton & Company.

Simon, James F. 2012. *FDR and Chief Justice Hughes: The President, the Supreme Court, and the Epic Battle over the New Deal*. New York: Simon & Schuster.

Solomon, Burt. 2009. *FDR v. The Constitution: The Court-Packing Fight and the Triumph of Democracy*. Walker Books.

Work

Donkin, R. 2010. *The History of Work*. New York: Palgrave Macmillan.

Gordon, Collin. 1994. *New Deals: Business, Labor, and Politics in America, 1920–1935*. Cambridge, UK: Cambridge University Press.

Huibregtse, Jon R. 2010. *American Railroad Labor and the Genesis of the New Deal, 1919–1935* (Working in the Americas). Gainesville: University Press of Florida.

Rees, Jonathan, and Jonathan Z. S. Pollack. 2004. *The Voice of the People: Primary Sources on the History of American Labor, Industrial Relations, and Working-Class Culture*. Hoboken, NJ: Wiley-Blackwell.

Rose, Nancy E. 2009. *Put to Work: The WPA and Public Employment in the Great Depression*. 2nd ed. New York: Monthly Review Press.

Taylor, Nick. 2008. *American-Made, The Enduring Legacy of the WPA: When FDR Put the Nation to Work*. New York: Random House.

Index

Page numbers in **boldface** indicate main entries. An italicized *f* following a page number indicates a figure.

AAA. *See* Agricultural Adjustment Administration
Adjusted Compensation Act of 1936, 20
Adkins v. Children's Hospital (1923), 192–93
AFL. *See* American Federation of Labor
Agee, James, 45
Agricultural Adjustment Act of 1933, 2*f*, 3, 156, 179, 230–37
Agricultural Adjustment Act of 1938, 5
Agricultural Adjustment Administration (AAA), **1–6**, 2*f*; Bankhead Cotton Control Act of 1934, 9; Federal Surplus Relief Corporation, 60; First New Deal, 66; Kerr-Smith Tobacco Control Act of 1934, 93; Peek, George Nelson, 118; Southern Tenant Farmers' Union and, 157–58; *United States v. Butler* (1936), 179; Warren Potato Control Act of 1935, 190
Agricultural Reform in the United States (Black), 2
Alabama, 251, 251*f*
American Earth (Caldwell), 25
American Farm Bureau Federation, **6–7**. *See also* organized labor; parity

American Federation of Labor (AFL), 113, 114
American Guide Series, 62
"American Individualism" (Hoover), 203–4
Amos 'n' Andy, 123–24
animated films, 64
antitrust movement, 16, 21, 164–65
Arnold, Thurman, 7
Ashwander v. Tennessee Valley Authority (1936), **8**. *See also* Tennessee Valley Authority
Association of Railway Executives, 126, 127

Bankhead Cotton Control Act of 1934, 4, **9–10**. *See also* Agricultural Adjustment Administration
Bankhead-Jones Farm Tenancy Act of 1937, **10–11**, 49–50. *See also* Farm Security Administration
Banking Act of 1933. *See* Glass-Steagall Act
Banking Act of 1935, **11–13**, 41. *See also* Federal Deposit Insurance Corporation; Federal Reserve Board

banking crisis, **13–15,** 66–67, 225–29
Bank of the United States protest, 214–15, 215*f*
bankruptcies, 27, 55–56, 102–3
Berle, Adolf, **15–17,** 21
Betty and Bob, 124
Bituminous Coal Conservation Act of 1935, 26
Black, John, 2
black cabinet, **17–18.** *See also* National Association for the Advancement of Colored People; Vann, Robert Lee; Weaver, Robert Clifton
Bonus Army, **18–20,** 19*f*
Brains Trust, **20–21,** 173
Branin, Carl, 175
bull market, **21–22.** *See also* stock market crash
Business Advisory Council, **22–23**
business conferences of 1929, **23–24**
Butler, William, 4

Caldwell, Erskine, **25–26,** 25*f*
California migration, 39–40, 39*f*
Carr, William G., 238, 239
Carter v. Carter Coal Company (1936), **26**
Catchings, Waddill, 121
cattle, 4
Chandler Act of 1938, **27.** *See also* Securities and Exchange Commission
CIO. *See* Congress of Industrial Organizations
Citizens' Reconstruction Organization, **27–28**
Civilian Conservation Corps, **28–29,** 28*f*
civil rights, 105
Civil Works Administration, **29.** *See also* unemployment; Works Progress Administration
Clements, Robert Earl, 170, 171
coal industry, 26
Cohen, Benjamin, **30,** 32

Committee on Economic Security, **30–31,** 37, 154. *See also* Social Security Act of 1935
Commodity Credit Corporation, 5, **31–32**
commodity dollar. *See* gold standard
Commonwealth Club of San Francisco speech, 215–25
Conference on Progressive Labor Action, 175
Congress of Industrial Organizations (CIO), 97–98, 114
Corcoran, Thomas, 30, **32–33.** *See also* Brains Trust
cotton, 3, 4, 5, 9
Coughlin, Charles Edward, **33–34,** 34*f,* 177, 178
court-packing scheme, **35–36,** 141, 143–44
crime/mystery radio shows, 125
crop insurance, 52
Cummings, Homer, 35

Dawes, Charles, 130
death sentence clause, 120
Death Valley Days, 125
Deere and Company, 117
DeMille, Cecil B., 125
Dewson, Mary, **37**
document-based essay questions: sample, 255–58; tips for answering, 259–60
documents, primary, 203–54; Agricultural Adjustment Act of 1933, 230–37; Bank of the United States protest, 214–15, 215*f*; Executive Order 8802, 252–54; "First Fireside Chat" (Roosevelt), 225–29; "Philosophy of Government, The" (Roosevelt), 215–25; "Principles and Ideals of the United States Government" (Hoover), 203, 204–11; "Rugged Individualism" (Hoover), 203, 204–2011; Social Security Act

Index | 287

of 1935, 242–50; "Teacher Faces the Depression, The" (Langdon), 237–41; "Veto of the Muscle Shoals Resolution" (Hoover), 211, 212–14; Works Progress Administration image, 251, 251*f*
Dos Passos, John, 38
Dracula, 64
Dust Bowl and California migration, **39–40,** 39*f,* 156*f. See also* Resettlement Administration; Steinbeck, John Ernst

Eastman, Joseph B., 43, 102
Eccles, Marriner, 11–12, **41–42**
Economy Act of 1933, **42,** 132
Edwards v. People of the State of California (1941), 40
elections, presidential: 1928 election, 203, 204–11; 1932 election, 139–40, 181; 1940 election, 196–97; 1948 election, 186–87
Electric and Farm Authority, 131
electricity, 141–42, 166–68
Emergency Banking Act of 1933, 14, 131
Emergency Farm Mortgage Act, 3
Emergency Railroad Transportation Act of 1933, **42–43**
Emergency Relief and Construction Act of 1932, **44,** 54, 130
Emergency Relief Appropriation Act of 1935, 199–200
essay questions, document-based: sample, 255–58; tips for answering, 259–60
Evans, Walker, **44–45**
Executive Order 8802, 252–54
Export-Import Bank, **45–46**

Fair Employment Practices Committee, **47–48**
Fair Labor Standards Act of 1938, **48**
Farm Credit Act of 1933, 49
Farm Credit Administration, **48–49**

Farm Mortgage Moratorium Act of 1935, 56
Farm Security Administration (FSA), 10, 45, **49–51,** 50*f,* 95
FDA. *See* Food and Drug Administration
FDIC. *See* Federal Deposit Insurance Corporation
Federal Anti-Price Discrimination Act of 1936, **51**
Federal Art Project, **51–52,** 150, 200. *See also* Works Progress Administration
Federal Crop Insurance Act of 1938, **52–53**
Federal Dance Project, **53,** 200. *See also* Works Progress Administration
Federal Deposit Insurance Corporation (FDIC), 11, 12, **53–54,** 72. *See also* banking crisis
Federal Emergency Relief Administration, **54–55.** *See also* Emergency Relief and Construction Act of 1932
Federal Farm Bankruptcy Act of 1934, **55–56,** 96
Federal Home Loan Bank Act of 1932, **56–57**
Federal Housing Administration (FHA), **57,** 107
Federal Loan Agency, 133
Federal Music Project, **58,** 58*f,* 200. *See also* Works Progress Administration
Federal Reserve Board, **59–60;** Banking Act of 1935, 11–12; banking crisis, 14, 15; Eccles, Marriner, 41; Glass-Steagall Act, 72; recession of 1937–1938, 127
Federal Savings and Loan Insurance Corporation, 107
Federal Security Agency, 133
Federal Surplus Relief Corporation, **60–61.** *See also* Agricultural Adjustment Administration

Federal Theatre Project, 53, **61,** 200. *See also* Works Progress Administration
Federal Trade Commission, 148
Federal Works Agency, **61–62,** 133. *See also* Public Works Administration; Reorganization Act of 1939; Works Progress Administration
Federal Writers' Project, **62–63,** 200. *See also* Works Progress Administration
FHA. *See* Federal Housing Administration
Fibber McGee and Molly, 125
film, **63–65,** 100
fireside chats, **65–66,** 65*f*; banking crisis, 15, 225–29; first 100 days, 67–68, 225–29; radio, 123. *See also* radio
"First Fireside Chat" (Roosevelt), 225–29
First New Deal, **66–67,** 146. *See also* first 100 days; New Deal
first 100 days, **67–68,** 140. *See also* banking crisis; New Deal; Roosevelt, Franklin Delano
Fischer, Irving, **68–69**
Fletcher-Rayburn Bill. *See* Securities Act of 1933
Folklore of Capitalism, The (Arnold), 7
Food, Drug, and Cosmetic Act of 1938, **69–70**
Food and Drug Administration (FDA), 69, 70
Foster, William T., 121
Frankenstein, 64
Frazier-Lemke Act of 1935, 56
Frazier-Lemke Farm Bankruptcy Act. *See* Federal Farm Bankruptcy Act of 1934
FSA. *See* Farm Security Administration

General Theory of Employment, Interest, and Money, The (Keynes), 94
Germany, 84
Glass, Carter, 71–72

Glass-Steagall Act, 11, **71–73.** *See also* Federal Deposit Insurance Corporation; Federal Reserve Board; Pecora Committee
God's Little Acre (Caldwell), 25
Gold Clause Cases, 74
gold standard, 59, 69, **73–75,** 188, 189
Gompers, Samuel, 207–8
Gone with the Wind, 63
Grapes of Wrath, The (Steinbeck), 40, 159

Hamilton, Alexander, 218
Hawley, Willis C., 77*f,* 78
Hawley-Smoot Tariff of 1930, **77–78,** 77*f*
Hays Code, 64
Helvering v. Davis (1937), **78–79.** *See also* court-packing scheme; Social Security Act of 1935
Henderson, Leon, **79–80,** 80*f*
Hickok, Lorena, **80–81**
Home Owners' Loan Act of 1934, 82
Home Owners' Loan Corporation, **81–82.** *See also* Reconstruction Finance Corporation
Home Owners' Refinancing Act of 1933, 81
Hoover, Herbert Clark, **82–84;** "American Individualism," 203–4; banking crisis, 14; Bonus Army, 18–19; business conferences of 1929, 23, 24; Citizens' Reconstruction Organization, 27; Emergency Relief and Construction Act of 1932, 44; Federal Deposit Insurance Corporation, 53, 54; Federal Home Loan Bank Act of 1932, 56; Hawley-Smoot Tariff of 1930, 77–78; "Principles and Ideals of the United States Government," 203, 204–11; Reconstruction Finance Corporation, 129, 130; Revenue Act of 1932, 135; "Rugged Individualism," 203, 204–2011; unemployment, 118–19; "Veto of

the Muscle Shoals Resolution," 211, 212–14; Wagner, Robert Ferdinand, and, 183, 185
Hoover moratorium, **84**
Hopkins, Harry Lloyd, 29, 55, **85–86**
horror films, 64
hot oil, 115
housing, 57, 106–7, 185
Howe, Louis, **86**
Hughes, Charles Evans, 2f, 143, 193
Hull, Cordell, 128

ICC. *See* Interstate Commerce Commission
Ickes, Harold, 17
Index of American Design, 52
Indian Currency and Finance (Keynes), 94
In Dubious Battle (Steinbeck), 159
Interstate Commerce Commission (ICC), 102, 172
Investment Bankers Association, 87
Investment Company Act of 1940, **87**. *See also* Securities and Exchange Commission

Jefferson, Thomas, 218
Johnson, Hugh Samuel, **89–90**, 108–9
Jones, Jesse, **90–91**
Jones, Martin, 10
Jones-Connally Farm Relief Act of 1934, 4
Jones-Costigan Sugar Act of 1934, 4
J.P. Morgan and Company, 101

Kennedy, Joseph P., 149
Kent, Atwater, 124f
Kerr-Smith Tobacco Control Act of 1934, 4, **93**
Keynes, John Maynard, **93–94**, 147

labor, organized. *See* organized labor
labor standards legislation, 48, 187
La Guardia, Fiorello, 47
Langdon, Eunice, 237–41
Lange, Dorothea, **95–96**, 95f

Lefkowitz, Abraham, 240
Lemke, William, **96–97**; Farm Mortgage Moratorium Act of 1935, 56; Federal Farm Bankruptcy Act of 1934, 55, 56; Union Party, 34, 177, 178
Let Us Now Praise Famous Men (Agee and Evans), 45
Lewis, John Llewellyn, **97–98**, 114. *See also* organized labor
Lilienthal, David, 168
Literary Digest, The, **98**
Lone Ranger, The, 124–25
Long, Huey P., 34, **98–99**, 99f, 177
Long Range Planning of Public Works, The (Foster and Catchings), 121
Lorentz, Pare, **100**
Louisville Joint Stock Land Bank v. Radford (1935), 55–56
Lux Radio Theater, 125

MacArthur, Douglas, 19
Major Bowes' Original Amateur Hour, 125
marketing agreements, 3, 4
McKee, Joseph V., 240
McNary-Haugen Bill, 1, 118
Means, Gardiner, 16
minimum wage, 48, 108, 192–93
Mitchell, Charles, 116–17
Modern Corporation and Private Property, The (Means and Berle), 16
Moley, Raymond, 20, 21
Morgan, Arthur, 167–68
Morgan, Harcourt, 168
Morgan, John Pierpont, Jr., **101–2**
Motion Picture Production Code, 64
Motor Carrier Act of 1935, **102**
movie musicals, 63–64
Mulford v. Smith (1939), 5
Municipal Bankruptcy Act of 1934, **102–3**
Muscle Shoals. *See* Tennessee Valley Authority
Muste, Abraham, 175

National Association for the Advancement of Colored People (NAACP), **105,** 145–46, 193–94. *See also* White, Walter Francis
National City Bank, 116–17
National Credit Corporation, 129
National Employment System Act of 1933. *See* Wagner-Peyser Act of 1933
National Farmers' Holiday Association, 3–4, 132
National Farmers' Union (NFU), 3–4, **106,** 132. *See also* organized labor
National Housing Act of 1934, 57, **106–7**
National Industrial Recovery Act of 1933: Fair Labor Standards Act of 1938 and, 48; National Recovery Administration, 108; National Resources Planning Board, 110; *Panama Refining Company v. Ryan* (1935), 115; Public Works Administration, 122; *Schechter Poultry Corporation v. United States* (1935), 143
National Labor Relations Act of 1935, 113–14
National Labor Relations Board, 113–14
National Recovery Administration (NRA), 66, 89–90, **107–9,** 115, 143
National Resources Planning Board, **110**
National Unemployed League, 175, 176
National Youth Administration, **110–11,** 111*f*, 195
Nation Magazine, 237–41
New Deal, **111–12**; Berle, Adolf, 16; court-packing scheme, 35; Fischer, Irving, 69; Hoover, Herbert Clark, 83; Morgan, John Pierpont, Jr., 101; National Farmers' Union, 106; Reconstruction Finance Corporation, 131; Roosevelt, Anna Eleanor, 138; Roosevelt, Franklin Delano, 140–41; unemployment, 177; Wagner, Robert Ferdinand, 183, 184*f*; Warburg, James, 188; Willkie, Wendell Lewis, 196.

See also First New Deal; first 100 days; Second New Deal
New York Stock Exchange, 21–22
New York Times stock index, 160, 161
NFU. *See* National Farmers' Union
Norman v. Baltimore & Ohio Railroad Company (1935), 74
Norris, Clarence, 145–46
Norris, George, 166–67, 211–12
Nortz v. United States (1935), 74
NRA. *See* National Recovery Administration

Of Mice and Men (Steinbeck), 159
oil industry, 115
Old-Age Revolving Pensions, Ltd., 170, 171
organized labor, 97–98, **113–14.** *See also specific unions*

Panama Refining Company v. Ryan (1935), **115**
parity, 3, 6, **116.** *See also* Agricultural Adjustment Administration
Patman, Wright, 20, 51
Pearson, Frank A., 189
Pecora, Ferdinand, 116
Pecora Committee, **116–17,** 147–48
Peek, George Nelson, **117–18**
Perry v. United States (1935), 74
"Philosophy of Government, The" (Roosevelt), 215–25
photographers, 45, 95–96, 95*f*
Pictorial History of Radio, A (Settel), 123
Pittsburgh Courier, 181
Plow That Broke the Plains, The, 100
polls, political, 98
potatoes, 4, 190
Powell v. Alabama (1932), 145
presidential elections: 1928 election, 203, 204–11; 1932 election, 139–40, 181; 1940 election, 196–97; 1948 election, 186–87
President's Committee on Administrative Management, 133

President's Emergency Commission on Housing, 57
President's Emergency Committee for Employment, 118–19
President's Organization on Unemployment Relief, **118–19**
price discrimination, 51
Prices (Warren and Pearson), 189
"Principles and Ideals of the United States Government" (Hoover), 203, 204–11
Public Utility Holding Company Act of 1935, **119–20**. *See also* Securities and Exchange Commission
Public Works Administration, **121–22**, 121*f*
Pure Food and Drug Act of 1906, 69

racial discrimination: Executive Order 8802, 252–54; Fair Employment Practices Committee, 47; National Association for the Advancement of Colored People, 105; National Youth Administration, 111; Scottsboro boys, 144–46, 144*f*
radio, **123–26**, 124*f*; Coughlin, Charles Edward, 33, 34, 34*f*; fireside chats, 65–66, 65*f*; Winchell, Walter, 197. *See also* fireside chats
Railroad Retirement Act of 1934, 126
Railroad Retirement Act of 1935, 126–27
Railroad Retirement Act of 1937, 127
Railroad Retirement Board et al. v. Alton Railroad Company et al. (1935), **126–27**. *See also* Social Security Act of 1935
railroads, 42–43, 171–72, 219–20
Randolph, A. Philip, 47, 252
reason, rule of, 7
recession of 1937–1938, **127–28**
Reciprocal Trade Agreements Act of 1934, **128–29**
Reconstruction Finance Corporation (RFC), **129–31**; banking crisis, 14, 15; Commodity Credit Corporation, 31–32; Corcoran, Thomas, 32; Emergency Relief and Construction Act of 1932, 44; Jones, Jesse, 90–91; Public Works Administration and, 121–22; Transportation Act of 1940, 172
Reno, Milo, **131–32**
Reorganization Act of 1939, 61, **132–33**
Resettlement Administration, 95, 100, **133–35**, 173
Revenue Act of 1932, **135–36**. *See also* Keynes, John Maynard
Revenue Act of 1935. *See* Wealth Tax Act of 1935
RFC. *See* Reconstruction Finance Corporation
River, The, 100
Roberts, Owen Josephus, 193
Robinson, Joseph, 51
Roosevelt, Anna Eleanor, 18, 80, 81, **136–38**, 137*f*
Roosevelt, Eleanor. *See* Roosevelt, Anna Eleanor
Roosevelt, Franklin Delano, **138–41**; Bankhead-Jones Farm Tenancy Act of 1937, 10; Banking Act of 1935, 12; banking crisis, 14–15, 225–29; Berle, Adolf, and, 16, 17; black cabinet, 17; Bonus Army, 19–20; Brains Trust, 20, 21; Business Advisory Council, 22, 23; Civilian Conservation Corps, 28; Committee on Economic Security, 30, 31; Commodity Credit Corporation, 31; Coughlin, Charles Edward, and, 33, 34; court-packing scheme, 35, 36; Dewson, Mary, and, 37; Economy Act of 1933, 42; Executive Order 8802, 252–54; Export-Import Bank, 45–46; Fair Employment Practices Committee, 47; Farm Credit Administration, 48–49; Federal Crop Insurance Act of 1938, 52; Federal Emergency

Relief Administration, 54, 55; Federal Housing Administration, 57; fireside chats, 65–66, 65f, 123, 225–29; first 100 days, 67–68; gold standard, 73–74; Hickok, Lorena, and, 81; Hopkins, Harry Lloyd, and, 85; Howe, Louis, and, 86; Keynes, John Maynard, and, 94; Lewis, John Llewellyn, and, 97–98; Long, Huey P., and, 99; Lorentz, Pare, and, 100; National Resources Planning Board, 110; New Deal, 111–12; "Philosophy of Government, The," 215–25; radio, 123; recession of 1937–1938, 127–28; Reconstruction Finance Corporation, 131; Reorganization Act of 1939, 132–33; Roosevelt, Anna Eleanor, and, 138; Rural Electrification Administration, 142; *Schechter Poultry Corporation v. United States* (1935), 143–44; Securities Act of 1933, 148; Shelterbelt Project, 150–51; Silver Purchase Act of 1934, 151–52; Social Security Act of 1935, 242–43; Soil Conservation and Domestic Allotment Act of 1936, 156–57; Temporary Emergency Relief Administration, 164–65; Tennessee Valley Authority, 167; Thomas, Homer, and, 169; Townsend, Francis Everett, and, 171; Tugwell, Rexford Guy, and, 173; unemployment, 177; Union Party and, 177–78; Vann, Robert Lee, and, 181; Wagner, Robert Ferdinand, and, 183, 185; Wallace, Henry Agard, and, 186; Warburg, James, and, 188; Wealth Tax Act of 1935, 190–91; Willkie, Wendell Lewis, and, 196–97

Roosevelt, Theodore, 220–21

Rosenman, Samuel, 20–21

"Rugged Individualism" (Hoover), 203, 204–211

rule of reason, 7

rural banks, 13–14

Rural Electrification Administration, **141–42**. *See also* Tennessee Valley Authority

Schechter Poultry Corporation v. United States (1935), 48, 109, **143–44**. *See also* National Recovery Administration

Scott, Howard, 164

Scottsboro boys, **144–46,** 144f. *See also* National Association for the Advancement of Colored People

SEC. *See* Securities and Exchange Commission

Second Hundred Days, 140

Second New Deal, **146–47,** 242. *See also* New Deal

Securities Act of 1933, **147–48,** 148–49

Securities and Exchange Commission (SEC), 27, 87, 120, **148–49**. *See also* Securities Act of 1933

Securities Exchange Act of 1934, 149

Settel, Irving, 123

Shahn, Benjamin, **149–50**

sharecroppers, 3

Shelterbelt Project, **150–51**. *See also* Agricultural Adjustment Administration; Civilian Conservation Corps

Silver Purchase Act of 1934, **151–52**. *See also* gold standard

Simpson, John A., **152–53**

slavery, 62

Smith, Gerald L. K., 177, 178

Smith-Lever Act of 1914, 6

Smoot, Reed, 77f, 78

Snow White and the Seven Dwarfs, 64

soap operas, 124

Socialist Party, 38, **153–54**

Social Security Act of 1935, 31, 37, 79, **154–55,** 242–50. *See also* Committee on Economic Security; Townsend, Francis Everett

Soil Conservation Act of 1935, 5, **155–56,** 156f. *See also* Agricultural

Adjustment Administration; Civilian Conservation Corps
Soil Conservation and Domestic Allotment Act of 1936, **156–57**
Southern Tenant Farmers' Union, 105, **157–58**
sows, 3
Special Committee on Farm Tenancy, 134
Steagall, Henry, 53, 54, 71–72
Steel Workers Organizing Committee, 114
Steinbeck, John Ernst, 40, **158–59**. See also Dust Bowl and California migration
stock market crash, 14, 59–60, 83, **159–61**, 160*f*
sugar, 4
sulfanilamide, 69
Symbols of Government, The (Arnold), 7

Tammany Hall, 139, 183
tariffs, 77–78, 77*f*, 128–29
tax legislation, 190–91, 248–49
Taylor Grazing Act of 1934, **163–64**
"Teacher Faces the Depression, The" (Langdon), 237–41
"Teachers and the Economic Situation" (Lefkowitz), 240
Technocracy, **164**
Temporary Emergency Relief Administration, **164–65**
Temporary National Economic Committee, **165–66**
tenant farmers, 3, 134–35
Tennessee Valley Authority (TVA), 8, **166–68**, 211–14. See also *Ashwander v. Tennessee Valley Authority* (1936)
thesis statements, 259
Thomas, Elmer, **169**, 230–31. See also gold standard
Thomas, Norman, 153–54
tobacco, 4, 5, 93
Tobacco Road (Caldwell), 25
Townsend, Francis Everett, 30, **169–71**, 170*f*, 177, 178

Transportation Act of 1940, **171–72**
trucking industry, 102
Truman, Harry, 186, 187
Tugwell, Rexford Guy, 20–21, 134, **172–74**. See also Brains Trust; Resettlement Administration
TVA. See Tennessee Valley Authority

Unemployed Citizens' League, 175
unemployed leagues, **175–76**
unemployment, **176–77**, 176*f*; Civilian Conservation Corps, 28–29; National Youth Administration, 110–11; President's Organization on Unemployment Relief, 118–19; Reconstruction Finance Corporation, 130
Union Party, 34, 96, **177–78**
unions. See organized labor; and *specific unions*
United Automobile Workers, 114
United Mine Workers, 97
United States et al. v. Bankers' Trust Company (1935), 74
United States v. Butler (1936), 2*f*, 4, 156, **178–79**. See also Agricultural Adjustment Administration
U.S. Housing Authority, 185
U.S. Justice Department, 7
U.S. Supreme Court: Agricultural Adjustment Act of 1933, 156, 179; Agricultural Adjustment Administration, 4, 5, 9, 179; Bituminous Coal Conservation Act of 1935, 26; California migration, 40; court-packing scheme, 35–36, 141, 143–44; Federal Farm Bankruptcy Act of 1934, 55–56; gold standard, 74; National Industrial Recovery Act of 1933, 109, 115, 143; Railroad Retirement Act of 1934, 126; Scottsboro boys, 145–46; Social Security Act of 1935, 79; Tennessee Valley Authority, 8. See also *specific cases*

Vann, Robert Lee, **181**
"Veto of the Muscle Shoals Resolution" (Hoover), 211, 212–14

Wagner, Robert Ferdinand, **183–84,** 184–85, 184*f*
Wagner-Connery Act of 1935, 113–14
Wagner-Crosser Railroad Retirement Act of 1935, 126–27
Wagner-Peyser Act of 1933, **184–85**
Wagner-Steagall Housing Act of 1937, **185**
Wallace, Henry Agard, 2–3, 49, **186–87.** *See also* Agricultural Adjustment Administration
Walsh-Healey Public Contracts Act of 1936, 48, **187**
Warburg, James, **188–89**
Warren, George Frederick, **189–90**
Warren Potato Control Act of 1935, 4, **190**
Wealth Tax Act of 1935, **190–91**
Weaver, Robert Clifton, **192**
West Coast Hotel Co. v. Parrish (1937), **192–93.** *See also* court-packing scheme
Wheeler, Burton K., 151
Wheeler-Rayburn Bill. *See* Public Utility Holding Company Act of 1935

White, Walter Francis, 105, **193–94,** 194*f. See also* National Association for the Advancement of Colored People; Scottsboro boys
Williams, Aubrey Willis, 111, **194–95**
Willkie, Wendell Lewis, **196–97**
Wilson, Woodrow, 221
Winchell, Walter, **197–98.** *See also* radio
Woods, Arthur, 119
Woodward, Ellen Sullivan, **198–99,** 198*f*
Works Progress Administration (WPA), **199–201**; Alabama, 251, 251*f*; Federal Art Project, 51; Federal Dance Project, 53; Federal Music Project, 58; Federal Theatre Project, 61; Federal Writers' Project, 62; Williams, Aubrey Willis, 195; Woodward, Ellen Sullivan, 198–99. *See also* unemployment
World War I, 1, 38, 84
World War II, 85, 91
WPA. *See* Works Progress Administration

You Have Seen Their Faces (Caldwell and Bourke-White), 25–26

About the Authors

James S. Olson is distinguished professor of history and department chair at Sam Houston State University in Huntsville, Texas. A Pulitzer Prize–nominated author, he has published more than forty books, including *Encyclopedia of the Industrial Revolution in America* (Greenwood) and *Historical Dictionary of the New Deal* (Greenwood) and *American Economic History: A Dictionary and Chronology*, with Abraham O. Mendoza (ABC-CLIO).

Mariah Gumpert is a writer and former acquisitions editor specializing in American history, world history, and popular culture.